GENRES OF CRITIQUE

LAW, AESTHETICS AND LIMINALITY

EDITORS
KARIN VAN MARLE
STEWART MOTHA

SUN PRESS

Genres of Critique: Law, Aesthetics and Liminality

Published by SUN PRESS

First edition 2013

ISBN 978-1-920689-02-5
ISBN 978-1-920689-03-2 PDF

Set in Serifa BT 9.5/12.5
Cover artwork: Andries Gouws: *"Ingrid's studio, Richter and phrenological head"*. Oil on canvas, 2011. 24 x 28 cm. Collection Murray la Vita, Cape Town. www.andriesgouws.com
Cover design: SUN MeDIA
Typesetting: SUN MeDIA

SUN PRESS is an imprint of AFRICAN SUN MeDIA. Academic, professional and reference works are published under this imprint in print and electronic format. This publication may be ordered directly from www.sun-e-shop.co.za.

www.africansunmedia.co.za
www.sun-e-shop.co.za

Produced by SUN MeDIA Stellenbosch

THE STIAS SERIES

The Stellenbosch Institute for Advanced Study (STIAS) was born from a simple but powerful conviction: in this part of the world special initiatives are required to create and maintain an environment where we can generate and engage with conceptual frameworks and knowledge that may guide us in tracking and co-shaping global academic developments and that will allow us to address the 'big' questions and issues South Africa and the African continent face, also in a global context.

STIAS has been moulded in the tradition of Institutes for Advanced Study across the globe. It distinguished itself by encompassing all disciplines from the natural to the social sciences and humanities (with a particular emphasis on research grounded in multi-disciplinarity), by maintaining a focus on the African and South African context, and by striving towards contemporary relevance, also by actively creating avenues for communicating the results of its research projects to a wider public.

The STIAS series publications are thus aimed at a broad public which will naturally vary with specific research themes. Straddling the academic world and the forum of an engaging public is a challenge that STIAS accepts; we trust that each STIAS publication will reflect the 'creative space for the mind' in which it is rooted, stimulate public interest and debate, and contribute to informed decision making at various levels of our society.

Further information about STIAS and its research programme may be found at www.stias.ac.za.

Hendrik Geyer
STIAS Director

Stellenbosch
June 2011

stias
PUBLICATION

This book is dedicated to

PAUL CILLIERS

25.12.1956 – 31.07.2011

ACKNOWLEDGEMENTS

- The editors would like to thank STIAS for giving us the opportunity to work and reflect on and discuss the thoughts that have culminated in the chapters included in this volume.
- We would like to thank assistants and academic associates in the Department of Jurisprudence, Faculty of Law, University of Pretoria, for invaluable editorial assistance.
- Thanks to Andries Gouws for graciously allowing us to use his artwork for the front cover and throughout the book.
- Finally, thanks to participants in the STIAS workshop held in 2010 and the workshop that took place at Birkbeck 2011 for sharing their views and comments.

CONTENTS

LIST OF CONTRIBUTORS

MARK ANTAKI

Mark Antaki is Associate Professor at McGill University's Faculty of Law. He is also a Fellow of McGill's Institute for the Public Life of Arts and Ideas, as well as a member of its steering committee, and is active in the Association for the Study of Law, Culture and the Humanities. Some of his recent and forthcoming publications include 'The Turn to Imagination in Legal Theory: The Re-Enchantment of the World?'; 'Genre, Critique, and Human Rights'; 'The Rationalism of Proportionality's Culture of Justification'; and 'Un-Stating Law'.

RICHARD BOWYER

Richard Bowyer is a lecturer in law at the University of Exeter, UK. His recent PhD thesis examined law in the writings of James Joyce. He also researches on psychoanalysis, legal theory, and migration.

PATRICK HANAFIN

Patrick Hanafin is Professor of Law at Birkbeck Law School, University of London, where he also directs the Law School's Centre for Law and the Humanities. His research engages with questions of law and the biopolitical, law and literature, human rights and citizenship, and the construction of community and identity. His most recent books include: *After Cosmopolitanism* (with Rosi Braidotti and Bolette Blaagaard) (2013); *Deleuze and Law: Forensic Futures* (with Rosi Braidiotti and Claire Colebrook) (2009); *Conceiving Life: Reproductive Politics and the Law in Contemporary Italy* (2007) and *Law and Literature* (with Joseph Brooker and Adam Gearey) (2004).

STEWART MOTHA

Stewart Motha is Reader in Law, School of Law, Birkbeck, University of London. He has published widely on questions of post-colonial sovereignty, indigenous land rights, political theology, and democracy. His research draws on visual art and literature in examining questions of memory, home, exile and political violence. His articles have been published in a variety of international journals, including *Griffith Law Review*, *Journal of Law, Culture, and Humanities*; *Theory, Culture and Society*; *Law and Critique*; *Journal of Law and Society*; and the *Australian Feminist Law Journal*. He is currently working on a book, *Archiving Sovereignty,* which is forthcoming with Michigan University Press in 2015.

GEORGE PAVLICH

George Pavlich holds a Canada Research Chair in Social Theory, Culture and Law, and is Professor of Law and Sociology at the University of Alberta, Canada. His research interests include the areas of social theory, socio-legal studies, restorative justice, sociology of law and culture, theories of governance and sovereignty, and critical criminology. He is the author of numerous journal articles and books in these areas, including *Critique and Radical Discourses on Crime* (Ashgate 2000), *The Paradoxes of Restorative Justice* (Glasshouse Press 2005), and *Law and Society Redefined* (Oxford University Press 2011). He has co-edited several collections, most recently a second edition, with Myra Hird, of *Questioning Sociology* (Oxford University Press 2012).

PATRICIA TUITT

Patricia Tuitt is Professor of Law and Executive Dean at Birkbeck, University of London. Her research interests span the fields of international refugee law and human rights, and post-colonial theory and law – with particular focus on European constitutionalism and the development of the European Union. Recent publications include 'From the State to the Union: International Law and the Appropriation of the New Europe' in Events: The Force of International Law, edited by F Johns, R Joyce and S Pahuja (Routledge 2010). She is also author of *False Images: Law's Construction of the Refugee* (Pluto Press 1996), and *Race, Law, Resistance* (Glasshouse Press 2004).

KARIN VAN MARLE

Karin van Marle is Professor of Law, and Head of the Department of Jurisprudence, Faculty of Law, University of Pretoria. Her research interests include feminist theory, critical jurisprudence, and issues of transformation, reconciliation and reparation within the post-apartheid context. She has published widely on these areas in international and national journals and books. Her most recent publication is a work with Drucilla Cornell on the jurisprudence of Albie Sachs forthcoming with Routledge. She is currently working on a monograph on post-apartheid jurisprudence.

INTRODUCTION

Stewart Motha and Karin van Marle

This project was conceived during the months of July and August 2008 and 2009 we spent at the Stellenbosch Institute for Advanced Study (STIAS). Our brief was to conceptualise a project that would involve a group of international scholars coming together to discuss and investigate. Throughout our time at STIAS Paul Cilliers gave invaluable support, inspiration, and direction. We hope that the chapters in this volume reflect in some sense his deep understanding of complexity, and his enthusiasm and generosity voiced during individual and group discussions. This volume is dedicated to him.

Genres of Critique seeks to open and explore the liminal space of critique at the intersection of law, aesthetics and politics. We elaborate and expand the meaning and significance of critique through aesthetic forms for responding imaginatively to legal and political problems. Although this endeavour has wider significance, our focus is primarily on South Africa.

These essays arose out of a process of reading, writing and discussion among visiting scholars at STIAS in 2010. The project responds to the limits of the transplantation of critical legal studies into different jurisdictions, especially South Africa. Aesthetics has been a significant form of critically interrogating law in many sites, and the discussions at STIAS were oriented towards the critical encounter between law and aesthetic forms. Another priority was to explore themes that had been only marginally present in critical legal scholarship in South Africa: problems of home, exile, belonging and the legacy of fractured community in the context of decolonisation and the inauguration of a new polity. The essays assembled here were subsequently discussed at the Birkbeck School of Law, University of London, in 2011. This not only expanded the number of participants and critical voices, but also served to maintain contact between debates in South Africa and those taking place elsewhere.

The essays in this volume develop an approach to critical legal thinking that is conscious of critique as a problem of genre. A genre relies on the presence of a trait which is used to assert a commonality that makes it distinct from a range of disparate practices and forms. Like all normative practices, then, the assertion of a genre is also marked by exclusions, silences and absences. We seek to open up this problem of genre in the context of critical legal studies.

Why does genre matter in the context of critical legal studies, especially in South Africa? It is now commonplace for scholars of law in many regions of the world to distinguish between positivist approaches to their subject on the one hand, and a plethora of interdisciplinary approaches – ranging from sociology of law or socio-legal studies to critical approaches – on the other (Constable 2007; Cotterrell 1984; Douzinas & Geary 2005). The former is generally privileged in law school curricula, although interdisciplinary approaches have been in ascendance since the 1970s. Much of this familiar story is an Anglo-American narrative that is assumed, typically, to be true for the rest of the world. Needless to say, that is not the case. How to engage critically with political and legal problems in South Africa is a pressing question taken up here.

South Africa was in the grip of a brutal colonial and racial state for much of the last 350 years, and certainly in the 1960 to 1970s, when civil and political rights became entrenched elsewhere in the world. In the 1990s, South Africa emerged as an exemplar of juridical and political renewal. After 1994, South Africa cut a different path from the anti-colonial revolutions of the 1960s, for a range of geopolitical reasons. By this time, the struggle for socialist national liberation that was a hallmark of other anti-colonial struggles in Africa, Asia and Latin America had given way to the 'new world order' and the 'Washington consensus' (Motha 2008). The ensuing 'transplant' of legal regimes drawn from multiple traditions consolidated liberal legalism as the juridical norm, and neoliberal economic relations as the horizon for the society in transition.

Karl Klare, in an influential article in 1998, declared that South Africa's new constitutional arrangements should be understood as carrying "post-liberal" potential (1998:146). The fact that the Bill of Rights in the 1996 Constitution contained elaborate provisions to guarantee social and economic rights was one reason for this measured optimism. But typically for an analysis centred on adjudication, the emphasis was on the culture and practices of lawyers and judges. This move to turn the problem of decolonisation into a constitutional project concerned with the interpretative practices of judges brings the problem of genre in critical legal studies to the fore in South Africa. A largely North American diet of rights talk, identity politics, the juridicalisation of intersecting political demands (of class, race, gender, sexuality, poverty, health, etc) and the importation of constitutional supremacy from Indian, German and other traditions came to dominate legal discourse in South Africa. What intellectual resources would a critical project employ to engage these developments? This is one manifestation of the problem of genre in critical legal studies that concerns us here.

One's optimism or pessimism about the constitutional transition in South Africa also depends on the critical stance adopted vis-à-vis a constitutional discourse that has come to dominate political discussions. Fifteen years after the transition from apartheid to a constitutional democracy, many are revisiting the question of what 'authentic liberation' from colonialism really means (Ramose 2007). The horizon of anti-colonial struggle has shifted, and may shift again. While all South Africans – black, white, 'Coloured' and Indian, etc – are racialised beings inhabiting a racialised time and space, the scope of racial analytics diminished after the transition in 1994. Black liberation and the non-racial political order championed by the ANC would come to be in inexorable tension. But a non-racial democracy is not a post-racial polity, and the problem of what a decolonised legal and social order should aspire to remains. Many would argue that this is a symptom of the post-1994 settlement being an effective recolonisation of a polity, or a case of 'neo-apartheid'. Others might retort that the 'Rainbow Nation' was a pragmatic compromise struck by a polity that wanted to avoid a protracted civil war at a geopolitical moment (the early 1990s) when the state-socialist horizon was in retreat. What does decolonising South Africa mean today? What critical approaches would help to address that question? We suggest that being reflexive about critique as a problem of genre will be helpful in addressing these questions. We also go on to re-articulate these questions as problems of inhabiting a liminal space and time.

Genres of critique in legal studies

How is critique a problem of genre? To speak of a genre is to draw a line, invoke a limit, mark a boundary. As Derrida pointed out, "when a limit is established, norms and interdictions are not far behind" (1992:224). A genre announces a line of demarcation, belonging, purity, but also the anomaly that lies beyond that limit. Even 'mixing' genres reiterates the line: a transgression that re-inscribes the norm, reinforcing difference. This is an axiom of the law of genre (*ibid*). To speak of genre is to become entangled in a law that demands faithfulness to the boundary, limit or line. Rather than simply being a description of what is, the enunciation of a genre exacts a promise and oath to respect the law of genre; a commitment to avoid contamination.

However, Derrida also suggests that it is impossible not to mix genres: "[W]hat if there were, lodged within the heart of the law [of genre] itself, a law of impurity or a principle of contamination?" (1992:225). Derrida called this principle of contamination "the law of the law of genre" (*ibid*:225,227). A genre is marked by various 'traits', conventions and protocols. Moreover, these traits may be 're-marked' within any instance of their iterations. For example, a novel, newspaper editorial, judicial decision or work of critique may indicate from within itself which genre or class it belongs to (*ibid*:229). So a work must bear the mark of its genre. But 're-marking' or 're-citing' these traits and conventions creates the possibility of designating, through the re-marking, an exteriority to the class or genre. The exteriority participates without belonging, takes part without being part of what is being delimited through genre: "the re-mark of belonging does not belong". As Derrida puts it, this happens in the "blink of an eye". According to Derrida, a "genre designation cannot simply be part of the work" (*ibid*:230). He gives the example of a novel, which may or may not be marked by the subtitle "A Novel". The designation is not "novelistic". The designation need not be explicit, but either way, it is neither clearly inside nor outside the corpus being designated. This is the topology of designating a genre. The designation occupies the space of a border, at once opening and closing, preventing the instance of the corpus from being either absolutely different or absolutely the same as the precedent.

How is a particular approach to studying or thinking about law different or distinct from another? We may begin by identifying two prominent genres of critical legal studies (CLS). Both approaches have been influential in the South African context. They may be broadly distinguished as being oriented by the relation of law to two cognate concepts: *politics* and *the political*. The first approach to CLS is the progeny of the American realist tradition of the early 20th century (Cohen 1935; Grey 1989; Holmes 1997). In the United States, CLS elaborates a notion of law as the site of wider ideological tensions that are manifested in the juridical order and legal judgements. In this sense, law is *politics*, and thus manifests underlying structural tensions of class, race, gender, disability and sexuality (Gabel 1984; Kennedy 1976; Tushnet 1979; Unger 1983). While CLS has its origins in the US, it has not been confined to that jurisdiction. Its influence ranges widely across the English-speaking world, the Commonwealth, and certainly in South Africa. This form of CLS challenges the conventional view that law is autonomous, free of wider social and political influence. These Crits see law as a reflection, indeed a mirror, of ideology. They also broadly subscribe to the view that law and legal practices have an underlying 'cause' that should be identified, interrogated and, where necessary, interrupted. Thus law is conflated with politics, and the work of critique is to expose the ideological biases and reorient the underlying determinants of law. The object of critical engagement is often the legal decision of a judge, or legislative schemes that disclose underlying political tensions, contradictions or hegemonic practices. The task of critique is then seen as exposing bias and, once cognisant of the defect, suggesting how the underlying problem might be averted. The orientation of this mode of CLS is regularly reformist in its outlook and tends to work within the purported institutional constraints of the legal system (Klare 1998). This leads to an overemphasis on adjudication and legal instruments as the site of political transformation and thus a juridicalisation of politics. It also results in the law being treated as the main site of politics.

In contrast, 'Euro-British CLS' draws heavily on contemporary continental philosophy to elaborate a theory of law as a linguistic phenomenon, a site of ethical contestation, an ontological problem of plural existence, or a problem of justice (Douzinas & Gearey 2005). Deconstruction of texts and close hermeneutic readings seek the paradoxes and slippages that ultimately disclose the instability of legal categories and expose the absent ground of legal authorisations (Constable 2007; Fitzpatrick 2001). There is some overlap here with US CLS and their emphasis on the ultimate 'indeterminacy' of the law. But Euro-British CLS – and their collaborators in South Africa – extend the indeterminacy thesis beyond the texts of law to the subject, community, identity and justice. Rather than law being a *transparent* site of politics, as with US CLS, here the emphasis is on the constitutive dynamics that determine the subject, community, identity, nation, and so on. By emphasising the centrality of *the political* as an ontological problem, the conditions of being a subject, being-in-community, being a nation and being plural have been interrogated. These phenomenological inquiries have emphasised the constitutive exclusions, sacrifices and necessary supplements that sustain the existence of subjects, communities and legal orders.

However, privileging the primacy of the political (as the problem of plurality) has neglected reconstructive demands. It is partly for this reason that we seek to recast critical legal studies beyond the primacy of 'law as politics' or 'law and the political'. It is here, we want to suggest, that attention to 'genre' in critical thinking will be of potential benefit.

The *Genres of Critique* project recast the problem of politics and the political in South Africa today. We identified the persistent problems in South African law and society as being those of belonging (in relation to land and home) and of subjects who emerge and exist between past and future (see Arendt 1977). In this regard, we reoriented the sense of 'politics' as the 'blindingly obvious' movement of determinant forces of capital (Lacoue-Labarthe & Nancy 1997:107-121). We also retreated from the sense of the 'political' as *telos* or 'destination'. The political as a site of plural existence is not a site of gathering for those with a common shared essence, but the exposure to the very problem of being with each other. In South Africa, this problem of re-treating the political is most powerfully presented in the problem of *home*. The 'un-homed' and 're-homed' subjects of decolonisation, exile and political struggle are an abiding concern in these essays, as are the subjects inhabiting the everyday spaces of urban and rural life. Literary texts and visual art increasingly feature as sites where these subjects and problems are re-presented. Aesthetic representation of political problems is itself, then, a question taken up in this project. We thus explore aesthetic forms as sites of juridico-political critique.

Critical Legal Studies in South Africa

In order to reflect on critique in post-apartheid South Africa, and particularly the influence of the US CLS and 'Brit-Crit' traditions, it might be useful to reflect briefly on the main jurisprudential approaches that played a role during apartheid. Hugh Corder and Dennis Davis (1988:2), reflecting on the jurisprudential models and debates of the late 1980s, noted the similarity with German lawyers in the 1930s in the "uncritical acceptance of a 'scientific' approach" to law. The authors explain that this scientific approach claimed to have "some kind of value-freedom" and adhered to a separation between law and "things 'political'" (*ibid*:3). This approach resulted in an inability to see law in a social context and thus the role that law played in the political crisis of the time. The authors note that legal science in South Africa at the time meant a specific process based on order, principle and a system inherited from Western Europe and their forebears that shifted away from English law. This shift must of course be understood in its historical context and against the background of the aftermath of a period of British colonialisation and the Anglo-Boer wars – in other words, the adoption of the legal science of Western Europe was simultaneously 'anti-English'. Quite ironically, this approach once again negated the majority of people living in South Africa and was beneficial only to South Africans classified as white. The "fetish" with Western European doctrine "assumed a life of its own". By separating law from morality, this scientific approach failed to provide any guidance concerning the "suitability or correctness"' of a rule. Instead, whether a rule fits into some greater abstract theory and the logical development thereof, or whether it could be correctly traced to its historical roots, were of significance (*ibid*). Corder and Davis note that jurisprudence or legal philosophy at the time focused on the main philosophers through the ages (the Greeks, the Romans, Augustine, Aquinas, Grotius, Hobbes, Locke, Calvin, Austin, and so on), with little or no attempt to ask how these theories might be relevant to the South African legal system. They include a number of authors focussing on some of these theorists and their relevance or application in the context of the time in their edited volume of 1988. The theorists who are taken up – Calvin, Kelsen, Hart, Fuller and Dworkin – illustrate something of the state of jurisprudence at the time. In his own contribution, Davis expands on Marx in support of what he frames as a 'non-instrumentalist' view of law.

Another significant essay on the state of jurisprudence during apartheid is of course John Dugard's 1971 challenge of the judiciary and their uncritical employment of positivism in the form of Benthamian command theory. Drawing on American Realism, Dugard exposed the 'inarticulate premise' of judges and the way in which the seeming intention of the legislator was found to justify legislation that limited individual freedom. Dugard observed an important tension between the ways in which judges approach private law and public law matters. Guided in the former by the legal scientific method described above, they were willing to develop the private law to ensure a better fit with science. In the case of public law matters, judges were overtaken by executive-mindedness, uncritically following the decisions of the apartheid government.

Very broadly and tentatively, the main approaches to law during apartheid can thus be identified as firstly, the scientific approach (legal formalism) adopted from a certain historical moment in Western-Europe, and secondly, the legal positivist approach of Bentham and Austin. We have noted Dugard's reliance on the insights of American Realism in exposing the ideology and indeterminacy of decisions taken by the apartheid judiciary. There are a few examples of legal scholars in the early 1990s who explicitly called for or drew on CLS method and theory to challenge aspects of the apartheid legal order. It must be noted that our focus here is critique levelled by academics. The activism of struggle lawyers who challenged the apartheid legal order in defending their clients is beyond the scope of this project. We refer briefly to the writings of John van Doren, CRM Dlamini, André van der Walt and Dennis Davis.

Van Doren (1989) is an American Crit who at the end of the eighties called for the incorporation of CLS into South African scholarship. He believed that the insights of CLS could be employed to expose the ideology of Roman-Dutch law and the contradictions of apartheid law. CRM Dlamini (1992), focussing on legal education, criticised the overemphasis on Roman-Dutch law and the neglect of apartheid legislation and customary law in the law curriculum. André van der Walt (1993), in the context of property law, challenged the neutrality and purity of Roman-Dutch law, which led to the law of property being taught in the abstract, devoid of social reality. In his early work, Dennis Davis also applied CLS critique in response to the challenge of legal transformation. In a 1992 article, he relied on the CLS critique about the indeterminacy of rights to argue against the inclusion of socio-economic rights in the South African Constitution. His fear was that there was no guarantee that socio-economic rights would be interpreted in a progressive manner.

In 1994, South African society underwent a major political and legal change that disclosed new possibilities for critique. Wessel le Roux (2002:25), in a chapter on natural law theories in which he discusses the various shifts that occurred in the natural law tradition through the ages, notes that there are two ways in which to address the question on how we should respond to these shifts within a post-apartheid society. Our sense is that the two ways suggested by Le Roux as a response to the natural law tradition illustrate something broader about the state of jurisprudence and critique in post-apartheid South Africa. The first response to the tradition identified by Le Roux is to regard the promulgation of the Constitution and the entrenchment of human rights as the "highest culmination of the Western natural law tradition" (*ibid*:28). From this perspective, the 'new' constitutional order is something to be optimistic about and celebrate as the final triumph of modern natural law thinking and liberal ideals. A second response, however, is less triumphant and more cautionary about the "universalisation of liberal democracy" (*ibid*). Writers sharing this perspective are concerned about the possibility of a liberal rights paradigm becoming dominant in post-apartheid South Africa. Broadly speaking, most responses to the new political and legal order may be divided into those that are mainly optimistic about the constitutional project and support liberal politics and notions of rights, and those that are sceptical about this project and liberalism. The latter group of course could be voicing their concern by relying either on CLS or a Euro-Brit-Crit line of critique.

As mentioned above, both US CLS and Euro-Brit-Crits have played a role in South African legal discourse, among others. Many other traditions and theories have also been employed in critical perspectives, for example deliberative/participatory democracy theory, Marxism/neo-Marxism, social movement theory, gender theory and environmental studies. Our aim in this chapter is not to refer to and discuss each and every one of the traditions that might have played a role in South Africa or to include the names of authors that have engaged with critique. Such an attempt would be dangerous and risky and would inevitably exclude many.

Given the focus of this project, we have confined ourselves to the two traditions mentioned above as the main traditions of critique. In doing so we do not attempt or claim to include all voices in the sense of providing a comprehensive overview. We merely sketch in a broad fashion some of the main instances of critique. One important thing to be noted, however, is the fusion of these two critical traditions in the context of South African legal studies. Critique in South Africa is not steeped in the purities of genre.

As noted above, CLS played a minor role in South African scholarship before 1994. In the post-apartheid context we see the continuance of US CLS, but also greater reliance on a Euro-British critical tradition. In 2000, a debate was conducted in the pages of the *South African Law Journal* between Dennis Davis and Johan van der Walt on the possible contribution of postmodernism and the meaning of postmodernism. Davis, in a book review of Duncan Kennedy's *A critique of adjudication* (1998), argued that postmodernism as seen in South African scholarship was "an imported academic fad, lacking in social conscience and unable to support democratic political action" (Davis 1992b:116). Davis was responding mainly to three texts previously published in the *Acta Juridica* and which later also appeared in an edited collection that had started out as conference papers delivered at a 1998 conference focusing on Critical Legal Theory in South Africa (Goosen 1998; De Ville 1998; Van der Walt 1998). Van der Walt, the main target of Davis' attack, responded by denying that his work is an example of postmodernism and proposing that it be read within the framework of artistic modernism instead. He also insisted that his writings are concerned with precisely the possibilities of democratic politics. (Van der Walt 2001). Davis has consistently voiced his concern that legal formalism and poststructuralism/postmodernism might stand in the way of legal transformation in South Africa. It should be noted that he has himself relied on poststructuralist approaches to challenge legal formalism. However, he is sceptical about the way in which poststructuralism has been used in legal writings, asserting that many of the writings are not politically grounded. In the decade following this debate there have been many other writings addressing the transformed South African context by drawing on poststructural philosophy and Brit-Crit work. (For examples from within South Africa, see among many others Barnard-Naudé 2008; Clarkson 2007; Le Roux & Van Marle 2008 and Van der Walt 2005, and for examples from outside South Africa, Cornell 2009 and Motha 2009, 2011). We think that it is safe to say that these writings are inspired by a concern for the possibility of democratic politics, transformation and reconciliation. To some extent, the *Genres of critique* project shares Davis' concern. It is interested in investigating aesthetic forms and how they might disclose possibilities for a grounded critique that is not concerned with textual free play, but rather social problems of identity, homelessness and poverty.

We have referred to Karl Klare's notion of transformative constitutionalism above. As mentioned, the main aim of Klare's project is to bring about socio-economic transformation through law, particularly constitutional adjudication. Crucial for his project is the transformation of the South African common law (private law) that controls and regulates socio-economic relations. By challenging the common law, Klare goes to the heart of the scientific approach/legal formalism of apartheid that continues to dominate post-apartheid law and society. Responses to the suggestion of transformative constitutionalism have also brought to the fore different jurisprudential positions and angles – from a pertinent realist view of social engineering, upliftment and reparation (Liebenberg 2010) to an explicit recasting of Klare's project in liberal terms (Roux 2009) and critical engagements with the impossibility of true transformation and the inevitability of a continuance of transformation (Van der Walt 2006).

Lastly, something about aesthetics in post-apartheid critique. In a 2006 publication, Wessel le Roux identifies the extent to which legal scholars rely on aesthetic examples as one of the most notable features of post-apartheid constitutional discourse. He regards this "aesthetic turn" as one of the ways in which scholars reject attempts to extend the legal formalism of apartheid law to constitutional discourse on the basis of legal science. One strand of aesthetic engagement is redemptive and concerned with "substantive constitutionalism", which involves, for example, a "reconfiguration of the public sphere as a republican sphere of deliberative (or communicative) interaction" (*ibid*:101). Le Roux also notes a second strand, namely writers who rely on the arts to highlight the limits of law, including constitutionalism. In contrast to the redemptive aim of the former examples, these writers emphasise the paradoxical or aporetic nature of these reconfigured spaces. One could ask whether it is possible to distinguish so neatly between redemption and paradox. Perhaps also, in engaging with aesthetics, as with the fusion between US CLS approaches and poststructuralism/Brit-Crit that we have seen in post-apartheid writings, post-apartheid critique stands in the guise of the palimpsest: "Constitutional Hill is a palimpsest. A palimpsest is a surface on which the original writing has been erased to make way for new writing, but upon which traces of the old writing remain visible" (*ibid*:116). In the context of post-apartheid critique we find not only new and old writings, but also different kinds, emanating from different strands.

Genres of Critique proceeds from the premise that what is central to forms of representation is how they stage a critical encounter. This encounter takes place in a liminal time/space in South Africa. In the early accounts of liminality in the work of Van Gennep and Turner, cultural spaces of transition, such as initiation rites, were used to describe processes of communal transformation (see discussion in Viljoen & Van der Merwe 2007:10-12). Liminality, in that anthropology of the 1960s, characterises forms of life that are at a midpoint of transition from one relative point of sociality to another: liminality is what comes after one form of sociality and before another. Rather than this anthropological orientation of liminality marking the space between one mode of commonality and another, we regard liminality as occupying the space and time of traversal and the impetus to hold that transformative zone open.

The chapters

We have included seven chapters in this volume: five authored by members of the group that convened at STIAS in 2010, and two authored by colleagues who participated in a subsequent workshop that took place in February 2011 at Birkbeck Law School's Centre for Law and the Humanities.

In the first contribution, Chapter 1, George Pavlich sets a critical path that departs from Klare's question of whether significant social change can be effected through constitutional or law-grounded processes. Pavlich's objective is to outline a type of critique that can inform transformative adjudication, but with sensibilities, reflexes and habits that defy formalism and scientific logics. This is the kind of critique that is apt for a liminal space, drawn from Gillian Rose, of active political struggle and engagements with law, which entail an unsettlement. Pavlich proposes a 'dissociative grammar' of critique that is able to work with the uncertainties and dynamism of constitutional openings and horizons. Disavowing reified images of legal practice and treating law as always a becoming rather than a being, Pavlich draws on literary and visual art works as illustrative of this grammar. Drawing on Wittgenstein's distinction between 'surface' and 'depth' grammars – articulated and readily accessible rules of language on the one hand, and unspoken conventions that emerge in the context of performance on the other – Pavlich extends these linguistic insights into practices of critique. Importantly, he connects these to resistant and defiant "forms of life":

> One might, for example, propose a kind of critique that works from a liminal threshold and is propelled variously through local engagements with the limits of social context, culture, language and legal framework to open up to new forms of life. The active gesture need not be one of founded judgement; rather, I suggest that critique could work through a 'dissociation' of familiar surface grammars and social processes in a quest to appropriate a future.

Drawing from William Kentridge's art and novels such as Ingrid Winterbach's *The Book of Happenstance* (2011), Njabulo Ndebele's *The Cry of Winnie Mandela* (2004) and JM Coetzee's *Disgrace* (1999), Pavlich explores how defiant forms of life emerge from disruptive events, the naming of contingency and the quest for residual knowledge at the limits of order. The characters in all these novels experience the limits of their being and have to face what seemed impossible before. By negotiating new accommodations, new grammars and lexicons emerge. There is a radical indeterminacy to these grammars. Kentridge's remarks on drawing as a contingent arrival of images is seen as a model of how lives are lived and judgements not based on 'founded' criteria might be made. Judgement would then have to be open to an indeterminate arrival. And a transformative constitutionalism would then have to embrace reasoning as 'contingently deferred chains of meaning' that are always in flux. Oriented in this way, judgement would have to remain ever open to contexts that impel reflection on limits, thereby foregoing the attachment to any given ordering.

In Chapter 2, Mark Antaki revisits the role played by the metaphors of the book and the bridge in post-apartheid legal discourse. He notes that although many scholars have relied on the bridge metaphor, the book metaphor received little attention. Antaki engages with André van der Walt's reinterpretation of the bridge metaphor and links it to Antjie Krog's refusal to write a novel. Like Van der Walt's wish for things to be different rather than better, Krog's refusal stands in the guise of opening something new, something other than a 'sovereign writing.' Antaki explains:

> A critical interpretation of this 'opening' would likely have to sever transformation from formation (Bildung) and, perhaps, even give up on, or radically reduce, the role of the imagination (Einbildungskraft) in bringing others and the future to clarity, in making them (re)cognisable. A critical interpretation of this 'opening' would lead in the direction of an acknowledgement of finitude – and hence of the givenness and gift of 'the open', even if experienced as an abyss or a gap – as an ontological truth of the human condition.

Antaki asks what book or novel we would turn to if it were possible to read the book metaphor differently, and briefly engages with the novels of JM Coetzee as examples of an acknowledgement of finitude. The chapter leaves us with the question: what legal form or genre is or would be analogous to this kind of literature?

In Chapter 3, Patricia Tuitt continues the exploration of the constitutive and transformative potential of aesthetic forms, but now with a critique of the colonial tropes in Antjie Krog's *Begging to be Black* (2009). If post-apartheid jurisprudence is going to draw on literary genres as a 'minor jurisprudence' for transformative ends, then Tuitt suggests that constitutional and subjective transformation must be mindful of not repeating the violent appropriations of all beginnings, inventions and grounds. Focusing on *Begging to be Black* as a work of 'literary non-fiction' – a designation that seeks to avoid the genre of novel and speaks through the genres of literary history, dramatised philosophy and political essay – Tuitt warns of the dangers that accompany the 'cut, closure and appropriation' of all *nomos*, thought and invention. Krog's regrounding and reinventing of herself as a white South African moves from the passivity of 'begging' to actively wanting an African perspective, wanting to be part of the country she was born in. Tuitt sets Krog's post-apartheid transformative becoming in the context of violent colonial appropriations – ones that usually required the making vacant of populated spaces and rendered indiscernible the beings who inhabited it (referring here to Krog's inability to understand Thabo Mbeki compared to German or Australian leaders). If the aesthetic is to have transformative potential, it must be 'alive to its ruinous origins' and suppress the temptation to be 'other than 'other'. Otherwise, rebellious invention would repeat the gestures of colonial discovery.

Stewart Motha elaborates the centrality of consciously false myths in constitutional narratives in Chapter 4. While the initial provocation is the post-apartheid constitutive myth that 'South Africa belongs to all who live in it', Motha traces the significance of the 'as if', the consciously false, for creating and sustaining a constitutional order. Is fiction essential to the constitutional form? Does law share the same condition of possibility as literature? Treating myth or fiction as a source of sense or value (after Jean-Luc Nancy), Motha examines how we might distinguish between 'degenerate myths' and nihilism. The response of critical thinkers to harmful myths that ground violence has been to orient ethical and political demands through a variety of 'forms of life' that are produced in the encounter between sovereign power and those subject to it (for example bare life, grievable life, vulnerable life, etc, by Giorgio Agamben and Judith Butler respectively). Motha explores the potential of liminal subjects as 'forms of life' represented in literature and argues that such liminal beings have the potential to occupy the frontier between past and future. Liminal beings inaugurate political life in societies that are grappling with deep divisions and violent colonial legacies.

In Chapter 5, Karin van Marle contemplates the notion of liminal landscape through an engagement with Lettie Viljoen's[1] 1996 post-colonial novel, *Landskap met vroue en slang* (*Landscape with women and snake*). Van Marle's main concern is the possibility of a space for critique within the present South African legal, political and social context. She places the relationship between the law and the humanities – especially between law, literature and critique – at the heart of this issue. For Van Marle, the possibility of critique lies in ambivalence, unfulfilment and uncertainty. She argues that a critical engagement with modernity and the rethinking of possible alternative modernities seem to be central to a critical project. Added to this are Hannah Arendt's notion of worldliness and a recognition of complexity and plurality. Van Marle calls for a sense of tragedy – rather than the Romanticism that often accompanies struggles

1 The pseudonym for author Ingrid Winterbach.

for freedom – to reveal opportunities for critical engagement, and links this sense of tragedy with humility and the acceptance of modest positions, slowness and attentiveness.

Patrick Hanafin engages with the notion of refusal, in particular 'a refusal to be constructed as an identity to be managed by the state', in Chapter 6. Hanafin claims that such a strategy of refusal to be constructed as 'an identity' has the advantage of allowing one to remain beyond the grasp of the state's ability to make visible and incorporate such identities into the biopolitical regime. He draws attention to how the refusal to be formed as an object of governance by the state constitutes an important mode of resistance to biopower. Focusing on JM Coetzee's 1983 novel *Life & Times of Michael K*, Hanafin considers its implications for a critique of the political within writing itself. He describes Michael K's performance as a testimony to being beyond the order of law, and argues that Michael K allows us to think of the paradoxical nature of political obedience and the subject's willed servitude to order: 'The action of refusing such servitude points to the beginning of resistance to biopolitical modes of production.'

In Chapter 7, Richard Bowyer takes up the theme of exile through James Joyce. Joyce has been regarded as apolitical, avoiding the turmoil of Ireland while living in exile in Paris. Bowyer shows how, despite being in exile, Joyce was closely engaged in a critique of colonial rule and imperium in Ireland. Moreover, through his displacement of 'home myths' in the process of writing fiction, the exiled Joyce is shown to be acutely sensitive to the 'myth' of home. Through a close reading of the Cyclops episode in *Ulysses* (1922), where the half-Jewish, half-Irish Leopold Bloom is pitched against the nationalism of the Citizen who is driven by Gaelic nationalism and culture, Bowyer opens yet another aesthetic formation of law, namely its musicality. Bowyer argues that Joyce uses music to convey ideas about nation and nationalism in the Cyclops episode. Elaborating the centrality of motif – specifically the motif of 'Jacob's biscuit tin' in the Cyclops episode – Bowyer argues for a conception of law as music. From Plato's treatment of music to the policing of contemporary urban concerts, music has been seen to bear a particularly threatening relationship to the state. Which genre of music is the state less or more threatened by? Music is also important, Bowyer argues, for the work of memory. Music can be a conduit for motifs that trigger memories, or memories can be carried through music. The power and force of music can be constitutive or destructive, contributing to processes of remembering *and* forgetting. Literary forms may in fact be seen as a musical genre. Through the biblical story of the brothers Jacob and Esau in *Genesis* (invoked by Joyce in the 'Jacob's biscuit tin' motif), Bowyer shows that a fraternal conflict between nation and birthright may be critically elaborated through the musicality of a literary text. What is at stake in the Cyclops episode is the standpoint and perspective of writers in exile, as well as the different genres and forms through which a law that resists imperium may be invoked.

Reference List

Arendt H. 1977. *Between Past and Future: Eight Exercises in Political Thought*. New York: Penguin Books.

Barnard-Naudé AJ. 2008. Beyond the brother: Radical freedom. In: AJ Barnard-Naudé, D Cornell & F du Bois (eds). *Dignity, freedom and the post-apartheid legal order*. Cape Town: Juta. 273-297.

Brink A. 2007. Stories of history: reimagining the past in post-apartheid narrative. In: S Nuttall & C Coetzee (eds). *Negotiating the Past: The Making of Memory in South Africa*. Oxford: Oxford University Press.

Clarkson C. 2007. The Time of Address. In: S Veitch (ed). *Law and the Politics of Reconciliation*. Hampshire: Ashgate.

Cohen F. 1935. Transcendental nonsense and the functionalist approach. *Columbia Law Review* 35:809-849.

Constable M. 2007. *Just Silences: The Limits and Possibilities of Modern Law*. Princeton, NJ: Princeton University Press.

Corder H & Davis D. 1988. Law and social practice: An introduction. In: H Corder (ed). *Essays on law and social practice in South Africa*. Cape Town: Juta. 1-30.

Cornell D. 2009. Ubuntu, Pluralism and the Responsibility of Legal Academics to the New South Africa. *Law and Critique* 20(1):43-58.

Cotterrell RBM. 1984. *The Sociology of Law: An Introduction*. London: Butterworths.

Davis D. 2000. Duncan Kennedy – A critique of adjudication: a challenge to the 'business as usual' approach of South African lawyers. *South African Law Journal* 117:697-712.

— 1992a. The case against the inclusion of socio-economic demands in a bill of rights except as directive principles. *South African Journal on Human Rights* 8:475-490.

— 1992b. Book review: Postmodern jurisprudence: the law of text in the texts of law. *South African Law Journal* 109:116-173.

Derrida J. 1992 (1986). The Law of Genre. In: D Attridge (ed). *Acts of Literature*. London & New York: Routledge. 221-252.

De Ville J. 2011. *Jacques Derrida: Law as absolute hospitality*. London: Birkbeck Law Press.

— 1998. Meaning, violence and responsibility: A response to Professors Van der Walt and Gutto. *Acta Juridica* 14:114-116.

Dlamini CRM. 1992. The law teacher, the law student and legal education in South Africa. *South African Law Journal* 109:595-610.

Douzinas C & Gearey A. 2005. *Critical Jurisprudence: The Political Philosophy of Justice*. Oxford: Hart Publishing.

Dugard J. 1971. The judicial process, positivism and civil liberty. *South African Law Journal* 88:181-200.

Fitzpatrick P. 2001. *Modernism and the Grounds of Law*. Cambridge: Cambridge University Press.

Gabel P. 1984. The phenomenology of right-consciousness and the pact of the withdrawn selves. *Texas Law Review* 62:1563-1599.

Goodrich P. 2008. Visive powers: Colours, trees and genres of jurisdiction. *Law and the Humanities* 2(2):213-131.

Goosen D. 1998. Deconstruction and tragedy: A comparison. *Acta Juridica* 14:21-40.

Grey TC. 1989. Holmes and legal pragmatism. *Stanford Law Review* 41:787-863.

Holmes OW. 1997 (1897). The path of the law. *Harvard Law Review* 110:991-1009.

Johannesburg Development Agency. 2006. *Number Four: The Making of Constitutional Hill*. Johannesburg: Penguin (South Africa).

Kennedy D. 1976. Form and substance in private law adjudication. *Harvard Law Review* 89:1685-1778.

— 1998. *A critique of adjudication*. Cambridge, MA: Harvard University Press.

Klare KE. 1998. Legal culture and transformative constitutionalism. *South African Journal on Human Rights* 14:146-172.

Lacoue-Labarthe P & Nancy J-L. 1997. *Retreating the Political*. London: Routledge.

Le Roux WB. 2006. The aesthetic turn in the post-apartheid constitutional rights discourse. *Journal of South African Law* 1:101-119.

— 1994. Natural Law Theories. In: C Roederer & D Moelendorf (eds). *Jurisprudence*. Cape Town: Juta. 25-59.

Le Roux WB & Van Marle K (eds). 2008. *Post-apartheid fragments. Law, politics and critique*. Pretoria: UNISA Press.

Le Roux WB & Van Marle K. 2004. Postmodernism(s) and the law. In: C Roederer & D Moelendorf (eds). *Jurisprudence*. Cape Town: Juta. 354-381.

Liebenberg S. 2010. *Socio-economic rights under a transformative constitution*. Cape Town: Juta.

Motha S. 2011. Rationality, the Rule of Law, and the Sovereign Return. *Constitutional Court Review* 4:113-136.

— 2009. Archiving Colonial Sovereignty: From Ubuntu to a Jurisprudence of Sacrifice. *South African Public Law* 24:297-327.

— 2008. Spectres of Communism in Post-apartheid South Africa. In: WB le Roux & K van Marle (eds). *Post-apartheid Fragments. Law, politics and critique*. Pretoria: UNISA Press.

Nancy J-L. 2000. *Being singular plural*. Stanford, CA: Stanford University Press.

Ndebele N. 2007. Memory, Metaphor, and the Triumph of Narrative. In: S Nuttall & C Coetzee (eds). *Negotiating the Past: The Making of Memory in South Africa*. Oxford: Oxford University Press.

Ramose M. 2007. In memoriam. Sovereignty and the 'new' South Africa. *Griffith Law Review* 16(2):310-329.

Roux T. 2009. Transformative constitutionalism and the best interpretation of the South African constitution: a distinction without a difference. *Stellenbosch Law Review* 20:258-285.

Tushnet M. 1979. Truth, justice, and the American way: An interpretation. *Texas Law Review* 57:1307-1359.

Unger R. 1983. The critical legal studies movement. *Harvard Law Review* 96:561-675.

Van Blerk A. 1996. Critical Legal Studies in South Africa. *South African Law Journal* 113:86-107.

Van der Walt AJ. 2006. Legal history, legal culture and transformation in a constitutional democracy. *Fundamina* 12:1-47.

— 1993. Reflections on teaching property law in future. *Stellenbosch Law Review* 4:88-99.

Van der Walt JWG. 2005. *Law and sacrifice. Towards a post-apartheid theory of law*. London: Birkbeck Law Press.

— 2001. The quest for the impossible, the beginning of politics: A reply to Dennis Davis. *South African Law Journal* 188:463-472.

— 1998. The language of jurisprudence from Hobbes to Derrida (the latter's quest for an impossible poem). *Acta Juridica* 14:61-96.

Van Doren JW. 1989. Critical Legal Studies and South Africa. *South African Law Journal* 106:648-661.

Viljoen H & Van der Merwe C (eds). 2007. *Beyond the Threshold: Explorations of Liminality in Literature*. New York: Peter Lang.

DISSOCIATIVE GRAMMAR OF CONSTITUTIONAL CRITIQUE?

George Pavlich

> Critique is essential to all democracy. Not only does democracy require the freedom to criticize and need critical impulses. Democracy is nothing less than defined by critique.
>
> – *Adorno 1998:281*

Adorno's words could be read alongside Klare's critical focus on the political and moral dimensions of adjudicative law-making generally, and South African constitutional adjudication in particular. Klare (1998:150) asks: "Can we describe a method of adjudication that is politically and morally engaged, but that is *not* illicit 'judicial legislation'. Is there a post-liberal account of the rule of law suitable to the political challenges South Africa has set for itself?" In response, he calls for politically engaged forms of constitutional legal adjudication that conform to legal process in their efforts to spur social changes on a scale greater than liberal reform, but short of revolution. Coining the phrase "transformative constitutionalism" to signify "an enterprise of inducing large-scale social change through nonviolent political processes grounded in law", he engages head-on a question that has dogged neo-Marxist approaches to law: "[Is it] possible to achieve this sort of dramatic social change through law-grounded processes?" (*ibid*).

Leaving aside the well-known details of Klare's affirmative response to this question, the following paper considers a type of critique that might inform transformative adjudication in contemporary democratic environments. It addresses an element of adjudicative legal culture, and engages specifically the critical dimensions of what Klare refers to as the "professional sensibilities, habits of mind, and intellectual reflexes" (1998:166). A focus on critique in the context of transformative constitutionalism is foundational, because, as Van Marle (2009:288) points out, this sort of constitutionalism is itself a critical process "committed to transforming political, social, socio-economic and legal practices in such a way that it will radically alter existing assumptions about law, politics, economics and society in general". If this recognition necessarily takes one beyond the confines of conventional legal theory or jurisprudence, it also implies a unique form of critique situated "within a liminal space and time, a precarious and uncomfortable space and time or, following Gillian Rose, a space of double anxiety and sustained equivocation, a broken middle. It must be a site of active political action and struggle, of active engagement with law; a site that entails an unsettled and unsettling approach" (*ibid*:297).

Here, Van Marle raises the theoretical stakes by inviting reflection on a "critique of critique" within the context of constitutional law (2009:297). It also appears to challenge Klare's critical legal approach with its attachment to normatively founded criticism and 'progressive' social transformation. By contrast, critique that occupies an always uncomfortable space, an unsettled 'broken middle', defies settled definitions of critical practice, social advancement or progress. Embracing this 'unsettled and unsettling' approach, a broad "aesthetic turn" in legal thinking (involving philosophy, history, art and literature) has challenged constitutional arenas not to tackle complex socio-political matters through formalist legal language games or simply framed technical, administrative and scientific solutions. As Le Roux puts it:

> [...] the aesthetic turn in post-apartheid constitutionalism could be interpreted as a direct response to the need for a non-scientific and non-formalised style of public reasoning. That the rejection of science as a model of constitutional law should have resulted in a turn towards art (traditionally regarded as the direct opposite of science) is not at all surprising. (Le Roux 2006:107)

In a related view, Van der Walt (2005) sees post-apartheid constitutional adjudication as a public, cultural space for deliberative democratic discussions vital to the future of a democratic society; it should thwart modernity's seemingly relentless push towards private law in constitutional thinking, as well as an emphasis on formalist legal reasoning and individual rights.

These unsettled critical slants take for granted the historically situated dynamism and provisional nature of constitutional law, recognising that democratic, transformative constitutions demand appropriate forms of adjudication to embrace – rather than deny by *fiat* – the contingency of constitutionally defined limits. This places a unique inflection on how to conceive of adjudication within constitutional arenas. It also raises an important issue: what 'grammar' of critique might attach to publicly spirited, democratic and transformative constitutional adjudication? In responding to this question, the following chapter draws on aesthetic (literary and artistic) sources to clear conceptual grounds for a grammar appropriate to contemporary legal critique. It begins by describing an influential, modern approach to critique (implicit too in Klare's formulation) that proceeded from founded judgements, before tackling the following question: what alternative critical grammar might work through the indeterminate dynamism of transformative constitutionalism, enabling practices of critique that operate by relentlessly reaching beyond current orderings? In response, I will propose a 'dissociative' grammar that conceives of critique as a practice not essentially tied to practices of founded judgement. In order to conceptualise the stakes of such critique, I refer to post-apartheid fiction and William Kentridge's ideas about his art.

If modern critique required critics to judge circumstances against absolute, ahistorical or universal criteria, the proposed approach points rather towards a dissociative grammar and practice of critique more able to work with the uncertainties, dynamism and intricacies of current constitutional horizons. At the outset, however, two caveats seem necessary. To begin with, this chapter's focus on such a critical grammar is rather ambitious on its own terms, enabling little more than an allusion to how that grammar might eventually inform transformative constitutional adjudication. Secondly, following Nietzsche and others, I consider law as always underway, a becoming and not a settled being (Pavlich 2011), so that the search for a dissociative grammar of critique explicitly attaches to dynamic rather than reified images of legal practice. In outlining this unconventional notion of critique, I refer to literary and visual art works to illustrate elements of this grammar, rather than offer an analysis of the works themselves. With these provisos in mind, how might one understand the notion of 'grammar' in context?

Grammar, critique and spades turned

> Essence is expressed by grammar. [...] Grammar tells us what kind of object anything is. (Wittgenstein 1983:371,373)
>
> Grammar, one may say, establishes the place of a concept in our system of concepts, and thereby in our world. It controls which other concepts, which questions and observations, are relevant to a particular concept. That is the sense, I believe, in which 'grammar tells us what kind of object anything is.' Grammar relates the concept of 'chair' to concepts like 'sitting' and 'mending' and 'lending'; which is to say that for something to be a chair, it must be such that a human being can sit on it, and sit on it in that way ... (Pitkin 1973:119)

Despite Wittgenstein's not always consistent use of the term 'grammar', one might infer from the above statements how, for him, grammar specifies ways to use particular words in a discourse, thus generating their meaning in context – that is, how words are used in given "language games" quite literally dictates their meaning (Wittgenstein 1983:107). Moreover, users learn how to use words in a language by getting to know the rules that specify appropriate ways of using words in particular language contexts (often by ostensive and performative definition, much like learning the rules of a game). This yields meaning for participants, and grammar encompasses the rules at hand. Through grammar, that is, rules for the use of words in language generate meaning and define 'essences' to frame how participants understand and relate to their worlds. But how might we understand the underlying grammar behind the meaning of a word like 'critique'? Wittgenstein's fleeting response provides that "[i]n their use of words one might distinguish 'surface grammar' from 'depth grammar'" (1983:664), and Kripke helpfully elaborates: "By Surface Grammar we actually refer to all the formal grammatical rules, while by Depth Grammar we refer to the circumstances and relationships that dictate language use" (1982:96). In other words, 'surface grammar' embraces formal and specific grammatical rules that define for language learners and users how to use words in a given language context. These rules specify how a given word is to be used in a sentence and, as Wittgenstein suggests, make it sound 'right' to language users:

> What immediately impresses itself upon us about the use of a word is the way it is used in the construction of the sentence, the part of its use [...] that can be taken in by the ear. (Wittgenstein 1983:664)

But if hearing correctly may be relayed through direct rules, Wittgenstein notes that there is a rather less accessible element to grammar: "[...] the 'deep' aspect of this matter readily eludes us" (*ibid*:387); that is, underlying surface grammars, one finds an elusive 'depth' grammar, which ordinarily resides in unspoken conventions. Emerging from relational performances and being with others in a given context, this depth grammar is obscure, because it operates in the shadows of language, in the unspoken relations and forms of life that yield communicative conventions. Its operation is mostly silent, hidden to language users, but it may become apparent when perplexing misinterpretations strike at the heart of ordinary communicative interactions:

> [...] the problems arising though a misinterpretation of our forms of language have the character of depth. They are deep disquietudes; their roots are as deep in us as the forms of our language and their significance is as great as the importance of our language. (Wittgenstein 1983:111)[1]

One might extrapolate from these brief references to Wittgenstein that a grammar of critique will contain more or less articulated surface rules that render the particular views of critics in context meaningful; at the same time, its depth grammar ties unspoken critical practices more directly to the unarticulated ebb and flow of convention that attend to particular 'forms of life'. In other words, both depth and surface grammars of critique are tied ultimately to the rules, conventions and forms of life associated with, and that give rise to, meaning in a given language. No grammar is therefore universally fixed or valid; moreover, its emergence is contingent upon conventions within given forms of life that defy absolute justification. As Wittgenstein notes, the quest to justify conventions is only possible up to a point; there is always a moment where we find ourselves without meaningful ways to provide ultimate justification:

> If I have exhausted the justifications I have reached bedrock, and my spade is turned. Then I am inclined to say: 'this is simply what I do.' (Remember that we sometimes demand definitions for the sake not of their content, but of their form.

1 This quote could also be taken to inform the 'deep' disquiet previously referenced in relation to legal theory's 'aesthetic turn' (Le Roux 2006; Van Marle 2003). Perhaps one might consider this turn as a deliberate attempt to render familiar meanings in constitutional legal theory strange and to work with 'misinterpretations' to develop a critical form of transformative constitutionalism. No doubt the implications for the forms of life that surround constitutional law could be profound.

> Our requirement is an architectural one; the definition a kind of ornamental coping that supports nothing.) (Wittgenstein 1983:217)

Wittgenstein's penetrating integrity on this matter faces head-on the contradictory and ultimately indeterminate yet 'architectural' requirement imposed upon many questions about the foundations of how we live and the meanings we promote. If nothing else, this demands caution from the outset: not everything can be articulated about critique or its grammar, and far less about whether one approach is necessary or not.

In sum, this Wittgensteinian-inspired formulation allows one to approach the grammar of critique with suitable modesty and without certainty; it also embraces the intractable indeterminacy of surface and depth grammars that generate the meaning of transformative, critical thinking. In exploring the indeterminate forms of life that spawn practices in the name of critique, any metadiscussion – a critique of critique – demands a certain diffidence. This attitude helps guard against an undue and yet pervasive conceptual arrogance that claims – with remarkable simplicity – the capacity to erect universally valid guidelines for accomplishing progressive social, legal and political change. Lest we forget, too many social disasters contain traces of such unwarranted assurances.

Judgemental grammars of modern critique

There is a constellation of signs – 'criticism', 'crisis' and 'critique' – whose surface grammar has over centuries been associated with images of judgement and the ability to specify privileged paths to true progress (Connerton 1980; Koselleck 1988). In modern contexts, the meaning of these words was increasingly associated with judging 'critical conditions', truth, and so on. Their surface grammar also reflected an enlightenment politics that contested the hegemony of divine revelation. Ultimately, the 'superstition', 'dogma' or 'despotic decrees' of religion and sovereigns were replaced by a reason-based regime of truth in which criticism served as a new, 'enlightened' master. It became the final arbiter of new truths. With this inflection, one might grasp the full significance of Kant's famous claim:

> [...] our age is, in especial degree, the age of criticism, and to criticism everything must submit. Religion through its sanctity, and law-giving through its majesty, may seek to exempt themselves from it. But they then awaken just suspicion, and cannot claim the sincere respect which reason accords only to that which has been able to sustain the test of free and open examination. (Kant 1958:7)

Basic to the 'enlightened' depth grammar implied here, critique revolved more and more around a critic's ability to serve as judge in matters of reason-based truth. As Connerton[2] succinctly puts it, with the landmark publication of Bayles' *Dictionnaire historique et critique* in 1697,

> Critique came to be seen no longer as a symptom of the sharpening opposition between reason and revelation. It was viewed as itself the activity which separated the two spheres. It was the essential activity of reason. (Connerton 1980:18)

[2] See Pavlich 2000:26-27.

Not surprisingly, perhaps, the idea of critique was subsequently associated with, even defined by, practises of judgement.

Yet the etymology of the term 'critic' suggests a rather different possibility, sharing as it does with 'critique', 'criticism' and 'crisis' a link to the Greek word *krinein*, which was associated as much with a capacity to decide as to judge (Ayto 1990). With its link to decision, *krinein* simultaneously connoted discerning, selecting, differentiating, sifting, and separating out (Koselleck 1988). Modern appropriations of 'criticism' or 'critique' tended to associate the practice with philological quests to find the authentic meaning of texts (Davis & Schleifer 1991), medical judgements about when the course of an unfolding illness had reached a 'critical condition' (Connerton 1980), and quests to judge the "justices" of particular events in legal settings (Pavlich 2000:25, 1996:18). Consequently, critical practices tended to be defined as ways to judge the truth or authenticity of something, or an "original condition" (Connerton 1980:17); hence, as Williams (1983:85) puts it, "[...] what is significant about the development of criticism, and of the critic and the critical, is the assumption of judgement as the predominant and even natural response".

In other words, as ideas about critique and criticism developed under modern conditions, so they came to be associated with practices of judging the truth, the authenticity, or the essence of given circumstances. Interestingly, both critics and judges were tasked with deciding on the truth of specified situations, diagnosing crises and intervening through legal remedy or prescriptive constitutional interventions. Traces of that judgemental critical grammar appear in Klare's critical legal studies: he articulates critique as a judgement that relies on 'progressive' criteria (for example, equality) to redress problematic social conditions through a 'transformative constitutionalism' that would assuredly guide society to an advanced state. Though different in appearance, both formalist and critical constitutional approaches proceed through not entirely unrelated models of founded judgement.

Although discussed in more detail elsewhere (Pavlich 2001, 2000), one might note here that modern criticism's emphasis on judgement dovetails with emerging disciplinary regimes of truth and their attachment to a gaze that operates through 'normalising judgement' (Foucault 1977a). To be sure, the association between legal judgement and normalising judgement is complex and context-specific. However, for our purposes here, suffice it to say that grammars of critique associated with founded judgement assumed an inordinately dominant position in modern contexts (Pavlich 2000). Moreover, the alignment between modern adjudication, critique and judgement, and between adjudicator, critic and judge, served to privilege the decisions as a cut, a litmus test; the point was not to reveal, but to judge the truth. The depth grammar is implicit: critique emerged as a practice of judging particular social conditions against criteria to advance a society's path to progress. That founding (if seldom articulated) grammar hovers almost imperceptibly over the unfolding Enlightenment conventions that came to define modern critique. But what surface grammar did those conventions enable?

Although multiple, modern surface grammars of critique tended to follow a three-fold rule structure that defined legitimate critical practices. To begin with, critics were to outline and formulate justified, founded and ahistorical normative criteria that defined 'ideal', 'progressive' or 'advanced' states of being (Benhabib 1986). Of course, there were many different ways to arrive at these criteria, and their content varied immensely from approach to approach. For instance, Kantian-inspired reflexive critiques sought metaphysically defensible and universally applicable ethical foundations – an approach echoed and yet developed by various critics. By contrast, praxis-orientated Marxists were more inclined to conceive of progressive critique as emerging from ideals generated through concrete historical struggles. Critical theorists, such as Habermas (1996, 1987), inflected a praxis orientation by calling for rational communicative practices of a 'discourse ethics' whereby participants of a 'deliberative democracy' delineate valid criteria. Though different, each of these approaches follows a surface grammar that requires them initially to define a progressive and/or rationally justified set of standards (ideals) as the markers, the foundational criteria, upon which any subsequent critical judgement will be based (Bernstein 1988). Thereafter, the surface grammar requires critics to describe – in analytically legitimate ways – a given social context or set of circumstances. Finally, critics were to *judge* context against criteria in order to prescribe change that would necessarily lead societies to more advanced orders. Even with many different conceptions of these stages, the underlying surface grammar remains, as does the attachment to practices of founded judgement. Without the latter, prospective critics are unlikely to be considered 'serious critics', or may even be deemed 'uncritical' (Pavlich 2005).

It is perhaps important here to review an associated critical promise to bring about social advancement through decisive critiques based on founded judgement. To be sure, this is an extraordinary promise to make, and one that is difficult to uphold. How could any ideal declare with certainty a universally valid guide to future social advancement or progressive social being? Even if one were prepared to overlook the inevitable imperialism of such conceptual certainty, it would be reckless to ignore the unparalleled bloodshed that over the centuries has flowed in the name of purportedly universal criteria: colonial images of 'civilization', eugenic science's racial hierarchies, Nazi visions of racial purity, Stalin's ideals of collective progress, apartheid's 'separate but equal' orders, etc ... These highly perilous yardsticks were not purged by modern grammars of critique; nor did the atrocities carried out under their auspices evaporate in an ethos of judgemental critique. Perhaps modern critics did not – and indeed could never – provide ahistorical guarantees against collective injustice, inequity, social exclusion or cruelty (Bauman 1994, 1987). Resilient beliefs in social progress assured by founded judgement may even have blinded participants to the dangers of asserting an intrinsic progress to modern social engineering (whatever visions might have driven the latter). Assertions of independently founded and progressive judgement also became increasingly difficult to sustain under what Bauman (1992:18) describes as social conditions fraught with an "ambient uncertainty". Whether referred to as postmodern or late modern, these conditions reflected an intractable disagreement about the very possibility of finding universal criteria and whether – as Lyotard's (1984) work argues – that quest is even vaguely credible.

Interestingly, one might note the extent to which Kant's critiques of aesthetic judgement (directed at beauty) appear to expand critical practices beyond that of founded judgement. As Kant puts it, to judge beauty, the critic must engage in a sort of reflexive analysis that empathises with other judges; it is not a matter of referring to Archimedean criteria, but to a more publicly minded quest that puts the critic in the shoes of another judge. Developing Kant here, Le Roux notes:

> Aesthetic judgements therefore require not the impersonal operation of logic, but rather an imaginative and self-corrective dialogue with others, otherness and difference. Seen in this light, good taste embodies a critical sense for the public or a public spirit. A reflexive judgement of this sort has as its essential precondition the existence of a plurality of viewpoints. It is a mode of judgement that not only celebrates dialogical openness, but depends for its possibility on a resistance to any drive towards the formalisation or closure of this dialogical openness. (Le Roux 2006:115)

In such formulations, one detects rumblings of another series of questions: Were the distended promises of judgemental criticism doomed from the outset? Could one instead leave room for a less totalising version of critique? Is it possible to reinvigorate ideas about criticism through a grammar not predicated upon practices of founded judgement, but which nevertheless pursue ways to open up new social, political, cultural and indeed linguistic horizons?

Critique without founded judgement?

As noted, the term 'critic' harbours etymological links with the Greek *krinein*, which connoted practices of separating, perceiving, dividing, discerning, etc. This suggests another possibility: critique need not be tied to practices of founded judgement, and might even be conceived as an indeterminate, interpretative practice that unravels textures of contextual meaning. In other words, one could reimagine critique as permanently opening up given representations, rationales and practices that become settled as 'necessary' within an order, and thereby remaining permanently open to other forms of life. No doubt, interpretative work of this kind cannot expect to provide certain or absolute assurances. It might be seen to disrupt (say) unjust, or exclusive, meanings or practices that ensconce specific forms of life, permanently projecting out towards other life forms. This interpretative work would reorder familiar meanings and question taken-for-granted, everyday ideas and practices, and its aim might be to expose underlying assumptive universes by naming diktats that operate from within the silent shadows of preconception. Clearly, this idea of critique taps into experiences that reach beyond what currently exists; it is less aligned with questions of how to be than of how 'to become' (Pavlich 2011).

One might note that Barthes, some time ago, also referenced an approach to critique without judgement:

> So long as criticism had the traditional function of judging, it could not but be conformist, that is to say in conformity with the interests of the judges. However, the true 'criticism' of institutions and languages does not consist in judging them, but in perceiving, in separating, in dividing. (Barthes 1987:33)

Though not wanting to echo his aspirations to retrieve an authentic ('true') form of criticism, I nevertheless endorse his observation that judgemental grammars of critique privilege the underlying 'interests of the judges'. Those interests are reflected in the (implicit or explicit) criteria used to make critical judgements. An alternative approach to criticism, says Barthes, might emphasise practices of perceiving over defining, separating over unifying, dividing over deciding, and discerning over judging. And he was certainly not alone it this view. Foucault echoes the call to envisage criticism beyond judgement in a rather lyrical passage:

> I can't help but dream of a kind of criticism that would try not to judge but to bring an oeuvre, a book, a sentence, an idea to life; it would light fires, watch the grass grow, listen to the wind, and catch the sea foam in the breeze and scatter it. It would multiply not judgements but signs of existence; it would summon them, drag them from their sleep. Perhaps it would invent them sometimes – all the better. (Foucault 1994:323)

Both positions refuse a modern blackmail that previously linked critique and founded judgement. They also point to the prospect of a different approach to critique, one that emphasises a reflective experience of becoming, and hence a kind of 'negotiating dissociation' from unfolding conditions that anticipate and welcome what might become. This approach involves a unique set of conventions and experiences of a different form of life.

The matter is, of course, complex. However, critical practices that do not define themselves through founded judgement suggest a different grammar. One might, for example, propose a kind of critique that works from a liminal threshold and is propelled variously through local engagements with the limits of social context, culture, language and legal framework to open up to new forms of life. The active gesture need not be one of founded judgement; rather, I suggest that critique could work through a 'dissociation' of familiar surface grammars and social processes in a quest to appropriate a future. As an event, the dissociative critique might strive to confront the indeterminate voids that support present limits and commence the always 'unsettled and unsettling' task of forging new horizons of meaning. To be sure, such an approach to critique can never offer the self-assurances of a firm *telos* that guarantees universally progressive societal transformation. Indeed, a dissociative grammar of critique deliberately works against totalising thought, including forms that claim to be necessary or universally valid. Its promise lies not in illusory universal ideals; instead, it remains forever open to other ways of thinking and becoming. Deluded closures may breed despotic acts. All this does not render an open grammar and experience of critique irrelevant to post-colonial contexts; on the contrary, it makes such critique pivotal. What that grammar might look like exactly, and how it could be articulated to legitimate the adjudicative processes of a transformative constitutionalism is a matter for continued discussion. However, echoing the 'aesthetic turn' previously noted, one might at least point to selected, but instructive, snippets of post-apartheid novels and art forms to help enunciate the outline of a grammar of dissociative critique.

Negotiating dissociation: a requiem for judgemental critique?

The comments below extend my earlier conceptions of (following Foucault) a governmental grammar of critique – 'how not to be governed thus' – and (drawing on Derrida) a deconstructive opening up to spaces beyond (Pavlich 2005, 2000). I continue to see congruent value in both trajectories; however, alluding to the surface and depth grammars of a dissociative critique that could be broadly attached to legal contexts, and transformative constitutionalism in particular, might extend them. As an initial gesture, my allusions will speak briefly to how versions of Wittgenstein's depth and surface grammars could shape a dissociative critique.

Depth grammar I: precipitating dissociative critique

Existing within an everyday social ethos, participants seldom reflexively examine or challenge the limits that constitute them as particular kinds of contextual beings. The depth grammars through which they come to engage meaningfully, make sense of, and act in a social context remain hidden. Yet, precisely at those moments where limits to particular forms of life are experienced as deeply problematic, subjects inaugurate unusual processes to name aspects of their subjection; at such moments, focusing on given limit-horizons becomes possible. To be sure, experiencing these limits is important for subsequent transformations. However, the precipitating event required for the dissociations that might eventually enable significant social transformation usually requires a more sustained engagement with – and dissociation from – the unspoken conventions of a context. One might say that critical forms of life start at a moment which Foucault elsewhere refers to as a "preface to transgression" (1977b:29) – the point at which subjects are sufficiently discontented to contemplate actively 'how not to be governed thus'.[3] Whatever else, Foucault's insights here reference a critical grammar that provokes subjects to imagine the dissolution of themselves and their current ways of being, and to consider ways to live outside of what they have come to be.

In legal arenas, various promises of justice, or conceptions of injustice, are mostly the spurs for dissociative thinking. Here one might recognise Derrida's (2002) important considerations of justice as an infinite promise; something that can never be rendered finite and yet requires calculation from within finite contexts. Perhaps too, the immediacy of 'phrasing injustice' in context may often serve as an incentive to open up to porous limits through which new forms of life may emerge (Pavlich 1998). In either case, the experience of disruptive – 'unsettled and unsettling' – moments within a given order is less abstractly captured through the development of characters in several recent South African novels.

For example, a central character of Ingrid Winterbach's *Die Boek van Toeval en Toeverlaat* (*The Book of Happenstance*) (2006), Helena Verwey is profoundly shocked by the incidental theft of her valuable and beloved shell collection. Yet this disruptive event leads to an unexpected reflection on her seeming abandonment between life and death. It propels Helena to an unyielding reflection on – and naming of – the contingency through which her current life moves along a path towards its eventual dissolution. Recognising the pervasive coincidence of all that she does brings her to a surprising realisation: the orders that have contoured her comfortable and often self-assured forms of life have emerged from accidental events, ironic concurrences and sheer chance. One might think that embracing the 'happenstance' quality of her life would prove disabling. On the contrary, however, Helena shows that the

[3] See Foucault in Kelly 1994.

very acknowledgement of a contingent way of being incites a renewed quest for another life. Thus we find her actively transgressing the anchors – including her past absorption with a shell collection – that had stabilised her former being. This renewed vitality yields a certain calm, and by the end of the novel she experiences, without consternation, feelings of loss and hopeful anticipation that at once project her through and out of the ordering formations of existing forms of life.

From a rather different vantage, but also signalling a form of life where a dissociative critique could operate, Njabulo Ndebele's *The Cry of Winnie Mandela* (2003) – a fictional characterisation of Winnie Mandela – questions how lives obsessed with order tend to drown out the chaotic foundations that contour their contingent existence. The fictional Winnie tells us that there is a link between "housekeeping and order", between the everyday practices, spaces and arrangements that eventually all get "structured into the mind and reproduce in cities that are built into grids of order" (Ndebele 2003:106). She continues: "I think this kind of order is one of the central features of whiteness. We were all 'civilised' into it" (*ibid*). The subtle (and not so subtle) elements that order a given form of life are indispensable to its continuation. Ironically, disruption may even work to preserve that order, because the effects of "[...] the disruptiveness of disorder on a mind structured into order" can be profound: "[D]eliberate disruption can be used as a device to make you desire more order. It ensures your perpetual compliance to some overriding law of control. You are deprived of order in order to desire is even more" (*ibid*:107). Here Ndebele insightfully shows how order often attaches itself so elementally to subject identities that it satisfies "daily personal needs". Order may even become a "natural law" and, "[a]t that point, the origins of man-made control disappear forever. Recalling those origins can become an act of resistance punishable by death" (*ibid*).

With that in mind, the words spoken by a fictional Winnie Mandela arrest her everyday reliance on the limits of an existing form of life, seeking a kind of death that simultaneously opens up to an "instinctual knowledge". This residual knowledge grows stronger as her torturers empty "order out of [her]". Ndebele's Winnie Mandela understands that jettisoning a past order required an "[...] emptying out of my life. My law of resistance emerged from the gradual emptying out of my life. Here was my law: embrace disruption, and then rage against order instead of longing for it" (2003:107). Ndebele artfully describes the fundamental exertions associated with a disrupted being, at the same time suggesting elements of a depth grammar for dissociative critique; that is, emerging from one form of life, resisting its deep hold, has profound implications for subjects who defy, dissociate and welcome new forms of life. This is not a matter of simple choice or fashionable opinion. It is a rather more profound disruption that, if successful, leads to a partial dissociation of past ways of being and an opening up to new forms of living with others.

In their respective ways, Winterbach and Ndebele help us to understand how a dissociated critique may be precipitated from within given limit-horizons or historical orders. Their selected insights suggest that this critique could assume multiple forms; however, it always involves a recognition that things might be otherwise, or that existing limits and orders of life are neither providential nor essential. This appreciation prompts difficult dissociative gestures that disrupt current orders and open up to the arrival of other ways of being. Reflective subjects who problematise their current lives concurrently welcome alternative futures and open up to what may yet come (Derrida 2000, 1999). If anything, this process involves liminal and disquieting events that lean permanently towards a future order recalibrated out of a variously rejected present. If there is a constant dimension to the depth grammar of a dissociative critique, it does not reside in specific reflections on limits, immediate calculations of injustice, or even the disordering of an order. Rather, it is the permanent recognition that any historical ordering may be dissociated. In fact, this could even be taken as an indeterminate 'law' of contingency, if by that we signal not regularity, but the perpetual and unforeseeable possibility of being governed otherwise. Thus, both order and its dissociation remain permanent possibilities; neither is ever fixed as a state or a law that cannot be undone. Recognising that disruption could invite stronger connections to an order, a dissociative critique may disrupt, but that disruption also reorders by installing new grammars and meanings. To change attachments to an existing order requires at least a recognition of their contingency, coupled with fundamental (life-changing) experiences through which other forms of life are actively sought. Ndebele's novel nicely exemplifies the indeterminacy of dissociative critique and emphasises – through the myth of Penelope who waits – the importance to social change of anticipation of another future, another form of life.

Depth grammar II: negotiating dissociation

Once precipitated, critique located at the threshold of ordering limits often involves undifferentiated experiences of the sheer voids beyond, negotiating a dissociation that taps into the chaos of what is deemed impossible from within historically ordered realms of possibility. An experience of this amorphous 'impossible' characterises a key moment of dissociative critique. The latter extends through the voids of porous limits of historical social orderings by naming contingent limit formations as somehow in need of change and iconoclastically opening up meanings to prospects of what may be. Such abstracted formulations of this aspect of dissociative critique's depth grammar may be illustrated by referring to the perceptive insights of selected post-apartheid fiction and visual art forms.

Consider, for example, David Lurie's disgraced life and fragile redemption in JM Coetzee's *Disgrace* (2000), as he confronts the crumbling order of his past academic world, the dissolution of apartheid structures, and the violent attack that signals so graphically the reordering of his daughter Lucy's farm. This attack, in which both are battered – Lucy is raped and Lurie set alight – provides a terrible allegory for disruptive events, which in this instance render the limits of an order porous and highlight in graphic ways the borders sustaining them. Facing up to the impossibilities of the absence that defined those borders, and contoured her past identity, Lucy fatalistically embraces what is to come, welcoming a responsibility to the absence-becoming-present of a disrupted ordering in the process of yielding to another future. Petrus, an erstwhile worker on Lucy's farm, whose status reverses in a new post-apartheid ordering, is initially silent on events, or uses words in a way that sounds odd to Lurie's ears. But as the narrative unfolds, Petrus' voice becomes confident and more easily understandable as conditions that once appeared 'impossible' gradually surface as more than possibility. Lurie's inability to face the once impossible meanings that take shape through the events around him, and the disgrace that has disallowed a return to any semblance of his past academic life, lead him to another form of life, where the clear distinction between 'the human' and 'the animal' blurs.

The sheer allegorical force of the book may overwhelm, but for our purposes here it offers a nuanced description of how different characters experience limits and confront what previously seemed impossible. Coetzee's book also highlights how disruptions propel a negotiation of new life forms. To be sure, disruptions are not always as extreme and violent as the ones depicted in the novel, but they likely involve a profound disorientation that glimpses chaos and propels a reordering. This unsettled threshold can be described as the place from whence dissociation is negotiated and attempts made to project reordered lives out of previously imagined voids. Coetzee provides glimpses into how various characters negotiate dissociation, disgrace and the difficult life-changing experiences required for fragile accommodations to new conditions. Through such negotiations, subjects actively appropriate new grammars and lexicons as part of receding or emerging forms of life. In parenthesis, Winterbach's novel also suggests how such negotiations may return to past uses of language to appropriate new horizons of meaning. For example, Helena and Theo Verwey embark on a project to compile a dictionary of Afrikaans words that are no longer used, but which variously help to open new literary possibilities and ways to assemble meanings in changing socio-political contexts. The recovery of such words forms a backdrop to the coincidental happenings (happenstance) that the book narrates – and one might also note here how a language (Afrikaans) faces radically altering forms of life by attempting to recover lexicons in efforts to find traction in a context of shifting limit formations and orders.

Equally, William Kentridge's art develops from the threshold of an experience that wavers between the order of existing meaning horizons and the chaos of days past or those yet to arrive. His fascination reminds us of contingent repetitions and the scope of the terrain at hand: "[...] there's a lot of change from chaos to order and order back to chaos. *Da Capo*".[4] Noting the ever-incomplete indeterminacy involved in ordering chaos, or indeed the dissociations that render order chaotic, it also indicates the porous and never-ending residues of emerging conditions. Kentridge uses a film technique that eventuates a threshold terrain between order and chaos:

> I suppose the possibility of reversing film or tape is so seductive because of its immediately revealing what the world is like if time is reversed, what it would be like if we could remember the future. [...] Tear a sheet of paper in half and it restores itself without the smallest crease. There is an extreme politeness of objects; pull a book out of a shelf and when you replace it, the books at each side at the last instance shift just the right amount to make space. From chaos there is return to order. The page of text returns letter by letter, word by word into the pen, leaving the load of ink pregnant with infinite possibilities.[5]

---

4 http://www.tate.org.uk/tateetc/issue15/kentridge.htm (Access date: 20 January 2011)

5 http://www.gallerytpw.ca/publications/pdf/1006-Kentridge.pdf (Access date: 5 February 2011)

Highlighting Kentridge's notion of 'remembering a future' in a context 'pregnant with infinite possibilities' provides a way to mark out the uncertainties of a threshold, dissociative topography. Having viscerally experienced disruptions to a limited ordering, critics at that threshold negotiate the prospect of moving beyond limit-formations by naming their contingent outlines and reaching out to other possible meaning horizons. These horizons are often framed as 'impossible' or infinite, without rules for language games, but as dissociative critics negotiate new orderings and rules for words, new sign constellations and associated forms of life, they engage a terrain considered chaotic from within a previous order. Kentridge's reference to *Da Capo* signifies the indeterminate, permeable, disordered, uncertain, unpredictable and relentless unfolding through which order and chaos contour social transformations. Often detected in words after the fact, this process traces an elusive depth grammar that negotiates dissociation and a redefined life calibrated out of a sustaining chaos.

Intimations of a surface grammar

Three illustrative techniques could transpire from such a depth grammar to become rules for a surface grammar and so guide practices of dissociative critique. First, Van Marle, in her discussion of Kentridge's potential insight for critique, points to the allegorical kinship between the indeterminate performances of criticism and drawing. She quotes Kentridge on this matter:

> I believe that in the indeterminacy of drawing, the contingent way that images arrive in the work, lies some kind of model of how we live our lives. The activity of drawing is a way of trying to understand who we are or how we operate in the world. It is in the strangeness of the activity itself that can be detected judgement, ethics and morality. Trains of thought that seem to be going nowhere but can't quite be brought to a conclusion. (Van Marle 2003:255)

The irresolute and scaled-down judgement referred to here is quite different from modern, criteria-based, 'founded' judgement. The indeterminate arrival of a drawing, an event that cannot occur without the practice of drawing, is allegorically akin to negotiating the dissociation of a social present and opening up to what is to arrive. In all this, there are no certainties, which means that all the more care, thought, or attention to detail and calculation are required as one pursues new orders from the backdrop of existing frames. But ultimately, the ethics to which Kentridge refers remains resolutely indeterminate. In this context, the practice of drawing could provide an exemplar for the sort of practices employed by dissociative critique in legal contexts.

Secondly, the required calculations involved in negotiated dissociations are contoured neither by absolute openings, nor by pointed judgemental closures. Here, privilege cannot be granted neither to closure, unity and gathering, nor to complete dissociation – none of these is ever fully possible, and they may even define death. However, in unfolding forms of life, the ever-contingent interplay between closure and openness, and the parasitic relations between order and chaos, critique and structure, are fully acknowledged. Techniques that recognise the heterogeneity involved in dissociative challenges to an order also thereby affirm their responsibilities to chaotic absent others who form the basis of all ordered sociality. One might here confront rules that recognise the tendency to order and yet always preserve the chaotic contingencies that enable any ordering (including the one here articulated).

Finally, as should be clear, dissociative grammars of critique are involved not with defining being in absolute terms or specifying how ideally to be; they are concerned with becoming (Pavlich 2011). Therefore, such critique requires particular techniques for indeterminate performances that allow a society to unfold, to become in ways that are other than those that support current orderings. Though these are likely to be multiple, one might refer to Motha's (2009) rules for initiating a contingent version of *ubuntu* to inspire a transformative constitutionalism of becoming. Equally, Fitzpatrick's (2001) determinacy-responsiveness couplet may be considered as an important technique for understanding the indeterminacy of all determined legal decisions, including those with constitutional inflections. In emphasising becoming, these approaches to legal adjudication embrace the indeterminacy of a given decision and the order that it seeks to gather. One might extract from them a key grammatical rule to guide critique's practices of becoming other by enunciating refusals, interpretative openings and negotiations that create new forms of life.

Provocation

By way of a provocation in lieu of a conclusion, I might repeat that the critical grammar assembled above does not license given universes of meaning to close themselves off from further discussion by claiming to be necessary, certain, inevitable, universal, absolute, and so on. The depth and surface grammars of a dissociative critique allegorically compare the critic to a nomad in constant search of new forms of life, for existence beyond the limits of what currently is there. This critic's task is not to judge; it is to challenge and negotiate a dissociation of contingent limits that are contextually framed as unjust, unequal and exclusive. Critical practice would thus involve continuous interpretation that separates out, discerns and opens conventional meaning horizons; it might also provoke dissociations of (or at least elements of) current social orders. As Adorno recognised, critique is not simply a matter of resisting for the sake of resisting; it is intimately tied to democracy and the never-ending process of thwarting totalitarian socio-political and legal formations. Equally, dissociative critique's promise is to pursue a different life in the name of such noble – if never fully calculable – ideals as justice, equality and democratic patterns of association. It is precisely *because* these virtues are ultimately incalculable that the critic's task of undoing any so-called necessities of totalising calculations may become urgent. Criticism has no end, and its vitality is basic to imagining the promises of just, anti-totalitarian and democratic collective futures.

Projected more directly onto constitutional legal horizons in post-apartheid settings, the proposed grammar of critique may ponder law's capacity to adjudicate more broadly and to conceptualise its 'reasoning' as contingently deferred chains of meaning that themselves are always in flux. This grammar could allow for critique to embed itself in adjudicative processes, thereby promising a much more tentative transformative constitutionalism than is implied by Klare's explicit calculations of a progressive order. It might call for contingent calculations that work with different preconceptions of justice, but which always remain attentive to the ways in which law limits, is limited by, and occupies an obdurately liminal place when it must decide or make its cuts. Whether this sort of posture could ever be 'licit' (far less 'orthodox') within the context of transformative constitutional adjudication remains, of course, to be conceived. Certainly, under current legal orders this would be a hard case to make. But there is another, perhaps more fundamental, matter. One must also recognise that any critical project associated with transformative constitutionalism – whether judgement-orientated or dissociative – always finds its expression at unique moments, namely those moments where events in context propel reflection upon limits, enable the 'phrasing of injustice', and entice a longing for the possible dissolution of, rather than an attachment to, a given ordering. Though the permanent possibility of this critical event happening must be preserved, I wonder whether the structure of critique isn't *essentially* parasitic, or at least residually dependent on the formation of order that grounds (by definition) any dissociation. To be blunt, without orderings of some kind, there is no critique, no critic, no criticism, and nothing to resist. One might then argue that dissociative critique could never be driven into the heart of transformative constitutional law. But I think, on the contrary, that it is precisely constitutional law's call to order – even in its transformative versions – that makes it such a fecund arena for the perpetual gaze of dissociative critique. The contours of dissociative critique's possible attachment to transformative constitutional adjudication may remain tenaciously undecided, but not so the democratic import of embedding its always unsettling thresholds into the heart of constitutional practice that 'cuts' and orders.

Reference List

Adorno T. 1998. *Critical models: Interventions and catchwords*. New York: New York University Press.

Ayto J. 1990. *Dictionary of word origins*. London: Bloomsbury.

Barthes R. 1987. *Criticism and truth*. Minneapolis, MN: University of Minnesota Press.

Bauman Z. 1994. *Alone again: Ethics after certainty*. London: Demos.

— 1992. *Intimations of postmodernity*. London: Routledge.

— 1987. *Legislators and interpreters: On modernity, post-modernity and intellectuals*. Cambridge: Polity Press.

Bayle P. 1952. *Selections from Bayle's dictionary*. New York: Greenwood Press.

Benhabib S. 1986. *Critique, norm and utopia – A study of the foundations of critical theory*. New York: Columbia University Press.

Bernstein RJ. 1988. Metaphysics, critique and utopia. *Review of metaphysics* 42(December):255-273.

Coetzee JM. 2000. *Disgrace*. London: Vintage.

Connerton P. 1980. *The tragedy of enlightenment: an essay on the Frankfurt School*. Cambridge: Cambridge University Press.

Davis RC & Schleifer R. 1991. *Criticism and culture: The role of critique in modern literary theory*. Essex: Longman.

Dean M. 1994. *Critical and effective histories: Foucault's methods and historical sociology*. London: Routledge.

Derrida J. 2002. The force of law: the mystical foundations of authority. In: G Anidjar (ed). *Acts of religion*. London: Routledge. 228-299.

— 2000. *Of hospitality*. Stanford, CA: Stanford University Press.

— 1999. *Adieu to Emmanuel Levinas*. Stanford, CA: Stanford University Press.

Fairlamb HL. 1994. *Critical conditions: Postmodernity and the question of foundations*. Cambridge: Cambridge University Press.

Fitzpatrick P. 2001. *Modernism and the grounds of law*. Cambridge: Cambridge University Press.

Foucault M. 2001. *Fearless speech*. Los Angeles: Semiotext(e).

— 2000. *Power*. New York: New Press.

— 1994. *Politics, philosophy and culture*. New York: Routledge.

— 1980. *Power/knowledge: Selected interviews and other writings 1972-1977*. New York: Pantheon Books.

— 1977a. *Discipline and punish: The Birth of the Prison*. New York: Pantheon Books.

— 1977b. *Language, counter-memory, practice: Selected essays and interviews*. Ithaca, NY: Cornell University Press.

Habermas J. 1996. *The Habermas Reader*. Cambridge, UK: Polity Press.

— 1987. *The Philosophical Discourse of Modernity: Twelve lectures*. Cambridge, MA: MIT Press.

Hutchings K. 1996. *Kant critique and politics*. London: Routledge.

Kant I. 1958. *Fundamental principles of the metaphysic of morals*. Indianapolis: Bobbs-Merrill Educational Publishing.

Kelly M (ed). 1994. *Critique and power: Recasting the Foucault/Habermas debate*. Cambridge, MA: MIT Press.

Klare KE. 1998. Legal culture and transformative constitutionalism. *South African Journal on Human Rights* 14:146-188.

Koselleck R. 1988. *Critique and crisis – enlightenment and the pathogenesis of modern society*. Oxford: Berg.

Kripke S. 1982. *Wittgenstein on rules and private language*. Cambridge, MA: Harvard University Press.

Le Roux W. 2006. The aesthetic turn in the post-apartheid constitutional rights discourse. *Tydskrif vir die Suid-Afrikaanse Reg* 1:101-120.

Lyotard JF. 1984. *The postmodern condition: A report on knowledge*. Minneapolis, MN: University of Minnesota Press.

Motha S. 2009. Archiving colonial sovereignty: from ubuntu to a jurisprudence of sacrifice. *South African Public Law* 24(2):297-327.

Ndebele NS. 2003. *The cry of Winnie Mandela*. Oxford: Ayebia.

Pavlich G. 2011. *Law and society redefined*. Toronto: Oxford University Press.

— 2005. Experiencing critique. *Law and Critique* 16:95-112.

— 2001. The art of critique, or How not to be governed thus. In: G Wickham & G Pavlich (eds). *Rethinking law, society and governance: Foucault's bequest*. Oxford: Hart Publishers.

— 2000. *Critique and radical discourses on crime*. Aldershot: Ashgate.

— 1998. Phrasing injustice: Critique in an uncertain ethos. *Studies in Law, Politics and Society* 18:245-269.

— 1996. *Justice fragmented: mediating community disputes under postmodern conditions*. London: Routledge.

— 1995. Contemplating a postmodern sociology: Genealogy, limits and critique. *The Sociological Review* 43(3):549-567.

Pitkin H. 1973. *Wittgenstein and justice*. Berkeley, CA: University of California Press.

Roux T. 2009. Transformative constitutionalism. *Stellenbosch Law Review* 2:258-285.

Truit P. 2004. *Race, law, resistance*. London: Glasshouse Press.

Van der Walt J. 2005. *Law and sacrifice: Towards a post-apartheid theory of law*. London: The Glasshouse Press.

Van Marle K. 2009. Transformative constitutionalism as/and critique. *Stellenbosch Law Review* 2:286-301.

— 2003. Law's time, particularity and slowness. *South African Journal on Human Rights* 2:239-255.

Williams R. 1983. *Keywords: A vocabulary of culture and society*. Oxford: Oxford University Press.

Winterbach I. 2006. *Die boek van toeval en toeverlaat*. Cape Town: Human & Rousseau.

Wittgenstein L. 1983. *Philosophical Investigations*. London: Blackwell.

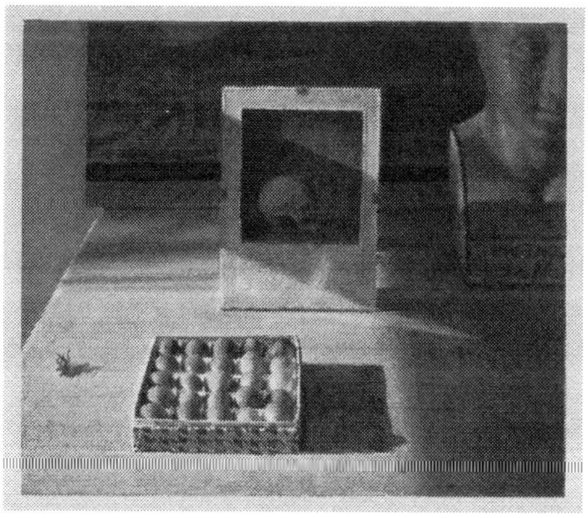

FROM THE BRIDGE TO THE BOOK

An examination of South Africa's transformative constitutionalism's neglected metaphor[1]

Mark Antaki

Introduction

The Epilogue to South Africa's Interim Constitution of 1993, entitled 'National Unity and Reconciliation', opens with one metaphor (the bridge) and closes with another (the book). It opens by describing the Constitution as a bridge between an apartheid past and a human rights future:

> This Constitution provides a historic bridge between the past of a deeply divided society characterized by strife, conflict, untold suffering and injustice, and a future founded on the recognition of human rights, democracy and peaceful co-existence and development opportunities for all South Africans, irrespective of colour, race, class, belief or sex.

1 I would like to thank the other members of the *Genres of Critique* project, the participants in a one-day workshop at the Stellenbosch Institute for Advanced Studies (STIAS), the participants in the iPLAI Artefacts of Memory seminar, and the participants in a Faculty of Law faculty seminar at McGill University (Montreal, Canada) for their comments, suggestions and help in framing some of this project. I would also like to thank Venetia Boehmer-Plotz, Karen Crawley, Ian Dahlman, Mireille Fournier, Jessica Magonet, Zain Naqi and Alexandra Popovici for their thoughtful help.

The paragraphs that follow underscore the need for understanding and *ubuntu*,[2] rather than vengeance, and instruct Parliament to adopt amnesty legislation. The Epilogue closes with a different metaphor, namely the book:

> With this Constitution and these commitments, we, the people of South Africa, open a new chapter in the history of our country.

South African legal scholars and judges alike have written about the bridge metaphor. Probably earliest and most prominent of these writings was Etienne Mureinik's. In 1994, he wrote:

> If this bridge is successfully to span the open sewer of violent and contentious transition, those who are entrusted with its upkeep will need to understand very clearly what it is a bridge from, and what a bridge to. (Mureinik 1994:31)[3]

The answer Mureinik supplied was that the bridge was a bridge from a culture of authority (and Parliamentary supremacy) to a culture of justification (and judicial review of legislation under constitutional supremacy).[4] Though the Epilogue characterises the *Interim* Constitution (my emphasis) itself as the 'bridge', the bridge rapidly became the dominant metaphor for a "long-term" (Klare 1998:150) South African project of 'transformative constitutionalism' (Langa 1996; Klare 1998; Ackerman 2004)[5] featuring the attainment of substantive equality and social justice. As André van der Walt writes:

> [T]he 'post-amble' was left out of the 1996 Final Constitution, but the image of the Constitution as a bridge between the old and the new social and legal order survived as a paradigm metaphor for constitutional transformation discourse in general. (Van der Walt 2001:259)

The South African Constitutional Court also seized on the metaphor, notably in its 1995 *Makwanyane* (declaring the death penalty unconstitutional) and 1996 *AZAPO* (upholding the amnesty) judgements. The metaphor of the bridge may even have led, and is certainly related, to a broader scholarly consideration of metaphors in South African law and legal discourse and of their relation to the requirements and possibilities of a transformative constitutionalism (Pretorius 1998; Botha 2003, 2002).[6]

---

2 On *ubuntu*, see, for example, Ramose 2002 and Cornell & Muvangua 2011.

3 Mureinik uses other metaphors as well. On p 32 he introduces "gardeners" and a "forest of apartheid statutes", and refers to the Bill of Rights as the constitution's "chief strut." On p 48, the Bill of Rights becomes a "weapon" for democracy.

4 Mureinik's articulation of a shift from a (political and legal) culture of authority to one of justification has been taken up in the global discourse of constitutionalism and, especially, judicial review of legislation. See, for example, Cohen-Eliya & Porat 2011.

5 The language of transformative constitutionalism suggests radical reform(ation) or even something akin to revolution, albeit achieved by way of law. For example, Ackerman (2004:646) refers to a "constitutional revolution", while Langa (1996:352) writes of a "social and economic revolution".

6 For example, in Part 1 of his two-part article, Henk Botha (2002:613) argues that "the reflective use of metaphors can help South African lawyers to break with the essentialism and reductionism of apartheid legal thought, transform legal theory and practice, and

By comparison, however, the metaphor of the book has received very little, if any, attention. Indeed, I have yet to find a more than cursory reference to the 'chapter' – or to the book of which it is presumably a part.[7] It is no surprise, then, that I have not come across works considering both metaphors together.

This article aims to remedy the widespread – and unfortunate – neglect of the book metaphor by taking the reference to the 'chapter' in the Epilogue as seriously as legal scholars and judges have taken the reference to the bridge metaphor. Rather than ignore the bridge metaphor, however, this article takes its cue from André van der Walt's thoughtful treatment of it. Van der Walt (2001) challenges the dominant interpretation of the metaphor as one of progress from one place (the apartheid past) to another (the bright, post-apartheid future) and raises the crucial and difficult question of what a truly transformative – as opposed to progressive – 'ethos' might look like. His critique of the forward-moving linearity of the bridge metaphor relies on a deep connection between openness to a future we cannot master and a (vulnerable) openness to (vulnerable) others.[8]

Inspired by Van der Walt's reworking of the bridge metaphor, I attempt to shed some light on the book metaphor. I do so by taking what may seem to be a strange focal point: Antjie Krog's account of her refusal to write a novel in her controversial *Begging to be black* (2009). The novel (book) she refuses to write, I argue, is akin to the dominant interpretation of the bridge outlined by Van der Walt. And the reasons why she refuses to write this book are rather close to Van der Walt's critique of the dominant interpretation. What is more, an examination of the rich and revealing metaphor of the book – understood as a novel – furthers the direction of Van der Walt's thought. Van der Walt's article hints at what we may call the co-constitution of ethics and art (or what we now call aesthetics). The metaphor of the book, particularly when interpreted in the light of Krog's refusal to write a novel, highlights the (aesthetic) question of 'genre', which accompanies or helps answer the (ethical) question of what a truly transformative 'ethos'[9] might look like. For example, as David Scott (2005) has

imagine more humane futures". Botha identifies the "container metaphor" as central to apartheid and follows André van der Walt in pointing to the complicity of Roman-Dutch property law in apartheid due to its emphasis on exclusivity and absoluteness. Botha argues that the Constitution requires a move away from legal formalism and its preoccupation with boundaries to a more relational understanding of rights. On a similar move away from formalism and boundary-talk in Canadian constitutional law, see Risk 1996. See also Meyer 2000, who argues for this kind of move in American constitutional rights adjudication.

7 For example, in his 1996 article, Cockrell adopts Dworkin's 'chain novel' metaphor and writes: "[T]he past year has presented an opportunity for the Constitutional Court to write the first chapter in the great South African novel of judicial review" (1996:1; see also Dworkin (1986:229)). However, Cockrell's article does not mention the Epilogue and it is difficult to see his turn to 'the novel' as anything more than a reference to Dworkin. For instance, he writes of a 'first' chapter, whereas the Epilogue refers to a 'new' one. What is more, Cockrell's 'novel' is one of judicial opinions, whereas the Epilogue's reference may be broader.

8 Cf the title of Lévinas 1987, *Time and the other*.

9 I am thinking of ethics in its primordial sense of 'dwelling place'.

suggested, tragedy, rather than romance, may be the genre, the narrative framework, which can best tell the story of the passage from the colonial to the post-colonial. It is counterintuitive, however, to think of tragedy as providing a transformative ethos, perhaps because tragedy does not appear to be about (trans)formation. Often, in tragedy, we witness the opposite: disintegration, deformation; even (self-)destruction.

Building on some of my previous and ongoing work,[10] I treat Krog's refusal of the novel as the refusal of a particular literary genre analogous to one of modernity's dominant forms of legality, namely human rights – in this case, human rights constitutionalism. Indeed, the close association between the novel and human rights[11] invites – if not warrants – a reading of the book of the Epilogue as a novel. Krog's refusal of the novel involves a refusal of at least two fantasies tied to a dominant version, and hence ethos, of human rights: the fantasy of identification or recognition (of knowing others or even oneself) and that of formation (of becoming a fully or well-formed – contained and finished – 'self'). Krog's refusal is at once the refusal of a novel that allows one to play out the fantasy of 'getting into' someone else's (or even one's own) head or heart, and the refusal of a novel that involves the movement of a protagonist towards a place where he or she arrives at a prefigured unity and maturity.[12]

Both Van der Walt's critique of the progressive bridge and Krog's refusal of the human rights novel invite a decentring of the will, and thus a simultaneous rethinking, or rather re-experiencing, of both futurity (human temporality) and alterity. Krog's refusal of the novel is akin to tragedy's refusal of the impossible combination of hero and author – of a hero who is also the author of his or her own story. This impossible combination appears as a prominent dream of modern constitutionalism and human rights. Problematising this hero/author and his or her story enables us to call into question the idea of the formation of this individual into a prefigured unity and maturity, as well as the possibility of knowledge of self and others that such an idea evokes and presupposes. Krog's refusal requires us to extricate the possibility of reciprocity from the horizon of a successful recognition or identification of self and other, a horizon which

---

10 This chapter builds on my previous work on Hannah Arendt, recognition and the imagination – see Antaki 2012, 2007 and Antaki & Kirkby 2009. It also builds on some of my ongoing work on global constitutionalism, specifically the rhetoric of proportionality (tied to a culture of justification), which should appear in 2013 in an edited Cambridge University Press volume, as well as some of my work on human rights and literary genres – work which was, of course, prompted by my participation in the *Genres of Critique* project of which this chapter is a product.

11 On this point, see Hunt 2008 and Slaughter 2007.

12 In this manner, the book metaphor complements and completes that of the bridge: the Epilogue discursively performs the unity and reconciliation the Constitution aims to achieve by ending with a paradoxical reference to an already united South African people (capable of) opening a new chapter in their own history. There are two prior occurrences of "the people of South Africa" in the Epilogue, but they do not have the same rhetorical force as this last one, in which the people of South Africa appear to undertake their first action as a "we" (cf Derrida 2002 and see also Honig 1991).

necessarily minimises or eliminates mutual vulnerability. Indeed, her refusal leads to a critical account of transformative constitutionalism, one that, paradoxically, involves transformation 'without' formation. To illustrate the implications of her refusal for both reciprocity and transformation 'without' formation, I conclude by briefly considering some of Robert Pippin's remarks about JM Coetzee's work. At stake in Krog's refusal of the novel she is invited to write is the possibility of reading the 'opening' of the 'new chapter' in the Epilogue as something other than the writing of – that is, both by and of – a newly sovereign, wilful author.

My reading of the bridge and the book suggests that these metaphors ought not to be grasped simply as South African metaphors or as metaphors of a historic South African moment or project. These metaphors are also, crucially, modern metaphors and metaphors of modernity. It is precisely for this reason that they resonate so easily and so deeply with many contemporary readers. These metaphors, like the South African Constitution's rights-guaranteeing provisions, contribute to making South African constitutionalism the exemplar of contemporary human rights constitutionalism, allowing jurists in South Africa and elsewhere to celebrate it as one of the world's most progressive constitutions. Indeed, many people apprehend South African constitutionalism as South Africa catching up to the rest of the world and, simultaneously, leading the way forward. Grappling with these metaphors may contribute to disentangling a South African story, or set of stories, from a broader story of legal and political modernisation and may complicate any superficial understanding, or hasty celebration of, a legal modernity. The scholars most invested in arguing that the South African constitutional order should be truly transformative are the scholars most interested in complicating a story of modernisation.[13] For many of them, the South African story must be more than the story of South Africa's socialisation into the civilised family of nations, characterised by human rights instruments and rhetoric, but also the institutions of global capitalism (Christodoulidis 2004).[14] It must be more than catching up with the 'end of history' (Fukuyama 1992) These scholars are on the lookout for a more critical understanding of transformation.[15] Examining the metaphors of the bridge and the book can help us catch a glimpse of this more critical understanding of transformation, that is, transformation without formation.

Before turning to Van der Walt, Krog, and company, I briefly review the appearance of the bridge and the chapter metaphors in *AZAPO* so as to show the judicial articulation of the bridge metaphor and the judicial dismissal of the Epilogue's chapter in favour of a book of accounts that must be closed. Are those who frame the book as a book of accounts to be closed implicitly rejecting the possibility of writing – or opening – a new chapter in the history of South Africa? Does one open a book (or a chapter), and of what kind, when one closes a book of accounts?

13 For example, Van Marle 2004:646.

14 Christodoulidis (2004:79) has already drawn attention to how the "liberalization" of constitutional law by way of human rights often conceals other liberalisations by way of global institutions such as the World Bank.

15 For example, Van Marle 2009:288.

The bridge and the book in *AZAPO*

While, as Pierre de Vos (2001:10) has noted, the South African Constitutional Court "first embraced the metaphor of the Constitution as a bridge in 1995 in *S v. Makwanyane*", *AZAPO* (1996) is particularly helpful in considering both metaphors and their relation to one another. In *AZAPO*, the Constitutional Court considered a challenge to s.20(7) of the Promotion of National Unity and Reconciliation Act (which authorised the Truth and Reconciliation Commission to grant amnesty) on the ground that amnesty to apartheid perpetrators violated the right of the victims to see the wrongdoers prosecuted and punished (s.22 of the Interim Constitution provides that "every person shall have the right to have justiciable disputes settled by a court of law [...] or impartial forum"). The Constitutional Court held that the (conditional) amnesty – that is, the granting of immunity from prosecution to offenders – and its purposes were constitutional. In so doing, it used the metaphors of the Epilogue. Whereas the Court, in a unanimous opinion penned by Mahomed DP, embraced the metaphor of the bridge, it transformed the implicit book of the Epilogue, of which the new chapter is a part, into a book of accounts that had to be closed.

The bridge metaphor appears four times in the judgement, and Mahomed refers to the bridge in (at least) three related ways: its erection or non-erection, its stability, and the comportment of those who walk over it. The first and probably most important reference is: "[...] but for a mechanism providing for amnesty, the 'historic bridge' itself might never have been erected" (*AZAPO* 1996:par.19; see also par.49). In other words, without a political decision to (legally) forget the past, a better and brighter future may not have been possible, because the "prospect of continuous retaliation and revenge" (*ibid*:par.19) would have been kept alive. The erection of the bridge, then, appears to stand for escape from a cycle of revenge, freeing South Africans from their past.[16] Second, had a bridge been possible without amnesty, "the bridge itself would have remained wobbly and insecure, threatened by fear from some and anger from others" (*ibid*). The bridge functions as a bridge not only because it connects two places, but because it does so securely. Third, keeping open "an abstract right to prosecution" without the necessary evidence would not do the victims any good, perpetuating their "legitimate sense of resentment and grief".[17] Under those circumstances, writes Mahomed,

> [...] both the victims and the culprits who walk on the 'historic bridge' described by the Epilogue will hobble more than walk to the future with heavy and dragged steps delaying and impeding a rapid and enthusiastic transition to the new society at the end of the bridge, which is the vision which informs the Epilogue. (*AZAPO* 1996:par.18)

16 This thought is worth comparing with Arendt's reflections on forgiveness in *The Human Condition* (1958). The erection of the bridge may even signal a metaphysical desire for an escape from a circular conception or experience of time to a linear one.

17 In other words, the political decision to (legally) forget the past is tied to a politics of memory, enabling the retrieval of a past. The use of "legitimate", particularly as an adjective qualifying "resentment" is striking. On the so-called legitimacy of resentment, see, for example, Minkinnen 2007 and Brudholm 2008.

Mahomed does not refer to the opening of a 'new chapter' in the history of South Africa. Nor does he treat the book of which the old and new chapters are a part as a history book or a novel. Rather, he treats the book of the Epilogue as a book of accounts that must be closed. As he writes:

> [...] it was realised that much of the unjust consequences of the past could not ever be fully reversed. It might be necessary in crucial areas to close the book on that past. (*AZAPO* 1996:par.2)

Later, he adds:

> Once the truth about the iniquities of the past has been established and made known, the book should be closed on them so that the catharsis thus engendered may divert the energies of the nation from a preoccupation with anguish and rancour to a future directed towards the goal which both the postscript to the Constitution and the preamble to the statute have set. (*AZAPO* 1996:par.59)

Indeed,

> The book would not be closed while litigation against the state proceeded throughout the land, accompanied by a constant fanfare of publicity and lasting much longer in all probability than the strictly limited period which, in the interests of putting an early end to unfruitful recriminations, the statute fixes for the work that it requires. (*AZAPO* 1996:par.59)

Mahomed's deployment of the book metaphor confirms both amnesty's politics of memory[18] and the unidirectionality of the bridge. The book of accounts must be written, filled out – but then closed. A good, hard look at the past allows one to leave it behind, to successfully exorcise it. The closing of the book of accounts (and the unidirectionality of the bridge) is tied to a perceived need to prompt a kind of collective purging of certain aspects of the past so as to allow for the constituting or forging of a new political community.

As we shall see in our discussion of Van der Walt, the metaphor of the bridge is tied to a one-way linear movement from a worse state of affairs to a better one. It creates a sharp contrast between the former and the latter, concentrating on the work of change, of attaining a better state of affairs, in the building and crossing of a bridge. The bridge, it seems, must be temporary and crossed only once – hence the affinity of the bridge metaphor with that of 'closing the book'. The bridge works to make the impossible possible – that is, the impassable passable and the difficult easy – by turning the most radical discontinuity into the smoothest continuity. The bridge is meant to allow those who walk on it to proceed as if there were no abyss below. The bridge metaphor then appears to combine a providential aspect (like the parting of the Red Sea (*Exodus* 13:17-14:29)) and a pragmatic, political aspect (without some significant measure of continuity between the past and the future, there may not have been a constitutional settlement). Both of these aspects may lessen the necessity of confronting the abyss *as* an abyss, and hence lessen the necessity of confronting the future as, somehow, radically other. This view or experience of the metaphor may be tied to the original identity of the bridge and the *Interim* Constitution (my emphasis).

18 Cf Cassin 2002.

As we shall see below, however, a more permanent bridge may invite a different view or experience.

The metaphors of the bridge and the book in *AZAPO* function primarily as metaphors of closure, and consequently (to echo Christodoulidis) of the containment of the 'risk' of futurity.[19] This containment of risk is manifest in the way both the Epilogue and the judgement presuppose what is to be achieved: a united South African nation, a 'we', a community. As Christodoulidis puts it:

> [...] talk of reconciliation all too often elides the distinction that matters by disposing of the dangerous non-communal type of conflict and assuming that conflict is always-already of the communal type. (Christodoulidis 2000:192)

The Epilogue (including the bridge metaphor) paradoxically appeals to the past in its construal of the future. On the one hand, the apartheid past is radically different from the human rights future. On the other hand, the human rights future is grasped out of a past – a past that never was. As Motha (2010:297) writes, the Epilogue is directed at "re-constituting a polity that did not exist" insofar as its aim is "the reconciliation between the people of South Africa and the reconstruction of society". And as Leebaw (2003:26) writes: "The TRC process would aim to deal with the past in order to 'restore' something that never was, a South African political community with shared values and goals." Re-conciliation, restoration, recognition and the like contain the risk of futurity by anchoring the future in a past, however problematic or imaginary (Antaki & Kirkby 2009). The *AZAPO* judgement, like the Epilogue, discursively performs the unity to be achieved by referring to a singular actor, 'the nation', whose energies ought not to be diverted from 'the future'. Indeed, Mahomed DP writes that the Act he is upholding allows the victims "to receive the collective recognition of a new nation that they were wronged" (*AZAPO*:par.17), even though the Act is meant to help bring about this new nation. Even when national unity is not presupposed, risk is minimised, because the 'new society' awaits on the other side of the bridge.

This minimisation of risk is built into teleological narratives where a protagonist becomes what he or she was 'always-already' called to be, where destination appears as destiny. This coming of age narrative undergirds much human rights discourse, both as grand narrative of world history (such that the horrors of the twentieth century can, somehow, be accommodated, if not treated as blips or opportunities)[20] and as the goal of human rights for each individual human being and nation: the opportunity to 'develop' his or her or its own distinctive capacities.[21] Needless to say, this kind of narrative, rooted in the formation of selves, appears far from a tragic wisdom rooted in the shattering of selves and is closely tied to the very modern (and impossible)

---

19 Christodoulidis (2000:179) argues that the TRC is a problematic combination of "public confessional and legal tribunal". The former aspect requires embracing risk, while the latter requires minimising it. One might say that Christodoulidis identifies a dangerous mixing of genres. There is an echo here with David Lurie in Chapters 5 and 6 of *Disgrace* (Coetzee 2000).

20 For a treatment of this narrative, see, for example, Douzinas 2000. For my response to the book as a whole, see Antaki 2003.

21 See, for example, Slaughter 2007.

combination, in the same figure, of the author and the hero.[22] Before turning to the book metaphor, we turn to Van der Walt's critique of the bridge metaphor, which raises the possibility of a more chastened – and open to risk – ethos of transformation.

Moving from the progressive to the transformative bridge

In 'Dancing with codes – protecting, developing and deconstructing property rights in a constitutional state' (2001), André van der Walt examines pre- and post-apartheid land law, a body of law that is key to any transformation worthy of the name. In particular, the article aims at "a critical assessment of the theoretical spin that mainstream jurisprudence places on the notion of a transition to a constitutional democracy" (Van der Walt 2001:258-259). 'Theoretical' here, I think, is to be taken literally, in line with its etymology: Van der Walt is concerned with how we see, envision and imagine transition and, therefore, with how we know, understand, even experience, it. He outlines and criticises the dominant progressive interpretation of the bridge metaphor, cautiously proposes metaphors of dance as alternatives, and concludes by articulating a truly transformative interpretation of the bridge metaphor. Throughout, Van der Walt engages in a critique of legal modernity that raises the question of what it would mean to have a truly transformative ethos. My reading of his article draws out this dimension in order, first, to contextualise and assist a subsequent interpretation of the book metaphor, and second, to highlight the modern character of both metaphors.

Van der Walt begins by analysing the dominant interpretation of the bridge metaphor as it appears in Mureinik's (1994) classic treatment of the metaphor. For Van der Walt, this interpretation yields "the abyss as an unavoidable but temporary problem to be overcome in an otherwise untroubled linear progression, and the bridge as an instrument of escape and liberation, of linear movement from old to new" (2001:260). According to this interpretation, explains Van der Walt, the crossing of the abyss is not a "goal in itself" (*ibid*:259) and the bridge is a metaphor "not for the destination of the journey but for an instrument that facilitates the transition" (*ibid*:259-260). What is valued is "getting from the one side to the other quickly and with minimum upheaval"; indeed, "the bridge is an emergency measure that loses its metaphorical and rhetorical significance as soon as the crossing has been made successfully" (*ibid*). The bridge is "the expression of a deep wish to break with the past and to open a new chapter in South African history, an expectation of a clean and complete transition from old to new" (*ibid*:260).[23] As I read him, Van der Walt's project involves problematising both the 'wish', which I believe he shares, and the 'expectation', which he does not.

---

22 See, for example, Bahktin 1990.

23 Van der Walt's analysis rings true with most of what we see in the Epilogue and in *AZAPO*: a 'new society' awaits at the end of the bridge. However, there is also a strand in *AZAPO*, albeit clumsy, that is compatible with the bridge being the destination, where crossing the bridge merely makes possible a long process of healing and the 'opportunity' to make good the constitutional commitments – and no more.

Before reinterpreting the bridge metaphor, however, Van der Walt proposes an alternative metaphor to understand the shift in South African land law and to theorise the transformation of land law promised or required by the new constitutional order: dance.[24] While he ultimately lets go of the dance metaphor in order to return to that of the bridge, his foray into dance serves to better illustrate the principal problem with the dominant interpretation of the bridge metaphor, namely that it confounds or confuses transition, a change in place or position, with transformation, a change in form, condition, or way of being.[25] Having illustrated the problem, Van der Walt is in a better position, so to speak, to reinterpret the bridge metaphor in a more critical way. As Michael Bishop (2007) points out, Van der Walt reinterprets the bridge metaphor as one of transformation, rather than one of transition.[26]

Rather than imagine "apartheid land law and post-1994 land reform" (Van der Walt 2001:261) as two static places or positions connected by a constitutional bridge, Van der Walt likens pre- and post-apartheid jurisprudence to "codes" one dances by (*ibid*:262). He turns to Afrikaner *volkspele* (folk dancing) and the *toyi-toyi* protest dance – "which played a role in bringing about a relatively non-violent political revolution in South Africa" (*ibid*:280-281) – as metaphors for apartheid land law and transformative jurisprudence, respectively. For instance, he ties the "enclosing" and "excluding" (*ibid*:265) of the *volkspele* dance, or wagon wheel dance, to the absolute and exclusive Roman-Dutch law understanding of ownership that prevailed during the apartheid regime (*ibid*:271).

Unlike the metaphor of the bridge, with its ostensibly very different points of departure and arrival, Van der Walt's turn to codes we dance by allows him to better see and describe continuity between pre- and post-apartheid jurisprudence. He situates post-apartheid land reform within "the rhetorical, ideological and aesthetic code of *toyi-toyi* jurisprudence":

> [L]and reform is essentially toyi-toyi jurisprudence, which tends to feed off the energy of confrontation with the very apartheid land law system that it is meant to reform, just like the toyi-toyi marches fed off the energy of the apartheid system which it confronted, demanding change, waiting for change. (Van der Walt 2001:292)

Van der Walt recognises that the "efficacy" of both the *toyi-toyi* marches and *toyi-toyi* jurisprudence is "beyond question", yet notes that "the meaning of this observation [of continuity] is not political or strategic or moral", but "aesthetic": "[T]he ghost of apartheid land law continues to hover over *toyi-toyi* jurisprudence" (2001:292). I take Van der Walt's 'aesthetic' observation to be about how one 'senses, or 'experiences', *volkspele* and *toyi-toyi* jurisprudence together. As he writes, his observation means that one cannot, or should not, experience "the two forms of jurisprudence" as "places or positions one can enter or leave" (*ibid*:294-295). While he asserts that the sense of his observation is not 'moral', I take the 'aesthetic' meaning of his observation of

24 In doing so, however, Van der Walt also cautions a critical consideration of all metaphors we use.

25 On 'position' vs 'condition', see Antaki 2003a.

26 Bishop also refers to Le Roux 2004.

continuity as ultimately moral, as ultimately 'ethical', concerning as it does an ethos, a sensibility, a manner of being-in-the-world. For instance, Van der Walt does say that the simultaneous experience of these two codes one dances by limits one's possibilities of being-in-the-world, limiting both the "energy and the options for change" (*ibid*:295).[27]

While Van der Walt prefers "rupture" with apartheid codes to change with minimal upheaval ("discontinuities are valued and embraced as potentially liberating alternatives" (2001:282)), his metaphor of dance, as opposed to the interpretation of the bridge that he criticises, tells of the difficulty of moving from the old to the new. While he does not elaborate this point, the metaphor of dance reveals memory as bodily, as a matter of habits that can stay with us wherever we go and however quickly we go there. Although we do not necessarily remember past experiences and practices, they leave their stamp on us, becoming a part of who we are, of how we do things. The dance metaphor drives home the entrenched character of legal forms, which Van der Walt derives from his reading of Robert Gordon (for example, *ibid*:261-262,296). Legal forms shaped by ideologies (such as apartheid) tend to survive even when those ideologies have ostensibly died or even been consciously disavowed. The dominant interpretation of the bridge metaphor appears to privilege the effectiveness of conscious, purposeful self-positioning, whereby an end is posited and then achieved, thereby making clean breaks and closure easier. The dance metaphor, in Van der Walt's account, requires us to carefully enquire into how we have been 'stamped' or 'formed' – that is, conditioned – to move in these or in those patterns. It reveals the great difficulty of achieving any kind of self-knowledge, insofar as we may think that we have 'moved past' something that has actually become a part of us. In other words, if one is to stick with the dance metaphor, we need to experience being 'out of step' in order to learn to dance differently. Van der Walt's use of the dance metaphor and the idea of 'haunting' calls into question the pretension of a once and for all successful exorcism of the past. While he is understandably quite keen on rupturing with the (ways of thinking and being of the) past, he tends to paint rupture as an arduous task (requiring a turn inward and not just outward, backward and not just forward) rather than an achievement, and worries about metaphors that let its nature as a task slip from view.

There are clearly echoes of Nietzsche and Foucault here, especially insofar as Van der Walt insists on the necessity of some archaeological or genealogical work for transformation to be possible. Specifically, he writes that the task of transformation includes the need "to unearth, destabilise and displace some of these remnants [of the jurisprudential apartheid codes] in order to liberate energy in order to imagine alternatives" (Van der Walt 2001:294). In this sentence, we may hear an echo of Mahomed's reference to the proper use of the "energies of the nation" (*AZAPO* 1996: par.59). However, the manner in which this energy is to be liberated does not

27 Van der Walt (2001:295) writes: "*Volkspele* and *toyi-toyi* tend to condemn us to the confrontational attitudes of struggle, in which both the energy and the options for change are defined by the confrontation between the reactionary exclusivity of rights as trumps and the reformist exclusivity of restitution demands."

accord with the security and stability afforded by the dominant interpretation of the constitutional bridge. In this respect, Van der Walt's turn to the imagination is also quite significant. While the language of 'imagining alternatives' suggests a wilful imagination, perhaps even a form of imagination as invention (Antaki 2012), both Van der Walt's turn to dance and his reinterpretation of the bridge metaphor make it difficult to see his turn to the language of imagination in this way, that is, as a tool at the service of conscious, self-positioning human beings. As he explains:

> The idea is not to devise or develop a new, third dancing code or jurisprudence, but to reassure ourselves that there will be opportunities to displace the normal and accustomed codes and to imagine the possibility that things can be different. (Van der Walt 2001:294)

We will revisit the language of imagination in greater depth when we return to Krog.

Accordingly, Van der Walt does not propose a third dancing code, but instead returns to the bridge metaphor, providing a reinterpretation of it that emphasises its relation to the abyss – a more permanent relation:

> The bridge metaphor allows for another interpretation, where the bridge is not simply an instrument for getting out of one place into another, but an edifice that is inherently related to the abyss which it spans. Here, the focus is not on the two spaces on either side of the abyss, but on the abyss itself – the bridge is functionally and essentially linked to and obtains its significance from the abyss beneath it, so that the bridge is not a temporary instrument for a single crossing, one way, but allows and invites multiple crossings, in both directions, since there is no inherent value attached to being on one side of the bridge rather than the other. In this alternative interpretation of the bridge metaphor, the danger is to stay on one side, while the bridge allows us to connect one side with the other. (Van der Walt 2001:295-296)

Van der Walt's reinterpretation of the bridge metaphor aims to do away with the fallacy "that we can rid ourselves of the legacy of the past", as well as with the fallacy "that we should be eager to get to the other side and get the whole thing behind us, leaving no room for imagining alternative futures" (Van der Walt 2001:296). Here, we see the possibility of imagining alternative futures, that things can be different, as tied to a willingness to remain on the bridge, with the abyss just below.

Van der Walt's reinterpretation of the bridge metaphor, and hence of futurity and human temporality, is intimately tied to the question of alterity. His reinterpretation of the bridge metaphor is meant to raise the possibility of not only a "non-linear vision of transformation", but also a "non-spatial jurisprudence of property rights" (Van der Walt 2001:302). A spatial jurisprudence of property rights describes property as "exclusive spaces for the development and protection of personal autonomy" (*ibid*:274). Under this jurisprudence, "rights are understood as secure places divided by boundaries" (*ibid*:291), just like the past and future are secured by the boundary of the bridge. Consequently, he ties a more relational understanding of the bridge to a more relational (or deconstructive) understanding of rights, one which he finds in Nedelsky, Michelman, Johan van der Walt and others (*ibid*:302; see also Nedelsky 2011). And so, Van der Walt identifies the closure of the present to the past(s) and future(s) with the closure of the self to other(s).

Indeed, Van der Walt's introduction of weakness, marginality and vulnerability into property law discourse is intrinsically bound up with his upending of the dominant interpretation of the bridge metaphor. Van der Walt's reinterpretation, by emphasising the permanence of the bridge, and hence of the abyss, calls attention to the bridge as also the potentially risky, vulnerable, liminal place in-between. His reinterpretation makes this in-between place more central, more permanent, precisely in order to unsettle the two ends of the bridge, which are apparently on solid land. Temporally or historically speaking, Van der Walt seeks to make the present more than a conduit between 'the' past and 'the' future. The present, the bridge, becomes the central place of human activity as the past and future become the sites of multiple visits, of comings and goings, thereby becoming more 'plural', more 'open', more 'indeterminate'. As human beings become accustomed to the liminal place of the bridge (that is, to the present), the past and the future (paradoxically) become unhinged from the present and lose their air of solidity. This 'experience' of the bridge is crucial to Van der Walt's wish that there be 'room for imagining alternative futures' and suggests, as I have mentioned, an imagination that is not a mode of human mastery.

That Van der Walt's article is a far-reaching and careful engagement with modernity becomes more apparent when it is brought into conversation with Hannah Arendt's own turn to the metaphor of the bridge. (While Van der Walt does not mention Arendt, his turn to Nedelsky on relational rights, as well as the tenor of his piece more generally, makes her a fitting interlocutor. See, for example, Beiner & Nedelsky 2001.) Arendt uses the metaphor of the bridge in her *Between past and future: Eight exercises in political thought* (1961), and particularly in the preface, which is suitably entitled 'The gap between past and future' (and was inspired by a Kafka story). She writes that modernity is defined by the breakdown of the "Roman trinity of religion, authority, and tradition" (1961:212). Tradition, specifically, "bridged over" (*ibid*:13) the gap between past and future; its breakdown points to the crisis of the modern world. This crisis, among other things, threatens the "world" – the "in-between" that "relates and separates men at the same time" (*ibid*:52) – and makes the "now" (*ibid*:212) a problem for modern human beings. We see here the same intertwining of the twin themes of alterity, of the relations of human beings to one another, and of temporality, of human historicity. Moreover, just like Van der Walt, Arendt sees the transformation of the 'now' into a problem as also an opportunity, perhaps even an opportunity for critique, for transformation.[28] While modern human beings may certainly despair at the breakdown of the bridge, their task is to, paradoxically and in whichever way, "settle" in the gap (*ibid*:76). The emergency, or 'crisis', of modern times leads to the need to give up the metaphysical comfort of the bridge. Being modern is being-in-the-gap, without the benefit of a metaphysical tradition that covers the gap. The hard to imagine habitability of the gap, of the 'now', makes the genuinely 'new' possible,[29] opens up a future. More radically, Arendt sees the gap as being constitutive of human

28 See generally Antaki 2007.

29 In English, 'modernity' comes from *modo* ('just now'); in German, 'modernity' (or *Neuzeit*) is tied to 'the new.'

being-in-the-world. Its exposure, then, also presents the possibility of, and the opportunity for, the reappropriation of one's humanity.

Were Van der Walt to dispense with the bridge altogether, of course, he would be dispensing with the very metaphor he is trying to critically reinterpret. However, his reinterpretation of the bridge metaphor may well be a kind of Arendtian embrace of the gap, of the abyss below the bridge. He too recognises the abyss or the gap, and the permanent relation of human beings to it, as constitutive of human being-in-the-world. Moreover, just as for Van der Walt a "dominant spatial logic of status and exclusivity" (2001:302) underlies both the dominant interpretation of the bridge and dominant approaches to property, for Arendt, our being-towards-others and our being-in-time are intrinsically linked. In Arendtian terms, bearing the burden of one in-between (that between past and future) is tied to bearing the burden of another in-between: the in-between human beings that she calls the 'world'.[30]

Along these lines, human finitude is constituted by being-in-the-gap, that is, the most radical exposure. This most radical exposure, implied in Van der Walt's critique of the dominant spatial logic, radically decentres the human will. Indeed, the ethos that properly belongs to being human is not one of mastering or holding on, tied to the illusion of the 'will' and the fantasy of 'sovereignty', but, at least in part, one of letting go (of Arendt's metaphysical bridge or of the dominant version of the bridge outlined by Van der Walt) and of learning to inhabit an uneasy, in-between place. Van der Walt participates in this displacement of the will when, for example, he refers to "a politics that would not be the subjective wish of what we want but a response to what is required of us" (2001:304). The displacement of will as a central human faculty severs or separates responsibility from mastery and thus challenges conventional understandings of transformation. With this separation or severing of responsibility from mastery, transformation is no longer something human beings do to a world grasped as an object, but rather something human beings 'let' happen to them as they respond to a call.

As I read him, it is precisely Van der Walt's philosophical engagement with modernity that leads him to end his article with the phrase it "can be different" (2001:311), rather than it 'can be better'. While he certainly criticises linear narratives – because they too quickly turn destination into destiny, promising difference but leading to repetition – in the name of true (as opposed to cosmetic) transformation, he must be fundamentally committed to the position that loosening the grip of 'the past' does not – indeed cannot – allow one to get a better grip on the future. Indeed, 'getting a grip on things' is the basic problem with the dominant spatial logic he criticises. If transformative constitutionalism is post-liberal, it cannot be super-liberal. For Van der Walt, releasing energy to imagine alternatives cannot be confused with unleashing human mastery.[31] For this reason, the 'different', as opposed to the 'better', captures the ontological underpinnings of this post-liberalism more accurately. At the heart

30 If the breakdown of tradition exposes us to the gap between past and future, the breakdown of authority makes us responsible for the world.

31 See my discussion of the transformative imagination in Antaki (2012:11-16).

of his discussion of alterity and of a relational understanding of rights, Van der Walt refers to understandings of rights according to which "the possibility of change is kept alive by a constant awareness of the possibility of otherness, that things can be different" (*ibid*).

The above engagement with the bridge metaphor, I believe, sheds some light on the more neglected metaphor of the Epilogue: the book of which the explicitly mentioned 'new chapter' is a part. Van der Walt sees the Epilogue's reference to 'opening a new chapter' as a wish for a clean break, analogous to the dominant interpretation of the bridge, which he criticises. However, the book need not be understood as a book of accounts to be closed. Indeed, read along the lines of the dominant interpretation of the bridge metaphor, the book can also be a novel in which the South African people are at once author and hero or protagonist.

If Van der Walt's reinterpretation of the bridge features alterity and futurity as problems of *habitus*, of ethos, taking the book metaphor seriously furthers his engagement with dance and aesthetics by highlighting alterity and futurity as problems of (literary) genre. Paradoxically, the genre that belongs to transformation might be that of the modernist novel or ancient tragedy, and not necessarily the early realist novel or the (idealised) *Bildungsroman* usually tied to human rights (and also such things as transformative constitutionalism and transitional justice). Transformation is not reducible to, and may not even include, formation. One may never get to the other side if getting there means attaining maturity, that is, the sovereignty of self-containment, of getting a grip on things. To read the book metaphor in terms of a transformation without formation would require reading and thinking through the 'opening of a new chapter' in the Epilogue as different from the writing of an author-hero.

The book as novel? Alterity and futurity as problems of (literary) genre

In his 2010 article on Antjie Krog's *Begging to Be Black*, Stewart Motha draws attention to a passage in Krog's book in which a philosopher, who is likely Paul Patton, asks her how she will present her conversation with him. Motha writes:

> Towards the end of her conversation with [Australian philosopher Paul] Patton in Berlin, Krog is asked whether she is writing a novel. She insists that she is not. Why so, Patton asks, when she could explore the inner psyche of characters – imagine being black, for instance? Krog responds that she does not want to give up on the 'strangeness' that can be preserved in non-fiction. It is a strangeness that is not invented: 'the strangeness is real, and the fact that I cannot ever really enter the psyche of somebody else, somebody black. The terror and loneliness of that inability is what I don't want to give up on' (Krog 2009:267). She goes on to state that at this stage, for her, 'imagination is overrated' (Krog 2009:268). Krog then says that 'to imagine black at this stage is to insult black. That is why I stay with non-fiction, listening, engaging, observing, translating, until one can begin to sense a thinning of skin, negotiate possible small openings at places where imaginings can begin to begin'. (Motha 2010:300-301)

Krog's assertion that 'imagination is overrated' is a response to a question from Patton: "But how will you live together in your country (or in mine) if you don't begin to imagine one another?" When she answers that 'imagination is overrated', he responds, "That's a terrible statement" and, a little later, "Am I hearing a suggestion that literature has failed you?" (Krog 2009:268).[32]

In these remarkable pages of her book, Krog ties her refusal of a literary genre, the 'novel' (however vaguely understood), to her refusal of the fantasy that one can, somehow, know others. As implied by Paul Patton's question, her acknowledgment of her inability to know others and her refusal to let go of this inability are potentially connected to a similar acknowledgment of her inability to master her own future in her own country. Krog's is a most peculiar holding on: she holds onto the impossibility of getting a grip on others, and this impossibility jeopardises the possibility of getting a grip on her future. Krog's refusal echoes those of Van der Walt. Her conversation with Patton brings to light the same connection between alterity and futurity as does Van der Walt's reinterpretation of the bridge metaphor.

While Van der Walt does not refuse the language of imagination as Krog does, his turn to imagination is not a turn to the form of mastery Krog rejects. Nevertheless, Krog's refusal of imagination as a form of mastery in the service of both reason (that is, knowledge of the other and hence of the future) and will (containment of the other and hence of the future) is a more visceral refusal of imagination's promise of mastery than Van der Walt's. For example, she gestures, cautiously, towards "small openings at places where imaginings can begin to begin" (Krog 2009:268).[33] In this phrase, imagination does not appear as a human faculty to be exercised. Human beings can 'negotiate possible small openings' at propitious places, but cannot, themselves, make imaginings happen. Krog's separation of imaginings from imagination reveals more than a concern that the imagination is 'overrated'. Her emphasis on 'imaginings' reveals a concern that a too strong belief in, or exercise of, the human capacity of imagination is a kind of self-deception whereby human beings fool themselves into thinking that imaginings are of their own doing. Whatever her level of philosophical sophistication, Krog raises questions of great import and does so in a way that brings to the fore their existential rawness.

Krog's refusal of imagination as a form of mastery issues from a discussion where she says: "I simply don't know enough about blackness, or birdness, or mountainness, or even Englishness for that matter, to imagine it in terms other than my own self or the exotic opposite of myself" (Krog 2009:268). Krog's refusal of imagination, then, appears to be a refusal of imagination as a remedy for the absence of knowledge proper: Krog refuses to make something unknown 'recognisable' or 'identifiable' to her by way of her imagination. She does not wish to use the imagination as a way to overcome her human finitude. Understood in this way, her refusal of the imagination as a form of mastery echoes political theorist Patchen Markell's argument in *Bound by Recognition* (Markell 2003). In an argument much influenced by Hannah Arendt, Markell ties the fantasy of knowing others and oneself to that of mastering one's future. He proposes that we approach "the politics of recognition through the lens of sovereignty" (*ibid*:15).

32 Krog's assertion that imagination is overrated for her "at this stage" (2009:268) leaves open the possibility of a future stage where imagination can – and should – do more.

33 These small places may be akin to Van der Walt's 'discontinuities' (Krog 2009:282,294).

Rather than think of sovereignty spatially, he argues that the problem with recognition as an ideal is "in the first instance a problem with its temporality – that is, with the way in which it expresses the aspiration to a sort of sovereign invulnerability to the open-endedness and contingency of the future we share with others" (*ibid*).

Markell's radical critique of the politics of recognition seeks to do away with "successful recognition", even "as a regulative idea" (Markell 2003:16,94).[34] In other words, accepting that successful recognition is impossible is not sufficient to accommodate his critique. One must, in addition, do away with successful recognition ('recognisability', 'knowability', 'identifiability') as one's horizon(s). According to Markell, recognition is not only "necessarily provisional", it is also "necessarily *retrospective*" (*ibid*:16). In his account, "the root of injustice in relations of identity and difference is not identity as such but rather the effort to make identity – the as-yet-unfinished and unpredictable story of one's life – into the ground of an impossible sovereignty over one's own future" (*ibid*:23-24). Seen in this light, Krog's refusal of the imagination may be a refusal to enlist the imagination in a politics of recognition. In Markell's terms, her refusal may even lead to a realisation that "the pursuit of recognition *is part of the problem rather than part of the solution*" (*ibid*:95). "On this account", writes Markell, borrowing the term 'acknowledgment' from Stanley Cavell, social relations of subordination marked by this pursuit "are to be understood not in terms of the failure of recognition, but in terms of the failure of *acknowledgment* – that is, the failure to acknowledge one's finitude, rooted in the condition of human plurality" (*ibid*).[35] Krog's holding on may be a holding onto human finitude and a refusal to exchange an acknowledgement of this finitude for an illusory recognition of others. And 'the novel' Patton proposes she write invites her to make exactly this exchange.

In literary terms, Markell's argument is that the hero can never be the author of his or her own story.[36] Markell turns to tragic *anagnôrisis* (or recognition)[37] precisely to call into question a politics of recognition "animated by a vision of sovereign agency, in which people are empowered by self-knowledge and by the confirming recognition of others to act in accordance with who they really are" (Markell 2003:63). Who we or others 'really' are is inaccessible to us, and so knowledge of these cannot ground our

34 On p 16, Markell writes that contemporary authors such as Honneth and Tully "treat recognition as necessarily provisional, but not as necessarily *retrospective*, and so they do not force us to consider the more challenging possibility that the pursuit of recognition, even when recognition is understood in this way as a regulative idea, might be an incoherent and therefore potentially costly enterprise".

35 See especially p 34 ff for Markell's turn to Cavell.

36 See also Bakhtin 1990.

37 Markell (2003:63) refers to Aristotle, who understands *anagnôrisis* as "a change from ignorance to knowledge, and *thus to either love or hate*, on the part of the personages marked for good or evil fortune". "From a tragic perspective", writes Markell, "efforts to achieve sovereignty are themselves ethically and politically *mis*recognitions – not misrecognitions of the identity of another, as that term usually implies, but failures to acknowledge key aspects of our own situation, including especially our finitude in relation to the future" (*ibid*).

actions. Our acts are not "our property" (*ibid*:64), Markell explains, and "the attempt to become master of our own deeds and identity is not only doomed to fail, but risks intensifying that suffering [the ineliminable possibility of suffering] unnecessarily, even demanding that we give our lives for what will turn out to have been an illusion of control" (*ibid*:65).

Markell's thinking echoes that of Van der Walt, Christodoulidis, and others. He writes:

> Given the relationship I have tracked here between recognition and notions of mastery and control, however, perhaps what is needed is precisely to think about democratic power and action outside the frame of sovereignty. This might involve translating democracy's egalitarian impulses into a new idiom in which risk, loss, and vulnerability are seen as constitutive features of political life rather than as burdens to be overcome once and for all. (Markell 2003:188)

The bridge and the abyss are symbols of risk, loss and vulnerability. Van der Walt's attempt to make the bridge more than an emergency measure is one attempt to see risk, loss and vulnerability as constitutive features of political life. For Markell, forgetting the tragic wisdom symbolised by the bridge and abyss is a fundamental ontological mistake regarding what it is to *be* human.

The extent to which Krog aims to avoid making this ontological mistake is not altogether clear, however. Is her holding on to the terror and loneliness of her inability to know others tied to her understanding of South Africa, the human condition, or both? Is 'blackness' qualitatively different for her than other forms of 'otherness'?[38] Does she believe that, one day, she might, or should be able or willing to, let go of this terror and loneliness? The answers are not clear. Nevertheless, Krog's refusal of the novel – associated as it is with her assertion that the 'imagination is overrated' and with her desire to hold on to the terror and loneliness of her inability to enter the psyches of others – appears as the refusal of the kind of novel which makes this ontological mistake. What kind of novel is this?

The kind of novel Krog intuitively rejects may very well be the literary analogue to the legal form of human rights and human rights-based constitutionalism. Of course, this is not to say that there are no literary genres (even fictional or novelistic), forms of writing, or ethics of reading that fit Krog's account: not all literature is about the penetration of psyches or relies on or encourages an ethics and a politics of recognition and identification. Some literature encourages its authors and readers to experience limits, including the limits of imagination, rather than simply seeking to transcend them. Krog's refusal of the novel involves, I think, a refusal of fantasies of recognition (of knowing others and even of self-knowledge) and of formation, of becoming fully or well formed. These two fantasies are tied to two standard tales about the intertwining of novels and human rights.

In *Inventing Human Rights*, Lynn Hunt (2008) explicitly ties the novel to the rise of human rights. In a chapter entitled 'Torrents of Emotion: Reading Novels and Imagining Equality', Hunt argues that eighteenth century novels such as Rousseau's *Julie, or the New Héloïse* "encouraged a highly charged identification with the characters and in

38 See, for example, the conversation entitled "Imagining Black" (Krog 2009:122).

so doing enabled readers to empathise across class, sex, and national lines" (2008:38). They taught their readers "to see others – people they did not know personally – as like them, as having the same kinds of inner emotions" (*ibid*:40). While Hunt focuses specifically on the epistolary novel, she writes that her "argument could have encompassed the 18th century novel in general" (*ibid*:41). Readers of these novels, she explains, did not "just follow" the character's actions. For example, a reader of Richardson's *Pamela* "participates in the blossoming of her personality as she writes. The reader simultaneously becomes Pamela even while imagining him-/herself as a friend of hers and as an outside observer" (*ibid*:45). Identification – seeing someone else as like oneself – taught equality, argues Hunt.

Krog's refusal of the novel may amount to a refusal of the authorial sovereignty that sets up a politics and an ethics of identification, itself dependent on the accessibility, even penetrability, of the psyches of others (and ourselves). Krog refuses this sovereignty in part because of her awareness of the limits of her own imagination and her incapacity to imagine otherness or blackness "in terms other than my own self or the exotic opposite of myself" (Krog 2009:268). Often, when we try to 'know' others, the best we do is to 'exoticise' the differences between us and them, such that we end up 'knowing' a projection of ourselves rather than these others. Understood in this way, Krog's refusal of the novel is also the rejection of a kind of voyeurism. Krog may also refuse this authorial sovereignty because she may question the very stability of 'self' and 'other' that allows them to be objects of knowledge or imagination.

The heading of the 'Conversation' from which Krog's refusal of the novel is drawn is 'Formation of the self' (Krog 2009:266). Before Patton asks Krog whether she intends to present their discussion by writing a novel, the discussion concerns the formation of a self and the relation of this formation to community and to the interconnectedness of human beings within a community. In response to Patton, who turns to Socrates and Kant as examples of thinkers who tied the unity of the self to a kind of being-with oneself, Krog reaches towards a criticism of the "Western moral self", which she, following Patton, also describes as created in conversation "with the self" (*ibid*:267), albeit meant as a criticism. For Krog, Patton's question about whether she intends to write a novel is "unexpected" (*ibid*:267). But his question is not at all foreign to the theme of their conversation. The novel, Patton implicitly recognises, is no stranger to the themes of selfhood and the formation of selves. Krog's refusal of the novel "follows" her refusal of what she takes to be the formation of the 'Western moral self' (*ibid*).[39] Whether or not her understanding of Socrates and Kant on selfhood is right, her refusal of the novel sheds light on the kind of 'self' and the kind of 'formation' she is rejecting or thinks she is rejecting.

Hunt's history of human rights ties eighteenth-century novels and the identification with others they helped cultivate to a "deeper cultural preoccupation with autonomy" and "self-determination" (Hunt 2008:60-61). Slaughter more probingly explores the connections between autonomy, self-determination, 'formation' and human rights. In his account, earlier novelistic forms, such as the sentimental novel, contributed to the

[39] See, for example, Taylor 1992.

rise of the *Bildungsroman* (Slaughter 2007:42), literally the 'formation novel'.[40] According to Slaughter, the *Bildungsroman* is "the novelistic genre that most fully corresponds to – and, indeed, is implicitly invoked by – the norms and narrative assumptions that underwrite the vision of free and full human personality development projected in international human rights law" (*ibid*:40). As he explains: "[H]uman rights law and the *Bildungsroman* are legal and literary regimes that imagine an idealistic scenario for the human personality to become the sovereign guarantor of its own development" (*ibid*:103). Slaughter insists on the "plot-logic of linear development" (*ibid*:107), which makes possible narratives of modernisation through which, for example, declarations of rights figure as "evidence of humankind's coming of age" (*ibid*). The linear development allows the protagonist, often retrospectively, to take responsibility, as author, for his or her own development.[41] The (however illusory) promise of the *Bildungsroman* is the achievement of "self-recognition" in a journey towards oneself (*ibid*:102). The linear development turns out to be circular: "The generic laws that rule all enabling narratives of subjectivation", writes Slaughter (turning to Butler), are inevitably circular and presuppose "the very subject" for which they must account (*ibid*:100). We saw this circularity in our discussion of the Epilogue and of the *AZAPO* judgement: the united South Africa that must be achieved is also presupposed.

Krog's struggles with 'the formation of the self' reflect how her thinking on blackness, and its inaccessibility, also makes impossible for her certain forms of self-recognition. Krog argues that 'blackness' taught her to be a stranger to herself: "Blackness released me from my white capsule [...] it has taught me how to become other than myself" (2009:268). Blackness did this, it must be said, without her 'knowing' or 'recognising' it, but simply by her experiencing it, however imperfectly. In Arendtian language, perhaps blackness taught Krog about the 'in-between' that is the world, an exposure that is itself a gift of "grace" (*ibid*:269) and which is, crucially, prior to reason and will (Meyer 2010) – the same reason or will that can enlist imagination in its service. Krog's refusal of the novel, then, may also be a refusal of the promised 'reconciliation', that is, the scripted return to oneself, of an idealistic and idealised formation or *Bildung*, itself tied to the possibility of self-recognition. 'I refuse to conceive of a formation of my own self that comes at the cost of a (necessarily violent) knowing of another', might run a Krogian sentence. This refusal is also an acknowledgment that any knowing of oneself is necessarily violent.

The 'novel' Krog rejects, I think, is a genre that thematises, performs, both self-formation and the knowing of the psyches of others, often tying them together. This novel may very well be the novel of the Epilogue. The Epilogue and the *AZAPO* judgement's presupposition of what they both aim to achieve, the dominant interpretation of the

[40] In *Kultur, Bildung, Geist*, Raymond Geuss (1999:38) identifies three elements of the *Bildungsroman*: the "development" of the hero's powers, the hero's "discovery" of his true wants, and the hero's "realistic acceptance of the world as it is".

[41] Unlike Markell's argument, however, this retrospective authorisation may take place at the moment of the attainment of maturity, when the hero retrospectively realises that he was author all along.

bridge metaphor, and the language of reconciliation all suggest that the book metaphor in the Epilogue points to a moment of self-recognition, of attainment of maturity, following which the hero and the author are one. This moment of self-recognition is the moment of the achievement of a form that allows the protagonist to retrospectively interpret his life story as a formation.[42]

Transformation without formation?

It may be impossible or very difficult to read the book metaphor in the Epilogue as referring to something other than the 'novel' Krog rejects, a novel analogous to the dominant interpretation of the bridge metaphor. The linear movement towards a 'we' that is presupposed, and the recovery of a past that never was, make it difficult to read the book metaphor differently. However, if a different reading were possible, it would require severing the author from the hero and, therefore, would mean placing a great deal of weight on the 'opening' of a new chapter as something other than the sovereign 'writing' of one. A critical interpretation of this 'opening' would likely have to sever transformation from formation (*Bildung*) and, perhaps, even give up on, or radically reduce, the role of the imagination (*Einbildungskraft*) in bringing others and the future to clarity, in making them (re)cognisable. A critical interpretation of this 'opening' would lead in the direction of an acknowledgement of finitude – and hence of the givenness and gift of 'the open', even if experienced as an abyss or a gap – as an ontological truth of the human condition. What book or novel would we turn to, were it possible to read the book metaphor differently?

Robert Pippin has written that, "with the somewhat fanciful suggestion of Hegel as a model", he wants to "suggest that [JM] Coetzee's novels represent unique, brilliant attempts at a kind of political self-knowledge" (2010:23-24). Pippin writes:

> [Coetzee's early novels] are, to a large degree, concerned with forms of physical and psychological disintegration. This disintegration in physical and mental illness is in turn clearly linked with a Hegelian theme that Coetzee, in several interviews and essays terms 'reciprocity' or, more exactly, the failure of reciprocity; in explicitly Hegelian terms, the failure to achieve any mutuality of recognition and so the perpetuation of relations of mastery and servitude in some form (including in relations to nature and to oneself). (Pippin 2010:24)

He adds:

> [T]hese repeated moments of disintegration suggest something about the internally 'self'-defeating exercise of unequal power that is not a moralistic

[42] This interpretation of the book metaphor resonates with some understandings of Hegel's account of reconciliation (see, for example, Lilla 2001) and drives home the belonging together of the ideas of recognition and *Bildung*. Markell's critique of a politics of recognition (while it involves a re-reading of Hegel) also amounts to a critique of certain conceptions of self-formation and *Bildung*, even as "regulative ideals". The impossibility of the hero becoming the author (or even spectator) is there in Nietzsche's critique of Hegel (in the preface to his *On the genealogy of morals*): "we are necessarily strangers to ourselves" and miscount the bell strokes that indicate noon, the moment of greatest clarity (1967:15; see also Kristeva 1991). As Arendt writes, "nobody is author or producer of his own life-story" (1958:184).

> critique but an internal one, one that does not presuppose at all a settled moral position brought to bear on the characters from an independent or external point of view. (*ibid*:25)[43]

Could it be that novels 'about' disintegration that also 'perform' that disintegration have something to tell us about transformation without formation, about an opening that is not a writing, about an imagination not at the service of making others and our futures (re)cognisable?

Whereas Pippin points to Coetzee's earlier novels, one could also take as exemplary cases Coetzee's more recent *Disgrace* (2000) or, for instance, Marlene van Niekerk's *Agaat* (2004; translated as *The Way of the Women*, 2010). Both novels thematise and perform the crushing or loss of will, the shrinking of horizons and of our power to see 'far'. They are both concerned, in whole or in part, with intimate relations of service – of service dedicated to, or received from, inscrutable others. In *Disgrace*, of course, Lurie's disgrace appears to lead to a radical shrinking of his world and to a life dedicated to suffering animals. In *Agaat*, we witness the physical disintegration of an ostensible mistress who cannot or does not know what her ostensible servant is thinking or feeling. In both these works, the possibility of an experience (but not knowledge) of grace emerges for both protagonist and reader in the shattering of sovereignty, in the dissolution of the hero-author – even, or especially, in disgrace, which is, in large measure, the difficult lesson of learning not to take the given for granted.

Indeed, the kind of political self-knowledge Coetzee's novels aim at may be, in Markell and Cavell's terms, acknowledgement of human finitude. What is more, while 'holding on' to the importance of reciprocity and mutuality, it may be useful to follow Markell and to locate the failure of reciprocity in a failure of acknowledgement rather than a failure of recognition. Strikingly, an emphasis on acknowledgement of one's human finitude may lead one to grope, as Krog does, towards reciprocity 'without' recognition. It may also lead one to recall reciprocity's roots in grace without always 'counting on' its (calculated) 'return'.[44] Indeed, the "failure of love" Coetzee speaks about (1992:96)

---

43 Pippin's readings are often insightful. For instance, he rightfully draws attention to the opening of JM Coetzee's *Waiting for the Barbarians* (1980), which announces the theme of recognition with Colonel Joll's sunglasses: these allow him to see others but shield him from their sight (and even from a full experience of the world as his skin is shielded from the sun). The book is filled with the incapacity to see and recognise others and does not deliver much hope with regard to proper sight. To the extent that a better seeing emerges, it is tied to the (de)formation of selves, for example the torture of the Magistrate. Now, it is certainly possible – and even desirable, following Pippin and Coetzee himself – to tie these failures of recognition to the colonial context of *Waiting for the Barbarians* and to South Africa. But, without leading us to celebrate deformation, these works also provide us with unique opportunities to let go of recognition and formation as (even regulative) ideals.

44 On grace, see Meyer 2010, which concludes with a careful and wonderful reading of Coetzee's *Disgrace* (2000) that focuses on coming to ground, but in a non-Hegelian, non-metaphysical way. On the roots of justice in grace, see Meyer 2010 too, but also Frank 2005, which provides an illuminating account of Aristotle's 'reciprocal justice'.

with regard to South Africa's master class may be more than a failure of 'recognition'. Coetzee's choice of words is telling.

Perhaps experiencing (dis)integration or (de)formation as a protagonist or reader is one way of not only grasping colonial contexts, but also of experiencing the givenness of 'the open' in a most radical exposure to and within it. If this is the case, things such as ancient tragedy or the modernist novel emerge as potentially 'transformative genres'. If this is true, it is highly doubtful that it will ever be possible to be 'post-colonial', if to be so involves removing oneself from any relation to the abyss, letting go of the terror and loneliness of being unable to truly know others, and finding oneself in a risk-free zone. Perhaps the virtue of some literary works emerging from 'post-colonial' contexts is to teach us this very lesson. Now, what legal form or genre would be or is analogous to this kind of literature?

Reference List

Ackerman LHW. 2004. The legal nature of the South African constitutional revolution. *New Zealand Law Review* 4:633-680.

Antaki M. 2012. The turn to imagination in legal theory: The re-enchantment of the world? *Law and Critique* 23:1-20.

— 2007. The critical modernism of Hannah Arendt. *Theoretical Inquiries in Law* 8:251-276.

— 2003a. The world(lessness) of human rights. *McGill Law Journal* 49:203-224.

— 2003b. Leading modernity (to) a – ground. *Australian Feminist Law Journal* 19:115-131.

Antaki M & Kirkby C. 2009. The lethality of the Canadian state's (re)cognition of indigenous peoples. In: A Sarat & J Culbert (eds). *States of violence: war, capital punishment, and letting die*. Cambridge: Cambridge University Press. 192-228.

Arendt H. 1965. *On revolution*. Harmondsworth: Penguin Books.

— 1961. *Between past and future: Eight exercises in political thought*. New York: Penguin Books.

— 1958. *The Human Condition*. Chicago, IL: University of Chicago Press.

Bakhtin MM. 1990. Author and hero in aesthetic activity. In: M Holquist & V Liapunov (eds). *Art and answerability: Early philosophical essays by MM Bakhtin*. Austin, TX: University of Texas Press.

Beiner R & Nedelsky J (eds). 2001. *Judgment, imagination, and politics: Themes from Kant and Arendt*. Lanham: Rowman & Littlefield.

Bishop M. 2007. Transforming memory transforming. In: W le Roux & K van Marle (eds). *Law, memory and the legacy of Apartheid: Ten years after AZAPO v President of South Africa*. Pretoria: Pretoria University Law Press. 33-49.

Botha H. 2003. Metaphoric reasoning and transformative constitutionalism (Part 2). *Journal of South African Law* 2003:20-36.

— 2002. Metaphoric reasoning and transformative constitutionalism (Part 1). *Journal of South African Law* 2002:612-627.

Brudholm T. 2008. *Resentment's virtue: Jean Améry and the refusal to forgive*. Philadelphia, PA: Temple University Press.

Cassin B. 2002. The politics of memory: How to treat hate. *Quest: An African Journal of Philosophy* 16:18-35.

Christodoulidis E. 2004. 'End of history' jurisprudence: Dworkin in South Africa. *Acta Juridica* Jubilee Edition:64-85.

— 2000. Truth and reconciliation as risks. *Social & Legal Studies* 9:179-204.

Cockrell A. 1996. Rainbow jurisprudence. *South African Journal on Human Rights* 12:1-38.

Coetzee JM. 2000. *Disgrace*. New York: Penguin Books.

— 1992. *Doubling the point: Essays and interviews*. Boston, MA: Harvard University Press.

Cohen-Eliya M & Porat I. 2011. Proportionality and the culture of justification. *American Journal of Comparative Law* 59:463-490.

Cornell D & Muvangua N. 2011. *Ubuntu and the law: African ideals and postapartheid jurisprudence* New York: Fordham University Press.

De Vos P. 2001. A bridge too far? History as context in the interpretation of the South African Constitution, *South African Journal on Human Rights* 17:1-33.

Derrida J. 2002. Declarations of independence. In: E Rottenberg (ed). *Negotiations: Interventions and Interviews, 1971-2001*. Stanford, CA: Stanford University Press. 46-54.

Douzinas C. 2000. *The end of human rights: Critical legal thought at the turn of the century.* Oxford: Hart Publishing.

Dworkin R. 1986. *Law's empire.* Cambridge, MA: Belknap Press.

Frank J. 2005. *A democracy of distinction: Aristotle and the work of politics.* Chicago, IL: Chicago University Press.

Fukuyama F. 1992. *The end of history and the last man.* New York: Free Press.

Geuss R. 1999. *Morality, culture, and history: Essays on German philosophy.* Cambridge: Cambridge University Press.

Honig B. 1991. Declarations of independence: Arendt and Derrida on the problem of founding a republic. *American Political Science Review* 85:97-113.

Hunt L. 2008. *Inventing human rights: A history.* New York: WW Norton & Company.

Klare KE. 1998. Legal culture and transformative constitutionalism. *South African Journal on Human Rights* 14:146-188.

Kristeva J. 1991. *Strangers to ourselves.* New York: Columbia University Press.

Krog A. 2009. *Begging to be black.* Cape Town: Random House Struik.

Langa P. 1996. Transformative constitutionalism. *Stellenbosch Law Review* 17:351-360.

Le Roux W. 2004. Bridges, clearings, and labyrinths: The architectural framing of post-apartheid constitutionalism. *South African Public Law* 19:629-634.

Leebaw B. 2003. Legitimation or judgment: South Africa's restorative approach to transitional justice. *Polity* 36:23-51.

Lévinas E. 1987. *Time and the other.* Pittsburgh, PA: Duquesne University Press.

Lilla M. 2001. Hegel and the political theology of reconciliation. *Review of Metaphysics* 54:859-900.

Markell P. 2003. *Bound by recognition.* Princeton, NJ: Princeton University Press.

Meyer L. 2010. *The justice of mercy.* Ann Arbor, MI: University of Michigan Press.

— 2000. Unruly rights. *Cardozo Law Review* 22:1-50.

Minkinnen P. 2007. *Ressentiment* as suffering: On transitional justice and the impossibility of forgiveness. *Law and Literature* 19:513-532.

Motha S. 2010. 'Begging to be black': Liminality and critique in post-apartheid South Africa. *Theory, Culture & Society* 27:285-305.

Mureinik E. 1994. A bridge to where? Introducing the Interim Bill of Rights. *South African Journal on Human Rights* 10:31-48.

Nedelsky J. 2011. *Law's relations: A relational theory of self, autonomy, and law.* Oxford: Oxford University Press.

Nietzsche F. 1967. *On the genealogy of morals.* New York: Random House.

Pippin R. 2010. The paradoxes of power in the early novels of JM Coetzee. In: A Leist & P Singer (eds). *JM Coetzee and ethics: Philosophical perspectives on literature.* New York: Columbia University Press. 19-41.

Pretorius JL. 1998. A response to Professors Michelman and Van der Walt. *Acta Juridica* 282-287.

Ramose MB. 2002. *African philosophy through ubuntu.* Harare: Mond Books.

Risk RCB. 1996. Constitutional scholarship in the late nineteenth century: Making federalism work. *University of Toronto Law Journal* 46:427-457.

Scott D. 2005. *Conscripts of modernity: The tragedy of colonial enlightenment.* Durham, NC: Duke University Press.

Slaughter JR. 2007. *Human rights, Inc: The world novel, narrative form, and international law.* New York: Fordham University Press.

Taylor C. 1992. *Sources of the self: The making of the modern identity.* Cambridge: Cambridge University Press.

Van der Walt AJ. 2001. Dancing with codes – protecting, developing and deconstructing property rights in a constitutional state. *South African Law Journal* 118:258-311.

Van Marle K. 2009. Transformative constitutionalism as/and critique. *Stellenbosch Law Review* 20:286-301.

— 2004. 'Meeting the world halfway' – The limits of legal transformation. *Florida Journal of International Law* 16:651-664.

Van Niekerk M. 2010. *The Way of the Women*. M Heyns (transl). Portland, OR: Tin House Books.

Case Law:

AZAPO (Azanian Peoples Organisation) v President of the Republic of South Africa 1996 (8) BCLR 1015 (CC).

S v Makwanyane 1995 (3) SA 391 (CC).

LITERATURE, INVENTION AND LAW IN SOUTH AFRICA'S CONSTITUTIONAL TRANSFORMATION

Patricia Tuitt

Introduction

Notwithstanding Edward Said's many works that draw attention to the 'worldliness' of literature (Said 1983) and, specifically, his searing – and as yet unsurpassed criticism – of the imperialist structure and content of the nineteenth century novel (Said 1994), the ability of certain narrative forms (fictional literature being a prominent example) to "project [...] new possibilities of existence" (Aristodemou 2000:17) is largely considered an evident good. Again, notwithstanding the many ruined peoples and cultures that have attended the search for 'new worlds' and new possibilities, the spirit of invention that is said to inhere in literature and other aesthetic forms continues to be applauded – and this by scholars who would not deny that literature produces action on the 'real world'. Indeed, any suggestion that the inventive imaginings of the aesthete should be compared to what we might call 'political invention' – the conquests and discoveries and other ways in which political life is renewed – may well be considered conceptually unsound. Yet, such a comparison is precisely the objective of this contribution, for it aims to reflect upon the encounter of the aesthetic with the world "as something yet to be invented" (*ibid*) against other (mainly colonial) projects of invention. This paper, then, implicates contemporary literature not in past projects of colonial affirmation, but in the invention of the post-apartheid South Africa. Although inspired by Said's legacy, this is far from a rehearsal of his ideas, for it draws – as Said could or would not do – on the discipline of legal theory as a means of exposing what I argue is the sovereign violence of all attempts at creation or invention, including creation or invention where the aesthetic provides the means.

The paper is in two parts. Part one provides a commentary on the relation between law and aesthetic forms and is informed by discussion of the grounds of law, referring, among others, mainly to four prominent legal and political theorists: Benjamin (1921), Schmitt (2006), Fanon (1961) and Derrida (2002). In part two, I bring the theoretical analysis of the first part to bear upon Antjie Krog's *Begging to be black* (2009) in order to show that the author's attempt in that work to reimagine her world is a very stark illustration of the structural violence of the law operating on the aesthetic realm.

The question of which category of literature *Begging to be black* may be said to inhabit is very much at issue in this piece. While the work exhibits certain features and characteristics of the contemporary novel, its narrative is equally propelled along by a strong philosophical impulse. The cross-fertilisation of literary genres and disciplines that Krog's work may be said to illustrate is addressed in the first part of this essay, which cautions against the danger of interdisciplinary forms working to create totalising discourses, rather than acting to facilitate the fracturing and interrogation of supposedly unified discourses, as they were intended to do.

South Africa's constitutional transformation

To begin, I situate my argument within the South African constitutional space and, more generally, within the broader concerns of this collection. In particular, the origins of this paper were prompted by a much remarked-upon feature of the process of so-called 'constitutional transformation'. This feature may be summarised as an explicit search for a new ground or grounds on which the emerging post-apartheid political community could rest. In a telling refusal of the logic of reparation that marked the beginnings of the post-colony in Canada, Australia and New Zealand (to name some prominent examples), it was the quest for reconciliation that was to help bring about the post-apartheid South Africa. Such a transformation could not, it seemed, occur in opposition to the usual constitutional theories, political tropes and legal conventions and practices that have served to authorise past political community, including apartheid South Africa. Constitutional transformation was thus contingent also on bringing to the most elite forces of the Constitution (including South Africa's higher courts) an entirely fresh impulse of thought – hence the somewhat unprecedented reach for aesthetic forms as a means to articulate how a constitution could come about without also bringing about a constitutional *settlement* in the classic sense.[1] Thus contemporary artwork, novels and other forms of literature – forms that incontrovertibly exist within the realm of aesthetics – were drawn upon in an effort to demonstrate the limitless shape in which a new arrangement between the South African state and its peoples should be negotiated. Implicit (and often explicit) in this newly interrogated

1 For this and more general discussion, see Le Roux 2004.

constitutional process is the position which asserts that within the aesthetic form is less likely to be found the determinative strains against which positive law and conventional politics operate or are engaged.[2]

It is this position (surprisingly categorical in itself) that I argue must be received with caution – or even suspicion – if only so that the aesthetic may reach its undoubtedly transformative potential.

Bringing us back to the objective that the early post-apartheid constitutional struggle was intended to achieve, a *transformed* South African constitution would be identifiable as one that could bring about the disturbance of law. By the disturbance of law, I mean the inauguration of a new law, marked not only by differences in the content and shape of its positive norms, but by a process of destabilising the original sense of law as a force that enters the world to determine definitively what is and is not legitimate.[3] Thus, early proponents held fast to the possibility of transcending the current dispensation – let's call that dispensation the biopolitical – by bringing about change without structural violence. If so much can be legitimately read into the process of constitutional transformation, then such a project surely calls for explicit analysis of the aesthetic's relation to violence. To state this position in another way, attention to the function of the aesthetic in the biopolitical age should be paid from a vantage point other than to assume the innocence of aesthetics in the forming and maintenance of the biopolitical sphere, as I suggest many accounts seemingly do.

Looking at the most publicised aspects of the early shaping of post-apartheid South Africa, one could indeed be tempted to suppose that something was emerging that, if not quite dispelling the biopolitical, was at least seriously challenging its fundamental structure. The law of Benjamin's account – in which there is a clear line between state (sanctioned) violence and individual (unsanctioned) violence – was the first certainty of the modern world to be interrogated through the truth and reconciliation process, which implicated more than the state and state organs and officials in the law-preserving violence that sustained the apartheid regime for almost half a century.

But it is not only (or especially) this coming, aspirant post-apartheid community's attempt to bring into question the force of law which Le Roux (2004) alluded to when he talked of an 'aesthetic turn'. Instead, commentators observed a change in the registers in which constitutional developments are usually couched. The language of rule, proposition, decision and command began to be replaced by expressions more oblique, intuitive, malleable, equivocal, questing and curious, offering the means for a potentially radical encounter with modern law. Even judges in South Africa's highest constitutional court were not immune from the aesthetic sensibility.

Yet, that fascinating moment when law and politics appeared to be deferring to art and other high culture was quickly in danger of passing into history. Even as our discussion was taking place in 2010 in Stellenbosch, South Africa, commentators noted

2 Exemplary works include Klare 1998, Mbembe 2008, Pieterse 2005 and Van Marle 2004.

3 Alluding here to Walter Benjamin's (1921) account of modern law as constitutive of a law-creating and law-preserving violence.

that the early appeal of aesthetics in the fashioning of South Africa's constitutional transformation had begun to wane and that the old familiar language of law – nuanced by the worldwide, encompassing frame of human rights discourse – was returning.

It was against this disappearing frame of reference in discourses around South Africa's constitutional transformation that I pondered two questions: First, how can one sustain the inclusion of aesthetics in the project of constitutional transformation? Second, and more pertinently, what is aesthetics to *do* exactly if it is to break new ground for South Africa's political community? Apart from a few general remarks, I leave the first question to other, more strategic, heads and focus the first section of my argument on the last question.

Law and the aesthetic

My tentative response to the first question is that to bring aesthetics into the constituting of the new South Africa is to foreground, or better still, insist upon (not understate or elide) the place of aesthetics in the advent or grounding of law. This would necessarily implicate aesthetics in the structures of the biopolitical. It would be to accept that aesthetics is caught in the spiral of violence, which, per Benjamin, is "the whole life of law" and which "ruins [law] in advance" (in Derrida 2002:273). As I hope to demonstrate, such acceptance is necessary if aesthetics is to realise its transformative potential. The form of violence of the aesthetic is such as to potentially bring into question the violence of modern law and thus of the biopolitical order.

In this regard, it must be understood that South Africa's constitutional transformation – however radical the frames within which it is presented – is not a gesture towards some kind of divine force that will bring about abruptly and irrevocably the violence of modern constituting. The ambition to see a new South Africa recognises that what Fanon (1961:64) refers to as a "numb violence" will always be in evidence. It is this lesser, tolerable violence that, at the time when Fanon wrote (and during much of South Africa's recent past), was to be replaced by an intolerable level of violence, which Fanon called "violence in its natural state" (*ibid*:48) – a state in which, to move to Derrida, the state's violence, which during normal times presents itself "through the substitute of a supplement" (1990:1015), is revealed in its naked form.

Of all contemporary writing, Peter Goodrich's monograph *Law and the courts of love* (1996) perhaps best captures the place of the aesthetic in the biopolitical when Goodrich speaks of literature as a "minor jurisprudence" and a "rebel", on the wrong side of the cut between what is sanctioned and unsanctioned, legitimate and illegitimate (Goodrich 1996). In this sense, it is possible to view literature and other aesthetics as potentially expelling a force that has value for a transformative project, not because it is non-violent – all force must always be conceived of as violent – but because its force is such as to occasionally confront the law with the law's own force and thereby undermine it. In theoretical accounts of the relation between law and violence, this (what I shall call) potency/impotence is given over to the perpetrator of individual violence – the great criminal – which both Benjamin (1921) and Derrida (2002) mused upon. In this essay, I would like to explore how productive a positioning of literature and other aesthetic forms as *criminal* might prove to be.

Since transformation – whether it be a transformed politics or something that exists on a lesser plane – can never be brought about by the intervention of an agent or force that is intractably different from that which is sought to be transformed (the exotic has no hope in urging transformation), to invest the aesthetic with a force that is structured within the law is not, as might at first seem, to compromise its potential in relation to the forces we might summon it to oppose, thereby rendering the aesthetic form inoperative in the process of transformation. On the contrary, it is the temptation to invest the aesthetic form with only the impulse toward openness – and to deny the closures that it must also bring about to assert itself as a jurisprudence (albeit a minor one) – that will eventually stifle its potentially transformative force. The aesthetic is not free of violence, for the unsanctioned, denied authority, denied the role of a major jurisprudence, can only be non-violent in *not being,* not speaking at all. Judged illegal at birth, it will have to *erase* itself entirely if it is to free itself of violence. But violence that is unsanctioned is 'impotent' violence; per Benjamin, it is an "impotent" violence that can yet "undermine" not just this or that law, but the very idea of law itself (Benjamin 1921:239).

The answer to the second question (I think) follows naturally from the first: the aesthetic must continue to expel its impotent violence, while knowing itself as violent *and* at the same time ultimately impotent. It must know that it can only aspire to be the violence that unsettles the "ground without ground" (Derrida 1990:943) on which the law sits, and not become itself a grounding. Such an assertion, of course, sits uncomfortably with any attempt to elevate aesthetics in any project of transformation, for a claim to a role in transformation is to begin to elevate aesthetics to a level beyond that of culprit or criminal – operating on the wrong side of the law – as I suggest is the proper place of the aesthetic in relation to law. Despite the fact that there might be some tension between the argument I pursue here and the rest of this collection, I would still want to suggest that in functioning as a potent/impotent force, aesthetics (along with other genres of critique) brings into question the order that Benjamin, Derrida, Schmitt and Fanon have described and analysed so compellingly. This bringing into question is precisely the deconstructive moment which a good deal of Derrida's work sought to keep alive – to maintain without the need to fill the notion of deconstruction with specific content; a task that sometimes proved to be beyond Derrida himself. As I hope this essay will show, especially in its second half, the ambitions that are sometimes invested in the aesthetic have the dangerous potential of closing spaces for contestation in situations of the kind of which apartheid South Africa is perhaps an extreme example. Deconstruction – the simple and unending questioning of positions of dominance and all that makes those positions possible – can sometimes appear a weak tool, especially in the face of the physical violence and loss of liberty that is frequently meted out to individuals in an effort to preserve desperate regimes. It is only once avenues of contestation begin to disappear that we see how politically important such an opening is. When freedom of the press is made vulnerable, this danger is apparent to all. Less immediately apparent is the danger of a discursive terrain that speaks freely, but fails to sustain the differences that emerge when the speaker announces his position from within the boundaries of disciplines and genres that knew their own limits and, therefore, knew how dependent they were on other disciplines similarly circumscribed. If we take Krog's *Begging to be black* seriously as a text that traverses several fields and genres of writing – the literary novel and the work of philosophy being prominent modes – it is worth exploring how these very features of the work contribute to what I argue is its grounding in a very modern conception of politics and selfhood.

A *nomos* of thought?

Taking Goodrich's analysis of literature in relation to law as a cue, I now move on to consider the fundamental ordering of the modern world and how the aesthetic relates to that order. This brings me to the core of my argument. At the advent of every political community there is a cutting, appropriation and closure. There is a violent determination of what is legitimate (permissible) and what is not. This advent has had a well-analysed impact on land distribution across the world – on who can claim sovereignty and who cannot. It has been exhaustively analysed in terms of the justification of force: when may violence be legitimately deployed as a matter of principle – irrespective of the cases of its use (Benjamin 1921) – and who may or may not deploy it?

But the advent of law is not just a marker of the legitimate sphere of *action*, but also of thought, expression and form. As I have argued elsewhere, Schmitt's first "measure"[4] (2006:67) of all political community – the cut, the appropriation, the closure – is evident in all forms of thought and expression, including political and social action.

Legal and political theory has accorded great attention to the violent actions that have assigned people to a particular order and distributed land in the furtherance of sovereign claims. Less attention, I argue, has been focused on the implications of these forceful political acts for what can be imagined and expressed even in those forms of expression (like the aesthetic) that would not obviously announce its complicity in the violence of settlement.

A true effort at constitutional transformation must then engage combatively not only with that which Schmitt describes as the *nomos* of the earth – the material present, the earthly community – but also with what I will call for now the *nomos* of thinking: how the original act of closure determines what can be imagined or thought about the future. Once stated, the foregoing appears obvious, but there is still a strong trend in theoretical analysis that seems disinclined to consider the structures of thought in ways which go beyond speculation over the causative relation between an author's biography and particular works, such as the effect of Carl Schmitt's prominent membership of the Nazi party on the scope of his work and how it should be read today.

Rather than explore what is read or otherwise digested in the mind as being circumscribed by the coincidence of its content being linked to certain life choices and

4 For Carl Schmitt, the beginnings of political community are marked by a division of land (or a 'land-appropriation', as he was to term it), which gives force to all social and political life, not least of which the positive laws (legislation) that govern (2006; see especially Chapters 4 and 5).

histories, I would entertain the idea that the advent of law of which Benjamin writes has implications for the whole of thinking: on what is possible to be thought and on available avenues through which thought can be expressed, be it thinking in writing, drawing, mathematics or musical notation.

Now, whether Goodrich was correct in ascribing to literature the status of rebel or 'minor jurisprudence' is immaterial; what is correct and material is that there are forms through which thinking is expressed that have 'outsider' or 'rebel' status: a status that is given as law enters the world. Until the advent of Benjamin's poorly elaborated 'divine' violence,[5] such 'rebels' can (much like individuals who deploy violence in defiance of a state monopoly on violence) offer only impotent violence to the law – that is, unsettle or deconstruct it. It is in this light that it may be useful to speak of aesthetics in the transformation of South Africa's constitutional order.

Thought and discipline

So, the question of whether aesthetics can play a part in South Africa's constitutional transformation is ultimately a question of *law*. In this regard, I would argue that while there may be avenues of escape from the constraints of positive norms – avenues which some Supreme Court judges (Sachs in particular)[6] have sought through reference to the aesthetic – there is no such easy escape from the force of law. When I argue that the role of aesthetics in South Africa's new constitution is a matter of law, I mean specifically that it is question of the form of thinking that was *authorised* in the advent of law. Law cut both thinking and acting into legitimate and illegitimate spheres and legitimated (or, less emphatically, made authoritative) thinking that represented/replicated the cut, appropriation, closure – the primary act of law, which is also a thought.

In this light, it is instructive to reflect upon what is implied in the oft-asserted claim that we inhabit a world structured according to a form of scientific rationality. What might such a claim have to do with law, or have to say about the operation of law? Such an exercise entails giving attention to the frame of thinking that characterises the scientific and, in doing so, recognising that if the natural and social sciences are dominant perspectives or frameworks of reasoning, analysis or consciousness, this is because aspects of these sciences obey the primary injunction of the law as it enters thought. To state the matter differently, the characteristics of some forms of scientific thought and processes represent the movement of law as it grounds itself in producing norms, rules, models, axioms, maxims and generalisations – measuring, observing, cutting, separating and discerning.

Consistent with the problem of dominance in modernity more generally, a dominant discipline within the academy or other spheres in which free or pure thought is

[5] Otherwise referred to as non-juridical violence, this is a form of violence that will end the biopolitical order through a force that is not recognisable within the frame of law-creating and law-preserving violence. Many writers have sought to elucidate the nature of divine violence, most recently Žižek (2008).

[6] For an interesting and moving analysis, see Sachs 2008.

nurtured becomes so only through being propelled by the force of law, enabling that discipline to attempt to comprehend the entire world. It is only through a slave-like obedience to law and its 'mystical' foundations that science can claim a foremost place in the means through which we comprehend our existence.

Let it not be said, however, that this obedience to law is peculiar to the discipline of science, for it has always been a marked feature of philosophy as well – a discipline that, following Bruno Latour's brilliant provocations in *We have never been modern* (1993) and other works, is a frame which also encompasses (literally!) all things in the world. How often, since Foucault, has it been said that critique (philosophical reflection) has always assumed the structure of laws. Derrida remarks that "[i]nsofar as it implies decision in the form of judgement and question with regard to the right to judge", the concept of critique "thus has an essential relation, in itself, to the sphere of law or right" (1990:983). The *nomos* of thinking/thought is the appropriation of thinking for the preservation (as well as the grounding) of law.

In this sense, if science is considered to be problematic to a transformative politics – at least in comparison to aesthetics – it can be so only because science sits on the legitimate side of the law, where, we must surely accept, it coexists most comfortably with philosophy.

To anticipate certain conclusions I will draw in the second part of this essay, Krog's interdisciplinary engagement in *Begging to be black* (2009) – which supposedly allows this work to elude characterisation as a simple novel – is argued in other chapters of this volume to be an element (among others) which lends it a quality that would justify the attention which has been paid to it by commentators on the new politics of South Africa. Yet, it is precisely the work that can speak to law, and speak through the language of law, which must, rationally speaking, command attention. It is the very juxtaposition of forms (including of dominant modes of thinking) – the seeming joining of the unfamiliar – in Krog's work that enables, in a seeming paradox, a very familiar tale about the origins of the modern European world to be uncritically related.

Law, philosophy, literature

Continuing in the vein of a preamble to the analysis of *Begging to be black*, in contrast to the minor jurisprudential status that Goodrich accords literature, philosophy is a major jurisprudence. Remembering literature as a feature of the origin of law may unsettle the law, but there is no unsettling relation between law and philosophy – that is to say, no major erosion of the force of law can come about through the interrogation of the languages and logics of law through the forms of thinking characteristic of the discipline of philosophy. There is, however, the appearance of fracture when philosophy is brought to the contemplation of law, which comes about with the disassembling of the *languages* of law, which are themselves a result of conventions far removed in time and space from the *origins* of law. Put more simply, philosophical thought and language have been very helpfully opposed to positive law and, indeed, have elucidated the character of the *nomos* from which these positive norms are derived. Yet the authority with which philosophy speaks is the authority of that very same law, and as such, it poses a very delicate challenge to any minor form which may be enticed into a seemingly fruitful alliance. Until we confront seriously the grounds of law, the cognitive and expressive order – that which determines how the world is perceived, analysed and reasoned, as well as the forms in which perception, analysis and reason are expressed – will replicate in varying but identifiable ways the first thought that came with law. Alternate thinking communities, therefore, can only rebel on the wrong side of the cut between what is permissible or impermissible, authoritative or illegitimate.

The inexorable logic of this analysis and my as yet not fully fledged criticism of Krog's work is that until we confront productively the grounds of law, it is also important to *keep* the rebels, the minor jurisprudences, as rebels and *minor* jurisprudences. If not, we expand the sphere of thinking that simply replicates law's original or primary thought, so that what are now dominant frames of reference will become totalising frames, leaving alive no possibility for the deconstruction of the law. It is with this caveat, this cautionary note, that we may bring aesthetics into the field of constituting and the project of constitutional transformation.

If aesthetics can properly be said to occupy the wrong side of the cut between what is permissible in thought and what is not (and this is a big if, because that particular case has not yet been made, in the sense of being proved rather than simply asserted), it now faces the particular challenge of remaining *minor*. And, as I hope I have made clear, being minor and remaining minor is not primarily a matter of guarding against a particular worldview – for example, a scientific worldview – but of guarding against the appearance of law in its originary form within *any* thought event.

The minor person or form always faces the great temptation of finding ways to cease to be minor. When such a quest is sought to be achieved in alliance with another minor person, thing or form, the possibility for contestation over means and ends remain. Whether the aesthetic can remain minor in the face of the allure of more totalising disciplines and the frames of thought common to them is thus crucial to the transformative potential of the aesthetic. Krog's work ceases to claim any minor, rebel status from the moment of its unthinking choice to eschew the simple form of the novel in favour of some speaking frame through which its author could speak with more influence, more authority, more persuasion – to speak, in other words, in the voice of the law.

Begging to be black

In the second half of this essay, I apply the arguments of the first half to what Motha has described as "a work of literary non-fiction" (Motha 2010:289).[7] Antjie Krog's *Begging to be black* (2009) is a text in which Goodrich's minor jurisprudence is engaged in what I hope to be able to show is a dangerous, and unfortunately not uneasy, alliance with what, again borrowing from Motha, is quite evidently a Deleuzian philosophical frame.

The question of being minor, remaining minor, and, more significantly, *becoming* minor, is one that is expressly posed in the book. And what I hope to show in this section of

7 The essay contains an excellent and balanced summary of the novel (pp 290-292).

the essay is that, from the title to the conclusion of the work, as well as in virtually every sentence and with virtually every utterance, Krog presents for us the process of the law's self-grounding.

The heart of this already widely-read work demands only a brief summary. It centres on the author's sense of displacement in the new, post-apartheid South Africa. The crisis of her being part of the white Afrikaner minority at the beginning of majority rule is brought to a head by her implication in the murder of a gang leader by ANC associates in 1992. According to Krog's account, she became involved in events following the murder after being asked by an individual she had associated with politically during the apartheid regime to dispose of a T-shirt, which she then discovered provided vital evidence relating to the murder. We learn also that further evidence of the murder – which, unlike the T-shirt, had not passed through her hands – was concealed on her premises. Forced to confront the moral, political and ethical questions attendant upon her decisions and actions, Krog sets out to discover whether she can live in a new relation with post-apartheid South Africa.

Invention

A significant aspect of this process of renegotiation is Krog's deep preoccupation in her work with King Moshoeshoe I's encounter with Boer and English settlers. Moshoeshoe was Sovereign over Basutoland, currently known as Lesotho, home to the Sotho people. We learn from *Begging to be black* that Moshoeshoe had, by the end of his life, lost more than half of this land to the Boers and the English. The King's life and his encounters with the English and the Boers, which included three wars (1851, 1865 and 1867) from which he emerged as victor, were narrated by the French missionary Eugène Casalis, who served as Foreign Adviser to Moshoeshoe during much of his rule.

I begin my analysis by noting that Krog seeks quite explicitly in this work to reinvent herself, a reinvention that, for Krog, must take place through a relocation of herself away from what she describes towards the end of the work as her "white capsule" to the (as we shall see) highly fetishised black body. Specifically, what she needed to reinvent for herself was "the life of a remarkable King" (Krog 2009:269). Thus, the *becoming of being* in the work follows an equivalent series of moves as the beginning of political community – and nothing that yet exists in legal and political theory has served to seriously unsettle Carl Schmitt's (2006:48)[8] claim that such a beginning is "not only logically, but also historically" preceded by an appropriation, which then serves as the source of all that follows in political life and culture. Krog's becoming (and perhaps all becomings, rather than beings or remainings) must also proceed from an appropriation – not the appropriation of land, but rather of another being, which must precede her entrance into 'blackness'. For more than half of the book, Krog (as she herself admits) lives vicariously through the life of the King. And while Krog's self-invention works upon the King's life, the work never reveals that she has any consciousness of what remains of his life as a result of her incursion.

[8] See p 48 for an effective expression of Schmitt's thoughts on the origin of political community.

At this early stage, it is also perhaps sufficient to note that more than half of *Begging to be black* is devoted to a recounting of how Krog lives the life of a 'remarkable' king who, ironically, had lost more than half of his land to Boer and English settlers by the end of his life. We might pause here to reflect on how Krog chooses to use the blank pages that stood before the published text. Just as during the age of colonial land acquisitions European settlers never encountered an expanse of land that they could not occupy and later seize, so Krog never hesitates in her conviction that the life of the 'remarkable King' was one to be ruthlessly reproduced and rewritten in aid of her own salvation or reawakening. Her conviction that the King's life may also accommodate her turbulent imaginings and yet remain a life is a remarkable and, in my view, disturbing presence in the work.

Paraphrasing the Deleuzian philosopher Paul Patton, who supposedly figures in the book as Krog's interlocutor, Motha (2010:299) questions whether *Begging to be black* is "another instance of the coloniser being convinced that the colonisers are utterly different", thereby "subtly keeping ingrained racism alive". Here Motha presents for us so seemingly banal and obvious a starting point for critique that one is in grave danger of resisting the invitation it carries. That one is tempted to resist it points to the innocence of violence which certain forms that draw on the aesthetic have been able to silently assert. Motha's casual invitation should not be resisted. Whenever those who hold a western worldview – the compass Krog identifies with (at least until she succeeds in becoming black, at around page 268 of the book) – declare an invention, a new beginning, a transformation or a *becoming*, every critical sense should be on the alert, for history is deeply encumbered with the impoverished lands and cultures that result from the Westerner's impulse toward invention.

Krog seeks to effect her renewal by 'begging to be black' – begging to enter the life of the 'remarkable King'. Moving from content to form, we must note that the structure of the book – whether deliberately so or not is hard to tell – captures the persistence of the beggar caricature. Each of the three parts of the book contains chapters where the reader is alternatively given Krog's inner musings as she journeys between her home in South Africa, her sabbatical stay in Berlin and her ostensibly 'humble' encounters with King Moshoeshoe. Thus, each time the reader scopes a chapter in which Krog appears to have moved out of the King's life, she returns to it in the next. She is as persistent a presence as the Boers and the English who, we recall, seized his lands but left his life intact. That she is free to come and go from Berlin to Lesotho is a remarkable conceit. Can Krog really have wanted by this narrative structure to remind us that free movement is a right that *European* citizens have always had at their command to effect radical change in various locations, and thereby to reinvent themselves? But here, it is Krog's imagination that *must* be free: as she says in 'Conversation 3: Imagining Black', she must be free to 'imagine black' (Krog 2009:122-123). Of course, Krog is not alone in entertaining the idea that to be free to imagine the world is the greatest thing that literature or the aesthetic can bring. Very often, such freedom to imagine is supposedly put to use in the service of the minor person. Per Aristodemou:

> [The] imagination is celebrated for making what is absent present, for freeing us from the constraints of the empirical world and for projecting new possibilities of existence. [...] A possible experience of truth is not the same as an actual experience

> of truth minus its 'reality value', but has something quite divine about it, as fire, a soaring, a readiness to build and a conscious utopianism that does not shrink from reality but sees it as a project, something yet to be invented. The power to surpass the self and the here and now invests the imagination with an ethical role: chief among its tasks [...] is to bear witness to forgotten or silenced voices, suppressed histories, and unsayable or unsaid past events. (Aristodemou 2000:17)

Yet we must not forget that most projects of invention are precisely projects of the *imagination*. It was the ability to imagine fully populated and governed spaces as desolate, deserted, uninhabited – as yet to be invented – that marked the so-called 'golden age' of discovery.

The constitutive act of land appropriation occurs at the beginning of every political community, but it takes many forms. It happens through wars and conquest, but as often, it occurs through the migration and settlement of peoples and the gradual acquisition of the lands and other possessions of those indigenous to the land. Although King Moshoeshoe's emerged victorious from his wars with the English and the Boers, these conflicts nevertheless depleted his territory. But territorial losses had already occurred much earlier, when, as Eugene Casalis records, the Boers arrived in the late 1830s under the guise of needy individuals seeking temporary shelter. Stories about leaders of indigenous tribes welcoming seemingly stricken European travellers and then being tricked into signing treaties agreeing to significant, yet lawful, land transfers are legion. Has this well-known process through which territory was appropriated ever been characterised as a strategy of begging? I do not think so, but one of the very few valuable things Krog gives us in this work is precisely a fitting framework within which to describe and analyse various practices of colonial imposition. Begging, according to the ever-instructive *Wikipedia*, is the practice of soliciting something, usually in a supplicating manner, *without having anything to offer in exchange* (my emphasis). But, initially humble, Boer settlers were soon (according to Casalis) "to throw of their mask" (Krog 2009:132), and within less than a hundred pages, the supplicating title of Krog's work is replaced by the insistent "I want": "I want an African perspective" (*ibid*:93); "I want to be part of the country I was born in. I need to know whether it is possible for somebody like me to become like the majority, to become 'blacker' and live as a full and at-ease component of the South African psyche" (*ibid*:93). And Krog will get what she wants, for make no mistake, her becoming is a 'discovery' in the sense of the old legal doctrine, which, according to Fitzpatrick (2001:161), remains "an impelling force in the treatment of peoples supposedly once discovered and in the self-identity of those who would claim to have once discovered them".

Let me make the point more bluntly: Krog cannot enter the life of that 'remarkable King' and his world until she clears away enough of that same world, namely the part that is populated by imaginings which are not hers, allowing her imagination to roam free, to imagine blackness. As we know all too well from history, the white man's journey to being black requires that he creates a significant amount of open space first – it is in the service of his self-invention that the fiction of *terra nullius* was devised. To relate this to begging, Krog's becoming means that she must not just intentionally move to inhabit the body and psyche of the King – covering so much incidental ground too on her journey – she must make of everything she sees during that journey an alien thing; she must make of the world she enters a desolate one, so that what she begs for seems so much less valuable than it really is. To provide a telling example, Krog writes as follows about former president Thabo Mbeki:

> [I]f Angela Merkel or the Australian prime minister says something, you do not sit dumbfounded thinking: God where did that come from? There is a traceable logic from within your framework to understand even if you passionately disagree with them [...] at times when my President speaks [...] and [Krog cannot resist saying] he is an intelligent man, I sit like somebody in complete darkness. It is not necessarily that I don't know what he is saying, I don't even know where it is coming from, from within what logic it wants to assert itself as 'right'. (Krog 2009:94)

Was Mbeki really that strange? That he made many an objectionable comment during his time in office is not in doubt, but had Krog really never encountered his 'logic' before during her energetic days in the ANC? Or is it rather that Mbeki's strangeness emerged (or had to emerge) only through Krog's invention? To remove Mbeki (and, crucially, all he represents) from her path of comprehension and conversation, she must make him strange, exotic. What she does with him (and all like him) then, outside of language, can leave little identifiable sign in the world.

There are other examples in the text where Krog appears to apply what I argue is the coloniser's strategy of begging – a strategy that begins with the coloniser reducing in value the object of desire. For example, in 'Conversation 5' (2009:184) and 'Conversation 7' (*ibid*:266), Krog reduces the philosophical horizon of black South Africa to the notion of interconnectedness. In contrast to the manner in which Krog approaches the philosophies of the West, little is provided by way of elaboration of this potentially expansive notion. The reader is left with the unmistakable impression that interconnectedness is a simple and self-evident concept, demanding limited intellectual engagement.

Having created her barren land – her wasteland, *her terra nullius*[9] – throughout the pages of the text, Krog arrives at page 268 to find what the reader could not doubt she would, as it is something that was found at the end of all the colonial journeys of old and, as such, for someone like Krog who merely retraces those journeys, could not have been otherwise: she finds "the grace and forgiveness of black people" (Krog 2009:269).

9 I invoke here reference to a particular technique of colonial governance which decreed that Europeans could settle in foreign lands that were uninhabited. The doctrine quickly expanded beyond its literal sense to justify the colonisation of lands that were inhabited by people deemed to be 'backward' in terms of their social, political and economic organisation. The expanded sense of the doctrine is in opposition to an appreciation that new political beginnings cannot always develop on fresh or virgin ground, but only through a process whereby inhabited land is claimed and represented as new. Recent post-colonial critique has effectively demonstrated how this particular colonial technique can only do its work by denying the existence, cultures and laws of those indigenous to the lands. It is this process of denial that allowed fully populated lands to be represented as empty. Krog's denial of the basic sense behind the former South African president is, I suggest, a contemporary instance of the process of creating a *terra nullius* in the expanded sense of the old doctrine.

Conclusion

Such a reading of *Begging to be black* as I have provided here might be thought by many to be ungenerous, for it goes very much against the grain of other assessments of the same work. I prefer the reader to dwell less on whether another version of Krog's mission could as plausibly be offered and to contemplate instead what possibilities of interpretation are opened or (conversely) are closed when the aesthetic or – if we are to accept the author's claim that *Begging to be black* is defiantly non-aesthetic – the work, which self-evidently strives to transcend the simple novel or simple philosophy, is read without the mantle of innocence that often attends such aesthetic or experimental works. For such is the point of this contribution: the aesthetic can have transformative potential (and can therefore be deployed effectively in South Africa's effort at constitutional transformation), provided that it remains alive to its ruinous origins and suppresses the urge to be other than 'other'.

Reference List

Aristodemou M. 2000. *Law and literature: Journeys from here to eternity.* Oxford: Oxford University Press.

Benjamin W. [1921] 1986. Critique of violence. In: P Demetz (ed). *Reflections: Essays, Aphorisms, Autobiographical Writings*. New York: Schocken Books. 277-301.

Derrida J. 2002. Force of law: the mystical foundations of authority'. In. G Anidjar (ed). *Acts of Religion*. New York: Routledge.

Fanon F. 1961. *The Wretched of the Earth.* London: Pluto Classics.

Fitzpatrick P. 2001. *Modernism and the grounds of law*. Cambridge: Cambridge University Press.

Goodrich P. 1996. *Law in the courts of love: Literature and other minor jurisprudences*. London: Routledge.

Klare KE. 1998. Legal culture and transformative constitutionalism. *South African Journal on Human Rights* 14:146-188.

Krog A. 2009. *Begging to be black*. Cape Town: Random House Struik.

Latour B. 1993. *We have never been modern*. Cambridge, MA: Harvard University Press.

Le Roux W. 2004. Bridges, clearings and labyrinths: the architectural framing of post-apartheid constitutionalism. *South African Public Law* 19:629-664.

Mbembe A. 2008. Passages to freedom: the politics of racial reconciliation in South Africa. *Public Culture* 20:5-18.

Motha S. 2010. 'Begging to be black': Liminality and critique in post-apartheid South Africa. *Theory, Culture & Society* 27:285-305.

Pieterse M. 2005. What do we mean when we talk about transformative constitutionalism?' *South African Public Law* 20:155-165.

Sachs A. 2008. *The strange alchemy of life and law*. New York: Oxford University Press.

Said E. 1994. *Culture and imperialism*. New York: Vintage Books.

— 1983. *The world, the text and the critic*. Cambridge, MA: Harvard University Press.

Schmitt C. 2006. *The Nomos of the Earth in the International Law of the Jus Publicum Europaeum*. New York: Telos Press.

Van Marle K. 2004. Lives of action, thinking and revolt: A feminist call for politics and becoming in post-apartheid South Africa. *South African Public Law* 19:605-628.

Žižek S. 2008. *Violence*. London: Profile Books.

AS IF

Constitutional narratives and 'forms of life'

Stewart Motha

On 16 August 2012, the South African Police Service opened fire and killed thirty-four striking mineworkers at the Marikana platinum mine near Rustenburg in north-east South Africa. Over seventy striking miners were also injured in the shooting. Many miners had been shot in the back, and some a long way from police lines. The killings have been compared to the Sharpeville massacre of 1960 and the bloodiest episodes of police violence unleashed by the apartheid state. A police force controlled by a black majority government of the ANC unleashed deadly force on its people. The mineworkers had been striking with a claim for higher pay and better conditions. The National Union of Mineworkers (NUM), allied with the ANC, and the Association of Mineworkers and Construction Union (AMCU) had also been vying for control of striking workers by using intimidation and violence. The NUM was formed in the 1980s to fight apartheid labour laws. Its leader was Cyril Ramaphosa, then a senior ANC labour leader and now a member of the board of Lonmin, the UK-based company that owns the Marikana mine. This combination of state violence, a political elite implicated as stakeholders in a privately owned mining industry, the interests of multinational mining corporations, and the post-massacre ANC statements to calm investors has left little to distinguish the 'post-apartheid' political order from the erstwhile racial state of the 1980s. A 'form of life' as citizen, worker and striker whose equality, dignity and right to life were laudably established in the post-1994 constitutional dispensation seemed all too readily extinguishable.[1]

The events at the Marikana mine serve to highlight a deep crisis in South Africa. The post-1994 constitutional order was meant to inaugurate an era of social and economic transformation. The political challenge was to hold together a racially and economically divided society that had been founded on more than three centuries of colonial violence and dispossession.

The long struggle against apartheid and the post-1994 constitutional dispensation were both oriented by a central myth. From the ANC *Freedom Charter* of 1955 to the preamble to *The Constitution of the Republic of South Africa* (No 108 of 1996), the founding assertion was that "South Africa belongs to all who live in it". This postulation – this 'as if' – was the basis for the 'post-racial' compact that the ANC was keen to see inaugurated in South Africa. Instead of the alleviation of poverty, or the nationalisation of mines and radical redistribution of property, a constitutional order was introduced that would seek to guarantee the equal citizenship of all South Africans. A bill of rights that included the guarantee of social and economic rights served to juridicalise and thus thwart the political demands for radical social and economic transformation. The newly democratic parliament was emasculated by the introduction of constitutional supremacy over parliamentary sovereignty (Ramose 2007). Racial equality was reduced to 'black economic empowerment', or a black minority's entry into the economic elite.

The Marikana massacre suggests that the assertion animating the post-apartheid constitutional dispensation – that 'South Africa belongs to all who live in it' – is a 'degenerate myth'.[2] What would it mean to do away with such fictions? What constitutional narratives would sustain more liberated 'forms of life'? The immediate retort might be that 'narratives' do not liberate; acting to change the social conditions in which life is lived does. However, the problem of status, class and the movement of the emancipatory agent from particular conditions to the general horizon of liberation will inevitably run up against the problem of imagining redemption (the messianic) and representation (at base a problem of language that is manifested also in politics).[3] Giorgio Agamben, preferring Jules de Gaultier's *Bovarysme* (after

---

1 See ss.9-12 of *The Constitution of the Republic of South Africa*, No 108 of 1996, which guarantee the right to equality, dignity and life. Trade union and labour rights are guaranteed in s.23.

2 Below I explore the distinction between myths and fictions through Frank Kermode's *A Sense of an Ending* (2000).

3 This compresses a much larger discussion of class and political agency and the relationship between state and civil society, which I have discussed elsewhere in Motha S. 2012. The Debt Crisis as a Crisis of Democracy. *Law, Culture and Humanities*, 8:390-397. There I discuss Ernesto Laclau's treatment of Karl Marx, 'Contribution to a Critique of Hegel's Philosophy of Law: Introduction' in J Butler, E Laclau & S Žižek (eds). 2000. *Contingency, Hegemony, Universality: Contemporary Dialogues on the Left*. London: Verso. p 44 ff.

Flaubert) to Vaihinger's treatment of the centrality of fiction and the 'as if', makes the point thus: "Because he is not anything in himself, man can only be if he acts as if he were different from what he is (or what he is not)" (Agamben 2005:37).[4] This puts fiction at the heart of inventing and reinventing who we are. Can a form of political life be sustained without the fictions that ground law and society? Can South Africa, or indeed any polity, abandon the 'as if' that grounds the constitutional order? What is the role of fables – of illusory or consciously false knowledge – in constitutional thinking?

There is something essential in the constitutional 'form' that requires a fiction – a consciously false 'as if'. The illusory (fiction) is a source of 'sense' – a response to the crisis of 'value' in the modern condition of being caught between disenchantment (the disavowal of myth) and nihilism.[5] The response from critical thinkers to exclusionary and harmful myths that buttress violence has been to chart and orient ethical and political demands through a variety of 'forms of life' that are produced in the encounter between sovereign power and those subject to it (for example, bare life, grievable life, vulnerable life, etc, by Giorgio Agamben (1998) and Judith Butler (2009), respectively). In the discussion that follows, I explore the potential of imagining 'liminal' subjects as a 'form of life' that occupies the frontier between past and future. Liminal beings inaugurate political life in societies that are grappling with deep divisions and violent colonial legacies.

My inquiry is a response to two persistent constitutional problems. The first goes under the banner of the 'paradox of constitutionalism' (Loughlin & Walker 2007). This is the problem of the 'we', or constituent power (*potentia*, law-making violence, etc). The paradox lies in the fact that the 'we' of a constitutional order comes second – that is, after the inauguration of what is constituted or done in their name (Lindahl 2007). The 'as if' is the dominant constitutional form through which a social compact sustains the contradiction that there is nothing before the law – nothing before the sovereign enactment of the law. In the discussion that follows, I trace the contours of this 'as if' in constitutional thinking.

The second constitutional problem is connected to the first. If the 'we' of a juridico-political order has no presence other than through the mode of constituting itself through sovereign violence and law, then what is to be done with the lives excluded in this process? Much of the critical writing on sovereignty and governance has been concerned with this relationship between sovereignty and political community. The inclusion or exclusion of a 'form of life' is at the heart of constituting a juridical order. Critical thinkers including Benjamin, Arendt, Fanon, Agamben and Butler have engaged the problem of sovereign violence through 'forms of life' that are the condition and residue of the sovereign inauguration of law and political community. Life intersects with law through a 'form' that cloaks subjects as citizen, slave, worker, woman, refugee, alien or abandoned being. To what extent can this 'form of life' – one that is conditioned in and through violence – be re-grounded through fictions that

4 See also 29-43 for a discussion of Marx's notion of class in these terms.

5 See Jean-Luc Nancy, *The Sense of the World* (1997).

are a *counter-archive* of constitutional thinking? This chapter sets out to explore how fiction – the 'as if' – archives the violence that grounds law. Law's counter-archive is to be found within constitutional fictions as well as the aesthetic forms that put the ethical and political limits of being into question.

'As if' – constitutional fictions

In a tradition as old as Kant's *Critique of Pure Reason* (1781), the 'as if' (the consciously false, illusory knowledge, or legal fiction) has been a motif deployed in critical engagements with law. The lawless origin of law was Kant's main political concern, and so he urged members of a civil state to proceed 'as if' the law was legitimately grounded on reason. The most influential legal theorist to adopt and elaborate this approach was Hans Kelsen, who proposed the *Grundnorm* ('basic norm') by way of a regressive attribution of the legal order to a higher norm (Kelsen 1991). This is nothing but another instance of the 'as if'. Kelsen was following in the wake of neo-Kantians of the nineteenth century such as Hans Vaihinger, who brought the 'as if' to bear on religion, physics, linguistics and mathematics (Vaihinger 1924). In the twentieth century, eminent literary theorists like Frank Kermode and philosophers like Jacques Derrida and Jean-Luc Nancy have all deployed the 'as if' in critical engagements with literary texts, sovereign events, and the future of the university.

Let us begin with the dominant animating fiction of the South African constitutional order, the 'as if' that informed the anti-apartheid struggle and now underpins post-apartheid law and politics and the 'new' constitutional order. This is the declaration of the ANC *Freedom Charter* of 1955 that "South Africa belongs to all who live in it". This performative declaration of commonality, equality, home, property, territory and belonging informs the regime of post-apartheid constitutional rights.

The words from the *Freedom Charter* are repeated in the preamble to the *Constitution* of 1996 (emphasis added in bold):

> We, the people of South Africa,
> Recognise the injustices of our past;
> Honour those who suffered for justice and freedom in our land;
> Respect those who have worked to build and develop our country; and
> **Believe that South Africa belongs to all who live in it**, united in our diversity.
> We therefore, through our freely elected representatives, adopt this Constitution as the supreme law of the Republic [...].[6]

A constitution is like and unlike other Acts or legislation. Derrida draws our attention to the multiple senses of the term 'Act': it is at once performance, legislative decree, mimetic action, a simulation and counterfeit, and the work of substituting as proxy on behalf of another, to stand in, to act as and for another.[7]

The *Constitution* is also believed to be the Act above all Acts. The question that always follows from this characterisation is: with what authority and in whose name

6 Emphasis added.

7 See epigraph, Derrida, *Acts of Literature* (1991:vii) – referring there to the OED definition of 'Act'.

is a constitution or constituted order created? This is often referred to as the paradox of constitutionalism. Would the 'people' who authorise the signature of him who signs on their behalf not already have to exist, and would such a 'people' not already have to be united by a legal order, for no other form can express the unity of diverse constituent parts (Kelsen *contra* Schmitt)?[8] The declarative act is a performative contradiction.

Additionally, the foundation, the act of constituting, is lawless. 'We the people' proceed 'as if' we already existed as such and could authorise our representatives to act on our behalf. The constituent assembly or force is only retroactively a constituent power of a constituted order. 'We' proceed 'as if' – that is, with the consciously false and the fictive at the heart of a constitutional order. The first Act, then, is an 'act of literature'. There is a long history to this account of the constituent event harbouring the 'as if'.

The question this formulation of law as literature raises is the one posed by Jacques Derrida (1991:187) in relation to Kafka's short story, *Before the Law* (1915): who judges, and by what criteria, that a particular narrative, myth, fiction, story or 'relation' belongs to literature? The homologous question follows in law: who decides, and by what criteria, that a particular act or narrative constitutes law? In reciting the constitutional narrative – in re-citing the law – law is as much a work of literature as literature is a problem of law (of genre for instance).

Derrida takes the problem back to Kant. Having reflected on whether Kant's account of practical reason harbours elements of the fantastic or of narrative fiction, Derrida asks: "what if the law, without itself being transfixed by literature, shared the conditions of its possibility with the literary object?" (1991:191). Derrida was referring to the formulation of Kant's second categorical imperative. In his *Groundwork for the Metaphysics of Morals*, Kant expressed the centrality of the 'as if':

> Because the universality of the law in accordance with which effects happen constitutes that which is really called nature in the most general sense (in accordance with its form), i.e. the existence of things insofar as it is determined in accordance with universal laws, thus the universal imperative of duty can also be stated as follows: So **act as if** the maxim of your action were to become through your will a universal law of nature. (Kant 2002:38 – emphasis added in bold)

The 'as if' enables Kant to reconcile practical reason with a 'historical teleology' and 'unlimited progress'. This 'as if' introduces narrative and fiction into the core of legal thought (Derrida 1991). The narrative and the law appear together: "[...] the story, as a certain type of relation, is linked to the law that it relates, appearing, in so doing, before that law, which appears before it". But nothing is presented in this appearance – we cannot experience the appearance of the law as such, we have no "proof or experience of it" (*ibid*:191). There is no history, genesis or derivation of categorical authority. What is concealed and invisible in law is the "being-law" of law (*ibid*:192).

---

8 See Derrida, 'Declarations of Independence', for an excellent reading of the US Declaration of Independence in these terms, and Hans Lindahl, 'Constituent Power and Reflexive Identity: Towards an Ontology of Collective Selfhood' in M Loughlin & N Walker (eds). 2007. *The Paradox of Constitutionalism*. Oxford: Oxford University Press. 9-24.

The narrative or fiction of the law takes the place of an uncertain origin that must be placed beyond scrutiny. Kant thus places the authority of the civil state beyond critique:

> The origin of the supreme power, for all practical purposes, is **not discoverable** by the people who are subject to it. In other words the subject **ought not** to indulge in **speculations** about its origins with a view to acting upon them, as if its right to be obeyed were open to doubt (**ius controversum**). For since the people must already be considered as united under a legislative will before they can pass rightful judgement upon the highest power within the state (**summon imperium**), they cannot and may not pass any judgement other than that which is willed by the current head of state (**summus imperans**). Whether in fact an actual contract originally preceded their submission to the state's authority (**pactum subiectionis civilis**), whether the power came first and the law only appeared after it, or whether they ought to have followed this order – these are completely futile arguments for a people which is already subject to civil law, and they constitute a menace to the state. (Kant 1991:143 – original emphasis in bold)

At first glance, this seems like the avoidance of contradiction – the people would already have to be united by a law which they then call into question. However, it is difficult to square this with the demand that everything must submit to critique. As Panu Minkkinen has put it, "critique is the sovereign philosopher-lawgiver's negative legislation in which he defines the legitimate boundaries of his self-knowledge" (2009:57). It turns out that critique is also submission. This of course leads to a "scandalous contradiction", as the 'philosopher-lawgiver' has to recognise the majestic sovereignty that constitutes the limits of his own reason – a contradiction whose productivity is civil peace (*ibid*). As we know, peace was not to be the legacy of this thought.

The most ambitious elaboration of the significance of the Kantian 'as if' was undertaken by the German philosopher Hans Vaihinger in *The Philosophy of 'As If'* (Vaihinger 1924). First published in 1911, Vaihinger had been working on the manuscript since the 1870s, when he was among the leading readers of Kant but also a philosopher who was confronting religious and ethical inquiries in the wake of Darwin and Nietzsche. For Vaihinger, his *magnum opus* was an attempt to write the complete theory, anatomy, physiology or biology of 'as if'. All of the implications of this work are beyond our scope here. Suffice it to say that for Vaihinger, the 'as if' or 'appearance', the 'consciously false' played an enormous part in science, mathematics, law, and indeed in life. (Vaihinger 1924:xli). He drew on his contemporaries, including Nietzsche, to elaborate the centrality of invention, creation, falsification, allusion and 'myth' – and by no means in religion alone.

Perhaps the most influential thinker of modern law to have drawn on the Kantian notion of the 'as if', especially as it was elaborated by Vaihinger, is Hans Kelsen. Kelsen distinguished between 'basic norms' and 'positive norms'. The former is 'basic' because 'nothing further can be asked about the reason for its validity' (Kelsen 1991). A positive norm, on the other hand, is posited by "a real act of will" (*ibid*:254). A basic norm is a norm presupposed in thinking – and in that sense it is a fictitious norm. The basic norm, or *Grundnorm*, is thus a fictitious and not a real act of will. Such a presupposed fiction, when used to authorise a moral (religious) or legal order (constitution), is not only a contradiction of reality (since there is no norm that is an actual act of will), it is also self-contradictory in that it does not emanate from an authority other than a fiction. In order to sustain this attribution of norms to a fictitious basic norm, Kelsen draws on Vaihinger:

> According to Vaihinger, a fiction is a cognitive device used when one is unable to attain one's cognitive goal with the material at hand (Vaihinger 1924:13). The cognitive goal of the Basic Norm is to ground the validity of the norms forming a positive moral or legal order, that is, to interpret the subjective meaning of the norm-positing acts as their objective meaning (i.e. as valid norms) and to interpret the relevant acts as norm-positing acts. This goal can be attained only by way of a fiction. (Kelsen 1991:256)

Kelsen, along with Vaihinger, distinguishes a fiction from a hypothesis. A fiction, in Kelsen's account, is accompanied "by the awareness that reality does not agree with it" (Kelsen 1991:256; Vaihinger 1924:85 ff). In the *General Theory of Law and State*, Kelsen speaks of the Basic Norm as a consciously formulated assumption. Kelsen's abiding concern to distinguish positive law from natural law is achieved by accepting the assumption that positive law does not produce "a material and absolute justification of the legal order" (Kelsen 2006:396). Reliance on this "hypothetical validity" (*ibid*) of positive law is essential for maintaining the separation between a science of law (positivism) and a metaphysical approach (natural law). Any attempt to push beyond the "relative-hypothetical foundations of positive law" (*ibid*) – that is, to move from a hypothetical to an absolutely valid fundamental norm justifying the validity of positive law (an attempt which for obvious political reasons recurs often enough) – means the abandonment of the distinction between positive and natural law.

This is not to say that we should readily equalise myths and fictions. Nor can we shy away from the ethical and political responsibilities that come with 'making sense' from invention, allusion or fiction (I use 'sense' here after J-L Nancy (1997) and Frank Kermode (1966)). For Nancy, our current predicament stems from inhabiting a space between myth and nihilism. Ethics, responsibility, value – that is the problem of 'sense' that we now face without the authority and certainties of myth, tradition and religion. How do we make sense, and can fiction be a source of sense?

The 'as if' as a source of sense

The 'as if' is not confined to the juridical realm, although there is already a deep and elaborate discourse on the fictions at the heart of speaking right, bringing a case within the law, or of establishing jurisdiction. The juridical order arises from a fiction – a "bare-faced lie", as Nancy put it in his essay 'Lapsus Judicii' (Nancy 2003:157). He went on to state that this 'as if' was one of the central motifs that Kant introduced to philosophy. What I wish to move towards is an elaboration of contemporary instances of the 'as if', or the fictive, as a site of critique.

Frank Kermode addresses this question by combining Nietzsche, Vaihinger and Wallace Stevens' insights on how fiction helps us to make sense of the world:

> After Nietzsche it was possible to say, as Stevens did, that 'the final belief must be in fiction'. This poet to whom the whole question was of perpetual interest,

> saw that to think in this way was to postpone the End – when the fiction might be said to coincide with reality – forever; to make of it a fiction, an imaginary moment when 'at last' the world of fact and the **mundo** of fiction shall be one. Such a fiction – the last section of 'Notes Toward a Supreme Fiction' is, appropriately, the place where Stevens gives it his fullest attention [...] **Mundo** is itself such a fiction. (Kermode 2000:36-37 – original emphasis in bold)

But then there is the problem that, if literary fictions are the same as all others, then what is to be done with their "dangerous relations" (Kermode 2000:37)? For Nietzsche, "the falseness of an opinion is not any objection to it", and all that matters is "how far the opinion is life-furthering, life-preserving, and species-preserving" (*ibid*:36-37). But what happens when this opinion is about furthering the 'German race', the 'American people', or any other of God's 'chosen' ones? Kermode states the conundrum well when he says that nature can always be made to comply with our fictions, which can be tested by their success in the world: "The validity of one's opinion of the Jews can be proved by killing six million Jews" (*ibid*:37-38).

For Kermode, this problem expresses the modern condition identified by Hannah Arendt – that man, "wherever he goes, encounters only himself" (Kermode 2000:38). How are we to make sense, then, of the humanly ordered and created picture of the world? There is tragedy and apocalypse in both *King Lear* and Buchenwald – both are horrible; both involve "rootless fantasies" (*ibid*) that are no more true or false than the other, except that the former does less harm than the latter. As Kermode puts it:

> The consciously false apocalypse of the Third Reich and the consciously false apocalypse of 'King Lear' imply equally a recognition that it is ourselves we are encountering whenever we invent fictions. There may even be a real relation between certain kinds of effectiveness in literature and totalitarianism in politics. But although the fictions are alike ways of finding out about the human world, anti-Semitism is a fiction of escape which tells you nothing about death but projects it onto others; whereas 'King Lear' is the fiction that inescapably involves an encounter with oneself, and the image of one's end. (Kermode 2000:39)

There is thus a distinction between fictions that help us to encounter ourselves, our being, and our birth and death, and those that project death onto others. Here Kermode draws a second and crucial distinction between 'fictions' (which change as sense-making changes) and degenerate 'myths' (ritualistic and unchangeable gestures). Myths are absolute; fictions call for conditional assent. We never think that *King Lear*, or any other work of fiction, is 'true'. Kermode thus endorses Vaihinger's suggestion of fictions as an 'as if' – the "consciously false" (Kermode 2000:39-40).

Taking stock of the role of fictions in constitutional thinking we are left with several tentative conclusions. Fictions are central to encountering the limits of being (ontology) and of knowing (epistemology). Constitutional thinking advances by way of fictions. A variety of accounts of law and its origins rely on fictions. We can distinguish between degenerate myths and fictions, to which qualified and tentative assent might be given. Such fictions can help to imagine and animate forms of political and ethical life.

'South Africa belongs to all who live in it' is an 'as if' that grounds a 'form of life'. Is the assertion that 'South Africa belongs to all who live in it' a degenerate myth (a merely ritualistic gesture), or a necessary fiction that inaugurates an as yet unrealised form of social and political existence? As a fiction, it asserts the existence of a 'form of life' of equal, non-racial citizenship and the relationship of such life to notions of 'home', place, territory and history. But it is also a 'form of life' that is buttressed by violence that renders this very life extinguishable. In the discussion that follows, I take up the point of the intersection between constitutional thinking on the 'political', the problem of sovereign violence, and 'forms of life'.

Norms, violence and 'forms of life'

A dominant analytic that has come to be called 'the paradox of constitutionalism' will either privilege the 'political' or 'legal' side of the binary between constituent and constituted power. The 'legal' tends to be privileged by liberals who see the legal order as an expression of the unity of collective existence (Kelsen). Other constitutional thinkers seek to keep open the democratic force of the political either through reflexive questioning of the conditions of collective selfhood (Lindahl), or by sustaining the transformative potential in revolutionary rupture through *dissensus* (Christodoulidis). (See the discussion in Lindahl 2007:9-24). However, Lindahl fails to attend to how the political is manifested as the 'eternal return' of sovereign violence within the legal or constitutional order (I return to this point below).

Another mistake among constitutional thinkers is to fall too heavily on the side of a crude Schmittian account of sovereignty as the foundation of the normative order. Even where there is a nuanced Schmittian account of sovereignty as a 'borderline' concept occupying the limit-point of the juridical order, there is generally a failure to account for the performative inscription of this sovereign place through a 'legal' decision, including the decision of the law to withdraw in the face of the exception. Let me elaborate the contours of the paradox of constitutionalism.

The paradox is regularly expressed in terms of the debate between Schmitt and Kelsen. As is well known, Schmitt asserted the primacy of the concrete decision on the political (the decision on friend/foe, and the exception) over the norm. For Kelsen, such political unification was never available, as, sociologically, populations are always diverse and split between economic, religious and national conflicts (Lindahl 2007). Only the state's legal order was capable of expressing the necessary unity. For Kelsen, collective subjectivity is attributed to a legal order. Whereas for Schmitt, political agency is at the beginning of the juridical order, for Kelsen it was the regressive end-point of attribution. As Hans Lindahl puts it:

> Whereas Kelsen's discussion of attribution moves from constituted to constituent power, Schmitt inverts the sequence, asserting that an act of constituent power is the indispensable presupposition of any legally meaningful sense of constituted power. (*ibid*:13)

The impasse produced by the Schmitt-Kelsen debate is that they are both unable to account for the 'we' of collective selfhood. Kelsen denies the unity of a polity and attributes collective existence to a norm, and Schmitt proposes an unpalatable ground for unity, which is in any case nowhere to be found. Lindahl proposes a solution to this problem:

> A collective can only act by re-acting to what, preceding it at every step, never ceases to confront it with the question, 'who are we?' Constituent power comes second, not first: from the very beginning, and as its beginning, collective selfhood is eccentric, decentred with respect to the other as well as the strange. Here, then, is the main contribution of the paradox of constituent power to an ontology of collective selfhood: the collective self exists in the modes of **questionability** and, by way of its acts, of **responsiveness**. (Lindahl 2007:21 – original emphasis in bold)

Collective selfhood is only possible by relentlessly posing and responding to the question 'who are we?' – a problem of inclusion/exclusion. A collective is never present to itself; hence the enunciation 'in the name of' is always attributive and performative. But who counts, and on what criteria? Does this not simply pose the problem of constituent power as a question of who gets to properly ask this question? Are we not simply returned to Schmitt here, or to that more deconstructive reading of 'friendship' by Derrida (2005)?

While the reflexive or deconstructive reading of the political (the problem of 'we') is important, my contention is that too much is packed into the claim that the paradox of constituent power can be understood as a reflexive question about the 'political' without considering the violence at the heart of the response to that question. Indeed, much critical thinking is occupied with the problem of the 'political' *per se* – and Lindahl's contribution is an instance of this.

The thinker who has arguably done more than any other to attend to the problem of the constitutive exclusion of life in relation to the political is Giorgio Agamben. Agamben's characterisation of the inclusive-exclusion of 'abandoned being' or 'bare life' from the political and juridical order interrogates the relationship between political-life (*bios*) and sovereignty (Agamben 1998). Life is included or excluded from the political depending on whether it is mediated by divine or profane law.

The political horizon offered by Agamben is the beautiful day of *zoē* – that is to say, *zoē* would need to become a 'form of life' "wholly exhausted in bare life and a *bios* that is only its own *zoē*" (Agamben 1998:188). This is the crux of Agamben's anti-nomian stance. Agamben proposes a 'form of life' emancipated from its dependence on normative regimes that mediate life. This new politics would require a shift from 'form of life' to 'form-of-life'. For Agamben, the former denotes the ostensible 'facts' of human life that are often expressed through the separation of 'naked life' (*nuda vita* or 'bare life') from the various forms in which it is represented or identified – usually citizen or subject (Agamben 2000:4). This abstract re-codification of life we find in a litany of social and juridical categories such as "voter, worker, journalist, student, HIV positive, transvestite, porn star, elderly, parent, woman" and so forth is disavowed by Agamben (2000:6-7). Agamben seeks to move away from the structures of representation in these categorisations. For him, they problematically separate political form from 'naked life'. A 'form of life' is then a human life mediated by political orders of representation. Such a 'form of life' is involved in submission to a sovereign (as in the Hobbesian compact) and forcibly assimilated in states of exception or biopolitical modes of power.

In contrast to these structures of political representation, Agamben proposes a 'form-of-life' that not only expresses facts of existence, but also the 'possibilities' of life. At stake is the possibility of a non-statist and anti-nomian politics. This is "a life for which living itself would be at stake in its own living" (Agamben 2000:9). However, one is left with the persistent problem that politics, the political, and violence go hand in hand. The constitutionalists give an account of normativity without theorising violence. The anti-nomian (Agamben) disavows legally mediated forms of life. Can we so readily give up on normative or constitutional frameworks of life and politics?

In contrast to Agamben's search for an anti-nomian expression for 'forms of life', one of the key contributions of Judith Butler's *oeuvre* is her attempt to address exclusion and misrecognition as an ontological question without surrendering normativity. Butler's essays in *Precarious Life: The Power of Mourning and Violence* (2004) and *Frames of War: When Is Life Grievable?* (2009) ask the ontological question 'what is life?' and the epistemological question of 'how life is intelligible'. Significantly for our purposes, she persists in asking the normative question of how we move from the recognition/apprehension of life, vulnerability, precarity, and so forth, to a politics and ethics that might address the violence of recognition/apprehension.

Another feature of Butler's engagement with the political has been her focus on the 'affective' character and constitution of being. Like Lindahl, she draws on how being is in multiple ways "ec-static" (inclined outside the self) (Butler 2004:24). Being is transported beyond the self by passions. What Butler attempts is an "insurrection at the level of ontology" (2009:33). As she puts it in the essay 'Non-Thinking and the Normative' in *Frames of War*, "any inquiry into [...] ontology requires that we consider another level at which the normative operates, namely, through norms that produce the idea of the human who is worthy of recognition and representation at all" (*ibid*:138).

An insistence on normativity thus seems central to Butler's work. But doesn't normativity, as it operates to generate subjects, identities and social and political orders, necessarily entail violence?

Butler responds to this question in her essay 'The Claim for Non-Violence' by pointing out how an ethical quandary arises when beings are formed by violence. Put simply, formative norms and their violence live on in us, but not in an absolutely deterministic way. The ethical problem is how to effect shifts and reversals when iterating the norms that have formed the subject – a determination carried within, carried by the subject. Butler asks:

> Can one work with such formative violence against certain violent outcomes and thus undergo a shift in the iteration of violence? Perhaps the better word here is 'aggression' or, less clinically, 'rage', since my view is that non-violence, when and where it exists, involves an aggressive vigilance over aggression's tendency to emerge as violence. As such, non-violence is a struggle, forming one of the ethical tasks of clinical psychoanalysis and of the psychoanalytic critique of culture. (Butler 2009:170)

In other words, a subject or a culture cannot eradicate the conditions of their own violent production, but they can assume the responsibility of contesting its determining power (Butler 2009).

Drawing on Levinas, Klein and Winnicott, Butler addresses the ethical imperative to safeguard the life of another while contending with ambivalence towards that other. There is a desire to kill, and an ethical necessity not to kill, the other. In Klein's account of murderous rage in the setting of mourning and loss, a lost other is internalised. Butler (2009:174) calls this a kind of "introjective cannibalism", which incorporates the object of loss and berates this object. A suicidal turn is possible here, where the subject attempts to preserve the other at the expense of itself. This melancholia might also, as Freud pointed out, lead to the emergence of a recriminating voice which speaks what the ego might have spoken to the other had she been alive to hear the admonitions. But this ego was always an ambivalent one, and so, anxiety, guilt and responsibility alert us to a relational subject that needs the other in order to survive. It is this shifting and fluid platform of the ego and its psyche that sustains an "ethical mandate" to find a "non-violent solution for rageful demands" (Butler 2009:177). Non-violence is not a principle, "but a practice, fully fallible, of trying to attend to the precariousness of life, checking the transmutation of life into non-life" (*ibid*). Precarious life and "injurability" are then elevated to a "generalized condition" and are not markers of a particular cultural identity (*ibid*:178).

Butler's refusal to relinquish the challenge of normativity, as well as her psychoanalytically informed discussion of violence, offer important insights for constitutional thinking. Social and political life cannot be entirely emptied of violence. While the fictions – the 'as ifs' – that ground law and society seek to inaugurate new forms of ethical and political life, they are future-perfect enunciations that harbour and hide the violent conditions of what is being inaugurated. The problem of precariousness and vulnerability persists at the level of inter-subjective, state-subject, or corporation-employee relations. How will this inform constitutional narratives?

Constitutionalism confronts the problem of 'archiving violence'. The juxtaposition of events I opened with – the Marikana massacre and the inaugural fiction that 'South Africa belongs to all who live in it' is one manifestation of how violence undergirds constitutional dispensations. While the fictions – the 'as ifs' – of a constitution are intended to offer the 'sense' that orients beings between myth and nihilism, we can look beyond legal instruments for counter-archives of violence. This brings us to the limits of critical theory and to literature as a *genre of critique*.

Critique: a singular literary and constitutional event

In moving beyond the legal archive of violence, I want to suggest that it is in literature, in the work of art, that the complexity of a political crisis, as well as the urgency and limits of critical responses, can be discerned. Think of the novel in dark times, the work of art in times of crisis. Is the novel or the work of art to stand in as a realist account of the crisis and what resists it? Must it serve as a true 'representative archive of violence'? Should the writer denounce the darkness and show the light? Must the novel or work of art be judged as being 'properly' with or against the 'cause'? Given the persistence of such demands, one crucial qualification is to insist that the *singularity* of the event of literature be preserved[9] – that is, literature or the work of art should

9 See generally, Attridge (2004).

not be deployed in an instrumental way that elides their singularity. That is a difficult challenge as we draw on literature to better understand a constitutional crisis.

JM Coetzee's novel *Disgrace* (1999) was published in the wake of massive constitutional transformation, the hearings of the Truth and Reconciliation Commission (TRC), and a new democratic dispensation in South Africa. The dawn of the 'new South Africa' was to be a time of hope, the charting of a post-racial future, and above all the shaping of a new society through juridical and political institutions. Some of the anger that greeted the novel, the official ANC response to the South African Human Rights Commission enquiry on racism in the media, and the missives of some literary commentators need to be seen in the context of the novel's massive disruption of the dominant constitutional narrative that we have discussed above (the assertion that 'South Africa belongs to all who live in it'). Far from a 'rainbow' or 'post-racial' nation, the novel depicts relations between people that remain explicitly racially divided. It also explicitly tackles the problem of living with sexual violence.

Disgrace unfolds through a third-person narrative voice, though the experiences and consciousness that we have direct access to is that of David Lurie. David Attridge (2004) points out that the relation between the novel and its historical and political context can be grasped through the references to 'the times' in which characters find themselves.

Disgrace begins with an economic exchange that stands in as a resolution for "the problem of sex". Every Thursday, David Lurie, a 52-year-old Professor of Communications at a university in Cape Town, meets Soraya, the "honey-brown" Muslim prostitute with whom he has a weekly arrangement. Later he discovers that she is the mother of two boys, with "a respectable suburban existence". This would be unusual for a Muslim, he thinks, "but all things are possible these days" (Coetzee 1999:3).

David Lurie specialises in Romance languages, but since the Classics and Modern Languages Department was closed down as part of the "great rationalisation", he is adjunct professor of communications, teaching courses such as "Communications 101, Communication Skills, Communications 201" (Coetzee 1999:3). I shall not recount the plethora of references to new, different, destabilising, and confusing 'times', but Attridge summarises it well when he says:

> [...] this narrative is not an attack on the new nation that emerged from the elections of 1994, and [...] it expresses no yearnings for the system of apartheid, but rather [...] it portrays with immense distaste a new global age of performance indicators and outcomes measurements, of benchmarking and targets, of a widespread prurience that's also an unfeeling Puritanism; and [...] it explores, by way of one invented life, some of the pains and strains of social and economic order reinventing itself against this background. (Attridge 2004:173)

The 'time' of reconciliation and a new democratic dispensation is under the spotlight in *Disgrace*.

David's affair with a 'coloured' student, Melanie, results in a committee of inquiry and his departure from the university. The committee offer him an easier route out if he would repent and apologise. David refuses. He pleads guilty, but refuses to offer "contrition" (Coetzee 1999:54) or a "spirit of repentance" (*ibid*:58). The committee insist on a public statement and suggest the following:

> I acknowledge without reservation serious abuses of the human rights of the complainant, as well as abuse of the authority delegated to me by the university. I sincerely apologise to both parties and accept whatever appropriate penalty might be imposed. (Coetzee 1999:57)

In refusing this demand to repent as a condition for being forgiven, David states:

> I appeared before an officially constituted tribunal, before a branch of the law. Before that secular tribunal I pleaded guilty, a secular plea. That plea should suffice. Repentance is neither here nor there. Repentance belongs to another world, to another universe of discourse. (Coetzee 1999:58)

So David Lurie clashes with the new ethos of juridicalising what he perceives as his nature, his servitude to Eros. The juridical plea was not enough – he had to give more, he had to lay bare his soul. The institution offered to accommodate him. David's stance challenges the conditions of that accommodation.

Another controversial aspect of *Disgrace* is the accommodation of violence and new distributions of power that Lucy, David's daughter, appears to accept after being raped. Lucy lives on a small holding in the Eastern Cape, growing flowers and vegetables and kennelling dogs for a living. She is raped by two men and a boy, all black. She refuses to report her rape to the police, and later finds out that she is pregnant and decides to keep the child.

There are at least three significant things that Lucy says about her experience of violence. The first is her explanation for why she has not laid charges:

> The reason is that as far as I am concerned, what happened to me is a purely private matter. In another time, in another place it might be held to be a public matter. But in this place, at this time, it is not. It is my business, mine alone. (Coetzee 1999:112)

Asked by David, "This place being what?"', she replies, "This place being South Africa". There is a withdrawal from the 'new public', the 'new South Africa', in this statement. Lucy asserts her privacy, invoking a sense of 'home' at the very instant when the safety and security of home has been attacked, when the home as well as her place in the nation has been rendered un-homely.

Louise du Toit, drawing on both Irigaray and Derrida, has written of the 'im-possibility' of a home for women in the face of masculine becoming. She also interrogates Derrida's comments in his essay 'On Forgiveness', regarding women who were raped in the course of the anti-apartheid struggle, but who were unable to testify openly to this before the TRC (Du Toit 2007). Derrida asserts that "the 'question of forgiveness' cannot even be posed publicly to these women" – suggesting a range of reasons, including the well-known fact that recounting the experience exposes women to another violence. But, Du Toit asks, why can't the question of forgiveness 'even be posed publicly' (or indeed privately, as Derrida acknowledges) to these women who were raped? Du Toit urges us to resist treating the rape of women and children as private. In analysing the work of the TRC and the overall erasure of the political nature of sexual violence against women, Du Toit concludes that they amount to a contemporary refusal to politicise sexual difference and to "allow women to speak as *women* within politics" (*ibid*:193). What is most powerful about Du Toit's observations is that she not only treats the political erasure of women and their sex-specific suffering during the years of struggle, she also brings her analysis to bear on the terminal present:

> [...] the marginalisation of women cannot be limited, 'closed off' or contained in an evil apartheid past [...] The oppression of women is still a structural part of the South African nation and political landscape [...] This may be another and perhaps the crucial reason why the question of forgiveness cannot (in the present tense) be posed to these women. Their oppression has not yet passed, has in fact not been acknowledged. A public shareable language has not yet been found in which to name 'it' (the large-scale sexual violation and rape of women and girls by men in this country) in a way that would make sense to women and men, rape victims and perpetrators, a language that would carry weight in a public-political, inter-subjective setting. It seems bizarre to ask someone to forgive even as the injustice transpires, in the very process of her being damaged and violated. (Du Toit 2007:196)

In *Disgrace*, Lucy's refusal to 'go public' about her rape invokes this crisis of *sense* in the new South Africa. Lucy, by drawing attention to how she occupies the limit of the political community, marks the *vanishing point* of law's capacity to provide an adequate response or archive of violence.

By 'vanishing point' I mean the conditions of possibility and impossibility, as Du Toit has explained, of having 'a public sharable language' for discussing large-scale sexual violence. Lucy occupies this vanishing point by inhabiting the space of the limit between the possibility and impossibility of representing violence. What would it mean to invoke the law in this situation if, as Du Toit explains, there is a "masculine-specific universal" of what is being attacked and threatened through sexual violence? She argues that rape is an act "*definitive* of the political", a means of "inscribing a masculine power struggle on female bodies" (Du Toit 2007:193).[10] Indeed, *Disgrace*, as an account of the disintegration of David's worldview, but one inscribed in and through Lucy's body, might be viewed in these terms. The very possibility of a public treatment of rape is put into question by Lucy's statement that what happened to her is a 'purely private matter'.

Lucy's second account of the violence is that it was possibly a form of debt collection in the 'new South Africa'. In response to David's suggestion that her attackers will come back for more, she says:

> What if that is the price one has to pay for staying on? Perhaps that is how they look at it; perhaps that is how I should look at it too. They see me as owing something. They see themselves as debt collectors, tax collectors. Why should I be allowed to live here without paying? Perhaps that is what they tell themselves. (Coetzee 1999:158)

[10] Du Toit's argument relates to the period of struggle against apartheid that the TRC attempted to address. But given what I have explained about Du Toit's assessment of the present, I am arguing that the masculine power struggle continues to be inscribed on women's bodies.

When David suggests that she is giving herself up for slavery, she replies, "Not slavery. Subjection. Subjugation" (Coetzee 1999:159). There is much that rides on the power of the 'what if' and 'perhaps' in this statement – '*what if* that is the price'; '*perhaps* that is how they look at it'; '*perhaps* that is how I should look at it too'.

These passages point once more to the limits of representing violence. There is the difficulty in identifying the crisis (the 'what if'); the setting out of its distinguishing features; the different subjective positions ('perhaps' this or that) – but above all the inscription of a subject that resists the terms of the current political dispensation. Rather than read this passage as suggesting that Lucy believes that she is the sacrificial figure in the new order, it might be understood to be putting into question a sacrificial logic. That is what is invoked in the power of the 'what if' and the 'perhaps' – a singular place beyond the sexual exchange-economy of a masculine-universal. The 'what if' and 'perhaps' invoke a capacity to question the terms of this exchange.

A subjectivity beyond this masculine arrangement of the political is discernible in a third crucial exchange between David and Lucy. David sees Lucy as humbling herself before history. In a letter to her father, Lucy replies:

> I am not the person you know. I am a dead person and I do not know yet what will bring me back to life. All I know is that I cannot go away. (Coetzee 1999:161)

In this powerful passage she insists that she is ungraspable, resists being assimilated by her father's disintegrating worldview, and points to the depths of the crisis that she sees in ways that no other character in her world can grasp. Here she is a 'dead person' who 'cannot go away'. She is at once passive and utterly resistant to attempts *to drive her out of her life*. It is, then, not property, land or political citizenship that is asserted in opposition to the violence of everyday life, but *life itself* – a life that says 'I cannot go away'; 'I refuse to leave'.

One of Lucy's means of coping with the precariousness of her life – the lack of security and the prospect of a child – is to accept the protection of her neighbour, Petrus. She decides to sign over her property to him:

> If [Petrus] wants me to be known as his third wife, so be it. As his concubine, ditto. But then the child becomes his too. The child becomes part of his family. As for the land, say I will sign the land over to him as long as the house remains mine. I will become a tenant on his land [...] No one enters this house without my permission. Including him. (Coetzee 1999:204)

At this moment when Lucy puts her own presence into question, we see a liminal space opening. It is another way of being-with each other. This is also the liminal space of critique – the place where the terms of the crisis are defined and redefined, where a subjectivity beyond existing juridical categories of proprietor, citizen and subject is inscribed.

As the agent of critique, as the person who sees the malady in the body-politic and whose existence is thrown into question, Lucy occupies the vanishing point of the legal archive. As the occupant, the tenant even, of this point of crisis, Lucy redefines the conditions of her existence along with her neighbours. It is an accommodation of changed times – hard, difficult, violent times – but an accommodation that disassociates sovereign rights from the terms of the compromise. But what is the point, one might ask, what is at stake in identifying the vanishing point of the legal archive in a singular event of literature?

Disgrace takes multiple instances of violence and interrogates these through characters who express shifting 'forms of life'. Socially inscribed roles and dominant subjectivities are seen in a process of transformation. I have only dealt with some of them here. Although our primary access is to David Lurie, his interaction with Lucy and her inaccessibility or alterity suggest what it means to put being into question from multiple gendered and raced standpoints. The accommodation that Lucy seems to be reaching with her neighbour Petrus offers a discomforting variation on the constitutional assertion that 'South Africa belongs to all who live in it'. Lucy seems willing to give up 'her' land, but seeks to preserve a sense of 'home'. She reopens the question of what it means to assert that 'South Africa belongs to all who live in it'.

Conclusion

The tragic events at the Marikana mine that we commenced our discussion with highlighted the problem of sustaining the narratives that undergird the post-apartheid constitutional dispensation. We examined the significance of the consciously false ground of law and the persistence of this 'as if' in modern forms of constitutional thinking. Fictions such as the assertion that 'South Africa belongs to all who live it' are an essential part of archiving erstwhile violence and inaugurating a new order. Whether such constitutional devices work as necessary fictions or dangerous myths was interrogated through the 'forms of life' that they sustain. Vulnerable and precarious lives ever subject to violence require that we not abandon a normative project in critical thinking. We observed, however, that a form of life that resists juridical categories can be drawn from literature.

The common perception is that literature and law are of a different order. After all, what of the world of law, what of its judgements, pain and death-dealing can literature accomplish, other than the re-presentation of the 'real'? At best, literature stands in through a cultural resemblance through metaphor or allegory. Adam Thurschwell (2007) challenges this subordination of literature to law. Drawing on Maurice Blanchot's 1948 essay 'Literature and the Right to Death', Thurschwell argues that literature should be placed at the very heart of law and jurisprudence.

Let us take as agreed that law's distinguishing characteristic is its capacity to express and legitimate the 'sovereign right to death'. Law has the capacity to impose the death penalty and to demand the sacrifice of citizens at a time of war. In order to compare literature with this legal/sovereign potential, we need to move beyond the familiar references to law's necessary fictions, the performative acts of foundation, or the meaning-creating act of a judge's interpretation of legislation (Thurschwell 2007). We need to show, as Thurschwell argues, that a "more fundamental point of contact between literature, law, and sovereignty can be discerned" (*ibid*:49). At the heart of the argument is that literature has the same *terminal* potential as law. Like law, literature has the capacity to put the question of being (including its own being) into question.

Reference List

Agamben G. 2005. *The Time That Remains: A Commentary on the Letter to the Romans*. Stanford, CA: Stanford University Press.

— 2000. *Means Without End*. Minneapolis, MN: University of Minnesota Press.

— 1998. *Homo Sacer: Sovereign Power and Bare Life*. Stanford, CA: Stanford University Press.

Arendt H. 1958. *The Human Condition*. Chicago, IL: University of Chicago Press.

Attridge D. 2004. *The Singularity of Literature*. London: Routledge.

Butler J. 2009. *Frames of War: When is Life Grievable?* London: Verso.

— 2004. *Precarious Life: The Power of Mourning and Violence*. London: Verso.

— 1997. *The Psychic Life of Power: Theories in Subjection*. Stanford, CA: Stanford University Press.

Coetzee J.M. 1999. *Disgrace*. London: Vintage.

Derrida J. 2005. *The Politics of Friendship*. London: Verso.

— 1991. *Acts of Literature*. New York: Routledge.

Du Toit L. 2007. Feminism and the Ethics of Reconciliation. In: S Veitch (ed). *Law and the Politics of Reconciliation*. Aldershot: Ashgate.

Kant I. 2002. *Groundwork for the Metaphysics of Morals*. New Haven, CT: Yale University Press.

— 1991. *Political Writings*. HS Reiss (ed). Cambridge: Cambridge University Press.

Kelsen H. 2006. *General Theory of Law and State*. Piscataway, NJ: Transaction Publishers.

— 1991. *General Theory of Norms*. Oxford: Clarendon Press.

Kermode F. [1966] 2000. *The Sense of an Ending: Studies in the Theory of Fiction*. New York: Oxford University Press.

Lindahl H. 2007. Constituent Power and Reflexive Identity: Towards an Ontology of Collective Selfhood. In: M Loughlin & N Walker (eds). *The Paradox of Constitutionalism: Constituent Power and Constitutional Form*. Oxford: Oxford University Press. 9-24.

Loughlin M & Walker N (eds). 2007. *The Paradox of Constitutionalism: Constituent Power and Constitutional Form*. Oxford: Oxford University Press.

Minkkinen P. 2009. *Sovereignty, Knowledge, Law*. Abingdon: Routledge.

Nancy J-L. 2003. *A Finite Thinking*. Stanford, CA: Stanford University Press.

— 1997. *The Sense of the World*. Minneapolis, MN: University of Minnesota Press.

Ramose M. 2007. In Memoriam: Sovereignty in the 'New' South Africa. *Griffith Law Review* 16:310-329.

— 2006. The King as Memory and Symbol of African Customary Law. In: MO Hinz & H Pateman (eds). *The Shades of New Leaves: Governance in Traditional Authority, A Southern African Perspective*. Berlin: Lit Verlag. 351-374.

Thurschwell A. 2007. Law and Literature and the Right to Death. In: G Hofmann (ed). *Figures of Law: Studies in the Interface of Law and Literature*. Tübingen & Basel: A Fracke Verlag. 45-62.

Vaihinger H. 1924. *The Philosophy of 'As If': A System of the Theoretical, Practical, and Religious Fictions of Mankind*. Abingdon: Routledge.

LIMINAL LANDSCAPE

Law, literature and critique in post-apartheid South Africa

Karin van Marle

Despite the consistency of the conventions employed, ideal landscape was neither a monotonous nor stereotyped form of art. It was capable of almost infinitely varied nuances of interpretation and several major differences of emphasis.

– *Kitson 1966:74*[1]

It is through the cultural processes of imagining, seeing, historicizing and remembering that space is transformed into place, and geographical territory into a culturally defined landscape.

– *Darian-Smith, Gunner & Nuttall 1996:3*[2]

Introduction

The thoughts regarding the ideas of a liminal landscape in this chapter are inspired by Lettie Viljoen's[3] post-colonial novel *Landskap met vroue en slang* (*Landscape with*

1 The quotation from Kitson is used as motto by Lettie Viljoen (Ingrid Winterbach) for the novel *Landskap met vroue en slang* (*Landscape with women and snake*).

2 As quoted in Viljoen 1998:74.

3 The pseudonym for author Ingrid Winterbach.

women and snake) (1996).[4] My main concern is the possibility of a space for critique within the present South African legal, political and social context. At the heart of this issue lies the relationship between the law and the humanities – especially between law, literature and critique. The general status of the humanities and what has been referred to numerous times as the 'crisis' of the humanities, globally and in South Africa, are closely linked to this concern. My specific interest is how to respond to this 'crisis' from the perspective of legal scholarship. Further aspects that play a role in my reflection are notions of modernity and how they relate to South African constitutionalism, post-apartheid jurisprudence and critique.

I focus on possible connecting themes between the Viljoen novel, post-apartheid law and critique. The story centres on artist Lena Bergh and her unfulfilled search for the sublime landscape. Lena is concerned with the works of the Baroque painter Nicolas Poussin – the title of the novel could already be read as a reference to one of Poussin's paintings, 'Landscape with two nymphs and snake', while the front cover shows a combination of his works 'Landscape with the ash of Phoicon' and 'Landscape with snake'. In *Mourning becomes the law: Philosophy and representation* (1996),[5] the late philosopher Gillian Rose critically reacts to an interpretation of 'Landscape with the ash of Phoicon' that attempts to avoid the political interpretation of the painting. For Rose, the painting signifies the search for political justice and the risks that come with it.

Post-apartheid law, similar to landscape, calls for a variety of nuances and interpretations. By reflecting on themes within the novel of Viljoen in the light of post-apartheid law and legal theory, I appeal for a stronger focus on the genre of literature as a genre of critique within the context of law as well.

Broadly speaking, three ideas voiced by academics working in South African constitutional law are significant to my argument: Stu Woolman's naming of the South African Constitution as the 'last modernist project' (2008); Wessel le Roux's identification of the 'aesthetic turn' in post-apartheid constitutional theory (2006); and Lourens du Plessis' work on constitutional authorship, narration and the memorial and monumental constitution (2008). The description of the Constitution as the 'last modernist project' discloses multiple ways of engaging with the constitutional project. Particularly given the post-apartheid context, it invites a reconfiguring of modernity, or rather 'modernities'. The notion of an 'aesthetic turn' in constitutional theory discloses ways for the arts, the humanities and literature of entering and coming into play. Du Plessis' reliance on literary metaphors is suggestive for the contemplation of critique in a post-apartheid context. He employs the metaphors of monument and memorial to reflect on the nature of the Constitution and argues in this vein for an aesthetic reflection on post-apartheid constitutionalism. Woolman's description may be regarded as an affirmation and embrace of Enlightenment ideals, and his understanding of 'modernist' accordingly linked to these ideals. Both Le Roux and

---

4 All translations of *Landskap met vroue en slang* (*Landscape with woman and snake*) from the original Afrikaans to English are this author's own.

5 The front cover of the book also features Poussin's 'Landscape with the ash of Phoicon'.

Du Plessis' engagements with post-apartheid constitutionalism could be regarded as critical of the ideals affirmed by Woolman. The notion of 'alternative' or 'Southern' or 'African' modernities could be of significance. Achille Mbembe and Sarah Nuttall's work on 'African modernity' could also open ways for reconfiguring legal modernity within the South African context.

The argument unfolds as follows: I start with Woolman's description mentioned above, followed by a brief discussion of the 'aesthetic turn' in post-apartheid constitutional discourse and Du Plessis' invocation of authorship, narration, monument and memorial as metaphors for the post-apartheid constitutional discourse. This is followed by a consideration of the notion of 'African' or 'alternative' modernities. Secondly, I turn to the 'crisis' of the humanities, and specifically the law's response to and engagement with the humanities. Thirdly, I highlight certain themes from the Viljoen novel and tentatively relate them to Rose's call for existence in this world. I then consider the notion of 'involved critique' and the significance for critique of recognising complexity and taking modest positions. In the final part of the chapter, I consider Hannah Arendt's response to modernity and her lamentation of the loss of the world in modern times, as well as her sense of tragedy. I conclude by tentatively putting forward a few markers for the notion of a liminal landscape as landscape of critique.

Truth, aesthetics and the African modern

In a chapter in the 2008 book *Constitutional conversations* entitled 'The South African Constitution as the last modernist project', Stu Woolman enters into a conversation with Albie Sachs in response to a remark made by Sachs on the role of legal academics in a post-apartheid South Africa. Woolman, understanding Sachs' remark as implying that although legal academics had played an important role during the transition, they would subsequently play a lesser one, reflects on how he (Woolman) conceives of the role of an academic.

Answering his own question regarding the phenomenological role of academics and what we do, Woolman says: "Well, we fix things" (2008:25). He continues, describing his job as an academic as similar to a that of a "mechanic", "therapist", "architect", "mason" and "critic" (*ibid*:27). Therapists, architects and critics who adhere to a different philosophical/theoretical tradition than Woolman might dispute the understanding of their work as being concerned with "fixing", offering solutions and making sense. But then, for Woolman, "such philosophical fashion has not yet taken root here [in South Africa]" (*ibid*:31). Therefore, South Africa "remains [...] the last great modernist project" (*ibid*:35), and academics should strive to "get things right. To get as close to the truth as possible" (*ibid*:28).

Part and parcel of this task is to "treat its [the law's] texts with respect" (Woolman 2008:27). Such respect entails that "we never for a moment deny the law its autonomy", which implies "the recognition that legal texts possess a logic and power of their own". From Woolman's description of the South African Constitution as the 'last great modernist project', one may summarise the following features of modernity that he ascribes to the constitutional endeavour (and prescribes for any such undertaking).

Firstly, "truth" – and as Woolman indicates, he means truth "with a capital T" (2008:31). Secondly, "rational political discourse", meaning that law shouldn't simply 'get it right' by producing the right answers, but also by "getting there the right way" (*ibid*), following a sound method. Thirdly, Woolman highlights the commitment to great ideals and the possibility of material transformation through law, or, to be more specific, through the constitution. Woolman refers to voices that challenge the potential of law to achieve all of this, but argues that this does not lessen the commitment to the "Enlightenment's commitment to truth", stating that such "philosophical fashion" has not taken root here [...] South Africa remains the last great modernist project" (*ibid*:35).

Wessel le Roux (2006) identifies as one of the most notable features of post-apartheid constitutional discourse the extent to which legal scholars rely on aesthetic examples. He regards this "aesthetic turn" (*ibid*:101) as one of the ways in which scholars reject attempts to continue applying the legal formalism of apartheid law to constitutional discourse on the basis of legal science. In contrast to legal formalists, those who engage with aesthetic examples are concerned with "substantive constitutionalism" that involves, for example, a "reconfiguration of the public sphere as a republican sphere of deliberative (or communicative) interaction" (*ibid*:103). Le Roux also notes examples of writers who rely on the arts in order to highlight the limits of law, including constitutionalism. In contrast to the redemptive aim of the former examples, these writers emphasise the paradoxical or aporetic nature of these reconfigured spaces.

In his exploration of the monumental and memorial features of the South African Constitution and constitutional jurisprudence, Lourens du Plessis (2008) is concerned with illustrating the contradictions and paradoxes of post-apartheid life: for him, 'logical' or 'rational' ways of addressing these contradictions will be of no use. Instead, he suggests "an aesthetic mode of coping with the dilemma of contradiction" (*ibid*:205), such as understanding the Constitution as both memorial and monument. Du Plessis distinguishes between 'monument' and 'memorial' by explaining that although memory is common to both, they treat it differently. Simply put, "a monument celebrates" and "a monument commemorates" (*ibid*:189). The differences between the two ideas are subtle but significant. Du Plessis does not argue for one of these modes to be overtaken by the other, but calls for the two to coexist.

Whereas Woolman explicitly connects the constitutional project to Enlightenment and modernity, both Le Roux and Du Plessis may be regarded as being more closely aligned to poststructural approaches – or critical engagements with the Enlightenment project and law as a product of legal modernity. Below I refer to Achille Mbembe and Sarah Nuttall's description of what they call "the African modern" (Mbembe & Nuttall 2008:1).

Mbembe and Nuttall describe Johannesburg as "the symbol par excellence of the 'African modern'", which they define as a "specific way of being in the world" (Mbembe & Nuttall 2008:1). They underscore the particular way in which 'worldliness' comes to the fore not only as an engagement with domestic cultural forms, institutions and ways of life, but also with those from elsewhere. (I shall return to the notion of worldliness as reflected on by Hannah Arendt below.) For Mbembe and Nuttall, modernity and worldliness in the context of Johannesburg have been "intrinsically connected to various forms of circulation – of people, capital, finance, and images – and to overlapping spaces and times" (*ibid*). In their work on Johannesburg, they address the way in which the global city has been approached by the dominant paradigm and argue that, quite often, a purely *functionalist* theory has been followed, neglecting the *complexity* of the city. They observe that "a true global city [...] is composed not only of flows of money, skills, knowledge [...] but also of ideas, people, images and imaginaries – a cultural economy" (*ibid*:3). I have previously (Van Marle 2009) reflected on the notion of 'transformative constitutionalism' (as suggested by Karl Klare more than a decade ago) – and particularly the ways in which South African legal scholars engaged with this notion – against the background of Mbembe and Nuttall's call for a complex understanding of the city. My sense was that the problems that we face as legal scholars are often approached in a way that neglects to pay sufficient attention to the complexity of these issues – what Mbembe and Nuttall refers to as the "cultural economy" (2008:3). For me, the notion of transformative constitutionalism (broader post-apartheid jurisprudence, as such, and narrower post-apartheid critique) asks for multiple approaches to law that do not necessarily subscribe to law's autonomy, if this means treating law and legal texts, including the Constitution, as if they have a life of their own. Mbembe and Nuttall, following the work of James Ferguson, note how most studies on African cities have relied on "an underlying meta-narrative of modernization, urbanization and crisis" (*ibid*:5). However, what has been neglected is the capacity of African cities also to attract certain forms of initially colonial and now global capital. For Mbembe and Nuttall, globalisation stands in the guise of exactly these paradoxes of "connection" and "disconnection and exclusion", following processes that are "refracted, splintered and cracked" (*ibid*). They are interested in ways of reading the African city that move away from the traditional paradigms, suggesting alternative readings. It is exactly these alternative readings that could also illustrate an alternative for traditional jurisprudence and open a space for critique.

Mbembe and Nuttall seek to read the city as more than "simply a string of infrastructures, technologies, and legal entities", wanting to show that it also consists of "actual bodies, images, forms, footprints, and memories" (Mbembe & Nuttall 2008:5). Their aim is to highlight the "artistic and aesthetic" elements of the city. Rather than opposing the 'formal' and the 'informal', or the 'visible' and the 'invisible', they call for a "more complex anthropology of things, forms, signs" (*ibid*). As noted before, it is such an approach that, in my view, should be translated and expanded to post-apartheid jurisprudence and critique. Such an approach also adds another angle to the argument of law's autonomy: without directly opposing it, it problematises, refractures the claim. For example, by acknowledging how the "'informal' itself expresses a 'form'", hiding and revealing rationalities, the multiplicity of law in all forms could come to the fore. Mbembe and Nuttall observe that many descriptions of Africa aim to characterise it as "otherworldly", "apart from the world", a "failed or incomplete example of something else" (*ibid*:9). Their aim is to problematise the sameness/difference dichotomy, making space for "the originality of the African modern, its capacity to produce something new and singular" (*ibid*) to become visible.

Mbembe and Nuttall observe that, in many writings, ...

> [...] modernity has been perceived as nothing more than the development of the capitalist mode of production and the processes by which capitalism as a socioeconomic formation in turn transformed social relations and the consciousness of black urban dwellers. (Mbembe & Nuttall 2008:11)

Charles van Onselen (quoted in Mbembe & Nuttall), for example, describes Johannesburg as a city caught up in self-interest, struggle and shallowness:

> [...] generations [who] have always felt more comfortable in the bank, the stock exchange and the sports stadium than they have in attending a church, sitting in a concert hall, walking through an art gallery, reading in a library or even serving in the ranks of their city council. (Mbembe & Nuttall 2008:12)

With some tweaking, these words could fit with how many people (legal scholars included) perceive law, legal practice and, sadly, legal scholarship.

Mbembe and Nuttall search to bring in other perspectives on Johannesburg too, exposing how the "city always operates as a site of fantasy, desire, and imagination" (2008:12). They describe how South African historiography tends to approach the city in a way that neglects to go beyond a certain point. The authors distinguish broadly between three approaches. Firstly, they point to a line that is concerned with spatial dislocation, class differentiation and racial polarisation, focusing for example on poverty and forced removals. These studies aptly describe racial forms of dispossession and exclusion, yet Mbembe and Nuttall note how these versions perceive the city merely as "a space of planning", and not as an "aesthetic project" (*ibid*). A second line focuses on institutional governance, the deracialisation of service provision and local politics, but fails to acknowledge that which goes beyond these, namely "city-ness as such". This approach views the city is a *problem* that must be *solved*, and in this vein prescribes what is to be done (*ibid*:13-14). A third line focuses on the spatial restructuring of the city, noting the construction of offices, complexes and upper-class residences. The authors critique these studies and highlight two aspects: firstly the need to formulate theories of race, class, labour and capital that are more sensitive to the underlying complexities, particularly the violent past of apartheid, and secondly, the failure of these theories to engage with the "city-ness" of Johannesburg, which could include a vast array of new perspectives. I have previously contemplated the extent to which these three features could be true also of approaches to law, and specifically approaches to transformative constitutionalism, placing all the emphasis on problem-solving, planning and restructuring in such a way as to render more complex theories and engagements with ideas and the imagination worthless (Van Marle 2009). An important notion that is highlighted by Mbembe and Nuttall's engagement with Johannesburg as metropolis is city life as such – how the city is lived, rather than how it is constructed (Mbembe & Nuttall 2008). This also discloses opportunities to become aware of suffering, alienation, rebellion and insurrection. Post-apartheid jurisprudence should take care not to neglect "scripts that are not reducible to the built form, the house facade, or simply the street experience of the metaphorical figure of the *flaneur*" (*ibid*:21). An engagement with the broad humanities, particularly literature, could be one way for legal theory to go beyond the mere abstract and technical, depending on the nature of that engagement.

The humanities, law and justice

During 2011, two reports (ASSAf 2011 and RSA DHET 2011, respectively) emanating from what is regarded as a 'crisis' within the humanities and social sciences were published in South Africa. The most important concern regarding both these documents – not only for the humanities and social sciences, but also for their relationship to law and the future of critical legal study – is the degree of functionality and utility ascribed to the humanities, without any regard for their intrinsic value. This view negates and undermines any intrinsic value that the humanities might have and could create an environment where there is no space for intellectual growth. The positive and direct value of the humanities, namely the intrinsic value of critique, is also negated through this approach.

In South Africa, as in many other countries, there is an overwhelming embrace of the approach of legal formalism, which stems from an approach to and an understanding of the law as autonomous, all-embracing and politically neutral. To the extent, if at all, that this approach engages with the humanities, it confirms rather than questions the sentiment of the two reports mentioned above, namely the affirmation of the strict functional value of the humanities, with no regard for their intrinsic value. The humanities are of use only to the extent that they may be utilised to strengthen the law. One result of this approach is the becoming of law as a "social-legal law", with the ultimate loss of the ideal of justice, as aptly described by Marianne Constable (1994:551).

A recent turn to the humanities under the mantra of 'multidisciplinary' work illustrates how law – here human rights law – can draw on the humanities for its own functional purposes, thereby undermining any intrinsic value that might be ascribed to the humanities. In the introduction to a collection entitled *Beyond the law* (2011), Frans Viljoen, the editor of the collection, explaining the notion of "disciplinary beyondness", starts by making a distinction between human rights and human rights law. He defines human rights as moral claims based on extra-legal sources of authority, such as a shared sense of humanity, religion, natural law, etc; human rights law, then, is the form in which these values have been made concrete in a legal document. Viljoen continues by lamenting the fact that human rights scholarship and approaches to human rights have been dominated by lawyers and legal scholars, and that there has not been sufficient engagement with non-legal scholars. He argues that it is surprising that human rights lawyers have not followed a more inclusive approach, referring to the "realisation that law coexists with other disciplines, and is applied in a context, together with other disciplines" (Viljoen 2011:xvi). Viljoen refers to the law and sub-disciplines – law and culture, law and semiotics, law and literature, and so on. He then continues to refer to the richness of the social sciences and the direct impact that, for example, political science can have by not only asking questions about context, but also providing empirically based answers to complicated questions about actual effect or impact (*ibid*:xvii). Turning to the title of the collection, he explains that although the notion of 'beyond the law' may invoke an image of lawlessness or disorder, this is not the intention of the collection. He refers to another meaning of 'beyond', one that denotes "over and above, not only but also" (*ibid*:xix), and says that it is rather this sense of complementarity which informs the collection. The other perspectives from other disciplines do not *substitute*, but rather *supplement*, law.

My concern with this approach is at least twofold. Firstly, it is premised on an understanding of law as an autonomous discipline, as if law actually functions in such isolation. Secondly, it draws on other disciplines only to make law stronger – not to question or, lo and behold, deconstruct law. This use of the social disciplines and humanities play directly into the hands of the two reports referred to above, in the sense that these reports value the humanities and social sciences solely for instrumental reasons. The premise of the *Beyond the law* project is the same: these disciplines are really of use in bringing to light the statistics, the empirical research that law needs to make a more convincing case.[6]

One chapter in the *Beyond the law* collection engages with the Argentinian film *The secret in their eyes*, set in mid-1970s Argentina (Van der Merwe 2011:235). The film tells the story of a young man whose wife is brutally raped and murdered and of how the legal system fails him. The author's purpose in referencing this film is to write about the rights of victims and offenders in the post-sentencing phase and to demonstrate that film is a useful tool to teach students the intricacies of criminal procedure law. But for me, the film is about much more than the workings of a country's criminal system. Even to the extent that the film may comment on law, it is rather a reflection on politics, ethics, life and complicity – and not a handbook or 'quick guide' to criminal procedure. My concern is that the narrow reading of the film as an example of multidisciplinary scholarship and education is in line with the broad aim of the *Beyond the law* project. Of course, one might say that this is at least better than merely presenting students with the relevant text book, Act and case law, but this is not multidisciplinary scholarship/education as critical scholarship/education – and more than that, it is a project that I fear might further harm or devalue critical scholarship and critical education by again underscoring the practical value of direct application.

In a reaction that forms part of a broader discussion regarding the crisis of the social sciences, Ulrike Kistner relies on Njabulo Ndebele, who encourages South African academics to move "boldly into the unknown" and "to run away from uni-dimensional characterisations of ourselves [...] nurturing imaginative thinking [and] the ability to embrace uncertainty from a position of intelligence and imagination" (in Kistner 2012:16). Kistner comments on how often commentators – even those concerned with the critique against the downgrading of social sciences – rely on a limited and determined view of social sciences, and criticises Lalu, who, in his critique of the South African National Research Foundation's one-sided focus on development, at the same time also reduces the social sciences to having a specific view of the human condition as identifiable by race, ethnicity, gender and class. One could liken this one-sided view with the line of critique stemming from the US CLS described in the introductory chapter. Kistner attributes this deterministic and limiting definition of

6 The edited collection referred to is directly linked to a master's course, 'Multidisciplinary Human Rights', where students are exposed to lectures from other disciplines to supplement – but not to question or challenge – their legal knowledge.

the human condition to the hesitancy of South African socio-historians to consider the unique philosophical idea of freedom and expresses concern about the reduction of the idea of freedom to that of liberation. Kistner relies on Hannah Arendt's separation of liberation and freedom:

> It may be a truism to say that liberation and freedom are not the same; that liberation may be the condition of freedom but by no means leads automatically to it; that the notion of liberty implied in liberation can only be negative, and hence, that even the intention of liberating is not identical with the desire for freedom. Yet if these truisms are frequently forgotten, it is because liberation has always loomed large and the foundation of freedom has always been uncertain. (Arendt 1963:22 in Kistner 2012:17)

Kistner suggests that a reopening of the differentiation between liberation and freedom – and more specifically, the embracing of uncertainty that is associated with freedom – will enable the humanities to return to their critical thinking role. Instead of focusing on the limitations of race, ethnicity, gender and class, another question could develop: "[T]he inquiry into the human of the human condition would have to reflect on its own conditions of possibility, which would locate it within the order of knowledge of modernity" (Kistner 2012:17). Kistner strives to create a space for critical social sciences to exist between nature and culture, the 'known' and the 'unknown'. Such a space will allow for the development of critical literacy, discursive transformation and reflective judgement. Kistner relies on Etienne Balibar to create the opening of social sciences as the "instant desire to know":

> It is not only a way of legitimating privileges or disqualifying competitors or continuing old traditions or reacting to situations of violence, it is a way of asking questions about who you are in a certain social world. (Balibar 1994:2000 in Kistner 2012:18)

Kistner explains that such a 'desire to know' is politically and historically earmarked, but can be investigated within the space of the critical social sciences as a third position. Her definition of this third position stands in close relation to the *Genres of critique* project's definition of critique as an in-between or liminal space.

Before turning to the novel *Landscape with women and snake*, I refer briefly to a recent publication, *No Foundations: an interdisciplinary journal of law and justice* (Boyd White 2012; Constable 2012; Hirvonnen 2012), dedicated to the rethinking of the possibilities of justice. The editors of this publication provide two reasons, based on law and social sciences, for choosing to focus on the relationship between law and justice. They firstly refer to the fact that the interdisciplinary movement is growing in Europe through the reconsideration of law in a way that opens dialogue with other disciplines, and, in doing so, confirm the view that the law is not complete as an autonomous discipline (*ibid*:ii). Secondly, this focus arises from the fact that this specific perspective, stemming from a relationship with the humanities, does not shy away from discussions regarding the injustices of the law. In contrast to the examples mentioned above, here the engagement with the humanities is not done in a functionalist way, employing the humanities in service of law.

James Boyd White, who is known for his work in the field of law and literature, authored the first article in *No Foundations: an interdisciplinary journal of law and justice* (2012:1).[7] Although his work does not focus solely on critical legal theory, it does offer a radical perspective on law and justice, rather than just the traditional one offered by many law faculties. I quote:

> What I shall say, in a phrase, is that law is not at heart an abstract system or scheme of rules, as we often think of it; nor is it a set of institutional arrangements that can be adequately described in a language of social science; rather it is an inherently unstable structure of thought and expression, built upon a distinct set of dynamic and dialogic tensions. It is not a set of rules at all, but a form of life. It is a process by which the old is made new, over and over again. If one is to talk about justice in the law, it must be in the light of this reality. (Boyd White 2012:1)

For Boyd White, to read and write is central to legal practice and is not only used in a strict or mechanical way, "but as the fullest and most important expression of a mind engaged in the world" (2012:4-5). He further describes law as "an activity of mind and language: a kind of translation, a way of claiming meaning for experience and making that meaning real" (*ibid*:5). He identifies seven tensions within legal theory that limit the workings of the law. These include the distinction between legal language and ordinary language; between different voices involved in the legal discourse; between the legal representatives who represent opposing clients; between opposing, but acceptable, interpretations of the law; between content and process; between law and justice; and between the past, the present and the future. Boyd White rejects not only the image of law as a system of rules and policy, but also the inherent view of law as an abstract, mechanical, impersonal and mainly bureaucratic system that limits the human potential to experience and gain insight and empathy: "To focus on the law as a system, and not on what happens when that system meets the world – and the people of the world – is to strip it of its difficulty, its life, its meaning, and its value" (*ibid*:17).

Marianne Constable's perspective on justice is to focus on the development of speech, and more specifically on the silences that derive from speech (Constable 2012:58). She repeats her previous argument, referred to above, regarding the taking over of a legal sociological global perspective. Her concern is the question of how one should approach law and justice, which differs from the empirical, measurable, instrumental strategies and techniques. Constable says that by only focusing on their social power and empirical impact, one negates the important insights that the social sciences bring to law and language. The answer to the question 'What is the law?' can be found in law's relationship to speech; the answer to the question 'What is justice?' can be found in speech and by the study of the silences within speech. For Constable, law and justice is an aspect of language, which is not based on logical or universal standards, but on grammatical and imperfect standards. She explains this statement by referring to the way in which subjects act continuously and imperfectly without being interrupted (*ibid*:59). Just as words are incapable of embracing a complex

[7] See in general Boyd White J. 1973. *The legal imagination*. Chicago, IL: University of Chicago Press and Boyd White J. 1990. *Justice as translation: An essay in cultural and legal criticism*. Chicago, IL: University of Chicago Press.

world, so too is the law incomplete and not fully describable or noticeable. This view of language stands in strong contrast to the argument that highlights the value of the social sciences, especially where language is required as a tool/component for students to understand mathematics or for law students to acquire the necessary skills to apply the law. Constable's view of language and the role of the social sciences in attaining a deeper/more inherent understanding of the law and justice not only provides an alternative to a positivistic understanding of the law and a functional understanding of the social sciences, but also allows for a richer interaction with justice. Speech escapes positive law. Our language recalls other laws. Our language and its – most gentle – law quietly raise issues that exceed the articulations and control of powerful states and the concerns of the most strategic and instrumental of social policies or positive law. These are the issues of justice (Constable 2012).

Ari Hirvonnen, in the same publication as James Boyd White's article, considers the possibility of a new humanism after Auschwitz (Hirvonnen 2012:144). He reflects on Kofman's (2007) focus on preserving humanism – and the ethical task that accompanies it – by transforming it and giving it a new meaning (*ibid*:164). According to this view, humanism, then, is not a coherent system of universal morality, but rather the responsibility to be human in the face of irreducible differences. Such a view does not exclude other views by denying differences and reducing them in the name of universality, but rather creates opportunities for thinking and creating communities on the basis of difference. Another view of justice is evident. Hirvonnen explains:

> We have to be careful here. Her [Kofman's] writing is not about justice. The subject of her writing is not justice. Justice is what takes place in her affirmation of surviving, in her attestation of existence, in her insisting and affirmative laugh. Justice is not something given to the victims – in the form of human rights, compensations or punishments of the offenders – but an affirmative force that insists on surviving. (*ibid*:168)

The above reflections are examples of how the law can respectfully deal with the humanities while allowing for the possibility of the rethinking of law, justice and critical legal study.

'Landscape with women and snake'

Landscape with women and snake (1996) is the last novel author Ingrid Winterbach wrote under the pseudonym Lettie Viljoen. The main character, Lena Bergh, a painter, moves with her second husband and child from the Western Cape to Durban, KwaZulu-Natal, where she finds herself within a sub-tropical landscape that does not appeal to her. Before I reflect on a few themes revealed in the novel, some remarks on landscape within the context of post-colonial literature.

Louise Viljoen (1998) notes that the post-colonial in Afrikaans literature is marked by ambivalence and heterogeneity. She explains that the Afrikaans language carries the double burden of being both colonised and coloniser. Afrikaans is the product of Dutch colonialism and a hybrid that developed in Africa. It performed the role of the oppressor, but was also a language in which the oppressed voiced their revolt, and it was simultaneously a supporter of Afrikaner nationalism and a symbol of struggle opposed to that same nationalism. The date that serves as marker for the end of colonialism in South Africa is also ambiguous: for most the era of colonialism came to an end in 1994, when the country had its first democratic election, but for some, 1961 marks the end of colonialism, when the country became a republic and British colonialism came to an end. Viljoen's concern is the role of landscape and place in post-colonial literature, and how it can contribute to post-colonial discourse. She is interested in the use of terms like 'geographical terrain', 'topography', 'space' and 'land'. In distinguishing between 'space' and 'place', the latter is seen as a "historically and culturally laden term" (1998:74). Viljoen recalls JM Coetzee's reference to the double meaning of 'landscape', denoting both geographical meaning and an aesthetic value or experience based on a European tradition of art that is connected to either the picturesque or the sublime (*ibid*:75; Coetzee 1988:61). She refers to work that questions the "natural connection" between place and identity, and quotes Carter: "[P]lace is space to which meaning has been ascribed" (Carter 1993:xii in Viljoen 1998:76). The uses of 'landscape' and 'place' in post-colonial studies can be distinguished from each other. As also noted by Coetzee, 'landscape' is steeped in a specific "philosophical tradition in which the objective world is separated from the viewing subject. Rather 'place' in post-colonial studies is a complex interaction of language, history and environment" (Viljoen 1998:76; see also Ashcroft, Griffiths & Tiffin 1995:391). Viljoen refers to the reading of 'place' as a palimpsest – a surface on which the history of various generations can be written and read so that the impact of factors such as race, sex and class are underscored.

Landscape(s)

As already seen from the title of the novel, 'landscape' plays an important role. The main character Lena's move from a town in the Western Cape to Durban, a port city in KwaZulu-Natal, is of significance. The Western Cape is historically associated with the first act of European colonisation, when the Dutch constructed a resupply station in Table Bay in 1652. KwaZulu-Natal was originally inhabited by the Zulu nation and was colonised by the British in the nineteenth century. Moving from the Western Cape to KwaZulu-Natal not only challenges Lena as a painter, but also on a psychic level. In contrast to the landscape of the Western Cape, which she finds easy to measure and control, the subtropical landscape of Durban is difficult to comprehend and predict. Viljoen recalls Ashcroft *et al*'s (1995) point that landscape is based on a philosophical tradition in which subject is easily distinguished from object. This can be linked to colonialism's aim to control, understand and appropriate (Viljoen 1998). She interprets Lena's longing for the order of the landscape of the Western Cape as a modernist one, in contrast to a postmodern experience of the fragmentation of the KwaZulu-Natal landscape.[8]

As a painter without inspiration, Lena concerns herself with the sublime landscape of the Baroque painter Nicolas Poussin, whose theme of longing for Paradise lost is

8 However, Willie Burger reads this novel (and also Winterbach's other work, for example, *Die benederyk* (2010)) as an engagement with modernity rather than postmodernity.

prominent. One finds a complex inter-relationship between the themes of displacement, distancing and the problem of adaptation in these new circumstances (Human 2010). Over and above her concern with the sublime landscape of Poussin, Lena also focuses on gardens and parks. By looking through the lens of the sublime landscape, she tries to build a relationship with her new environment, only to realise that the KwaZulu-Natal landscape can be experienced in ways other than the sublime. By recognising the ambivalence in Poussin's landscapes, and through discussions with her friend Maria Darboven (meaning 'from above'), Lena comes to the realisation that experiencing beauty/the sublime is impossible without acknowledging ambivalence and insecurity (Human 2010).

The use of language in the novel in itself creates a sublime landscape, as well as a specific experience of the sublime for the reader. The novel can be interpreted as an attempt to create a landscape – a landscape as narrative – particularly a Poussinian landscape (Human 2010; Viljoen 1998).

Time

The historical context of the novel is 1996, two years after South Africa's first democratic election, the year the 'final' Constitution is adopted. The theme of the past, and how to deal with the past, runs through the novel. Jack, Lena's spouse, says to her, "You don't have to leave the past behind [...] but don't get too attached to it" (Viljoen 1996:148). Lena dreams of a place where everything is desolate, "as if nothing happened; or as if there was no history" (*ibid*:151).

Human notes that Poussin wanted "his late landscapes to be viewed slowly, deliberately and with unbroken concentration" and quotes Pierre Roseburg, the former director of the Louvre:

> He wanted the time one might spend reading and absorbing a text in understanding its significance or its message to be spent contemplating his paintings, with the same complete attention, the same concentration, the same emotional engagement. (Human 2010:60)

One can observe here that the reading of Viljoen's novel requires similar attention and concentration. Below I return to the notion of slowness.

Patriarchy

In this novel, as in Viljoen/Winterbach's other novels, there is a strong feminist element present. In her search for the sublime landscape, Lena Bergh rejects the centrality of the father, the dominant masculine figure. Lena is, for example, unsuccessful in finding her father's grave. The male teachers of her past could not help her in this search, nor is Jack able to replace her father: "But even Jack's love fails to free her from her own limits" (Viljoen 1996:191). One of her former teachers has gone dumb, which could be seen as a symbol of the male discourse that has been silenced (Burger nd). There are two dreamscapes that should be read within the sociopolitical context – both the king and the general lose their positions of power and have to accept new positions (*ibid*). The acceptance of these new positions of power reminds me of Njabulo Ndebele's challenge regarding the embrace of uncertainty, and his call for giving up certainties

(Ndebele 2007); further on, I also refer in the same vein to the late Paul Cilliers' call for "modest positions" (2005:255). The absence of simple solutions is important: patriarchy is in no way replaced by matriarchy/a feminine centre. Kistner's reminder of Arendt's distinction between liberation and freedom is of importance. There are no signs of easy answers or one-sided replacements that could be associated with liberation: "The foundation of freedom has always been uncertain" (Arendt 1963:22 in Kistner 2012:17).

Liminality/the middle ground

I referred earlier to Poussin's wish that his landscapes be read 'slowly', noting that the same may be said concerning the reading of the novel. Viljoen (1998) suggests that the novel should be read in the same way as a Poussin painting, particularly as it consists of several levels that portray a progression in time. The paradise-like background/ sublime landscapes could possibly be regarded as a pre-colonial landscape. The 'middle ground' represents the landscape in all its dimensions – political, social and historical – as well as Lena's daily routine. As in the interpretation of Poussin's paintings, Lena is confronted with the ambivalence and equivocation of the middle ground – a space where the colonial cannot be contemplated separately from the post-colonial (*ibid*). The foreground is a violent one, where everything is portrayed clearly and sharply. However, the events in the foreground are influenced by the landscape of the middle, which is both close and far away. According to Viljoen (*ibid*), the main character, through her engagement with the different layers of the Poussin landscapes, comes to understand aspects of her situatedness in South African history, from the pre-colonial to the colonial and post-colonial (Human 2010:54).

Gillian Rose's 'broken middle'

The late Gillian Rose's work deals with the relationship between critique and postmodernism and, in particular, a rejection of rationalism and the search for a new ethic. She is concerned with a rethinking of reason, politics and justice. In her work *Mourning becomes the law: Philosophy and representation* (1996), Rose links Poussin's 'Landscape with the ash of Phoicon' – as an expression of never-ending love – with a certain postmodern rejection of modernity and rationality in favour of a new ethics. She problematises such a rejection of modernity, as well as politics, risk and the embrace of a new ethics. Rose insists on an aporetic reading of the Western tradition. She rejects the interpretation of the painting as an attempt to escape political involvement and transcend the law and the city (Athens as symbol of justice). Rose supports the notion of equivocation and laments the low tolerance for it in the modern world: "Wisdom works with equivocation" (Rose 1996:3). In another work, *The broken middle* (1992), she describes a space of anxiety and equivocation and focuses on three Jewish women – Rahel Varnhagen, Rosa Luxembourg and Hannah Arendt – as examples of women who lived in such a space and were involved in multiple struggles without resorting to the safety of community, identity and transcendence. According to Rose, none of these women accepted either Athens or Jerusalem, but acted and died at the border of the "third city" (*ibid*:39).

The story of Lena Bergh's unfulfilled search for paradise and the absence of easy solutions could be regarded as a similar embrace of modernity and the aporia of modernity. The character realises that the desire for transcendence is futile and that she has to struggle to find a place in this world; however, this is no homecoming in the traditional sense. I regard the novel, particularly when read with Rose in mind, as suggestive for a contemplation and investigation of liminal critique.

Critique

In a recent article in reaction to a debate that developed in 2010, after Media24, a large South African media house, announced that in future there would be only one national book page rather than a number of such pages in its various regional publications, Willie Burger pleads for "involved critique" (2012:52). He sets the crisis of literature and the social sciences (in general) against the backdrop of specific occurrences: the end of humanism, the interpretive turn, and the rise of cultural studies and theory. He describes the reaction to the critique of literature as twofold: firstly, as one of immigration to the "Republic of the Arts", which manifests as either a return to humanism or an embrace of deconstruction, and secondly, as a rejection of critique in favour of culture. Burger suggests 'involved critique' as an alternative and calls for a literary critic "who is passionate about literature" (*ibid*:60). This call, however, is not one for a romantic return to humanism. He pleads for interpretation and, like Kistner (2012; referred to above), expresses concern about the discussion of mere gender inequalities, patriarchy and so on, which boils down to a reductive reading in which the value of the literary text as a work of art is lost (Burger 2012). Central to Burger's idea of 'involved critique' are also "literature as thought" (*ibid*:60) and "aesthetic concepts as existentialistic concepts" (*ibid*:63).

Burger describes literary art as something that can be seen as a way of thinking and calls for "aesthetical thought" (Burger 2012:60). With reference to Ernst van Alphen (2005), he argues that artworks should be seen as opportunities for discussion, interpretation and participation. An artwork is always more than an expression of culture, identity or a specific historical period; it is a reflection of the artist's thinking. He invokes Milan Kundera's reliance on Arendt's reference to Nietzsche as an example of somebody thinking "experimentally", in support of his argument that the author of the novel also thinks in this way (Burger 2012:61). What is important is the way of thinking and that which is generally accepted as questionable, as this creates alternatives. Kundera supports "authentic novel-like thought" (*ibid*), which for him is similar to experimental thinking, as both are unsystematic and undisciplined. Burger admits that one should not be too quick in believing in the ability to break free from power structures, but argues that one should believe in the imagination's ability to uncover other ways of thinking. In fact, perchance it is the unexpected, unplanned relation between things that is seen by the artist and then brought into a work of art, where the possibility of something new lies. Burger draws on an interview with Marlene van Niekerk, as well as the work of Paul Riccour, to emphasise the argument that the thinking of the reader is formulated by the artist and can leave a trail in this world. This notion of leaving a trail in this world could be linked to the work of Hannah

Arendt (1958), especially the emphasis she places on the possibility of natality/new beginning and the importance of plurality in the public sphere. I return to this below. Burger (2012:63) also refers to Breyten Breytenbach's reference to a "middle world", which can be linked to the liminal critical social sciences, Rose's 'broken middle' and Lena Bergh's situatedness in a 'middle ground'.

Burger recalls Pamuk's statement that "[n]ovels are only as valuable as the questions they raise about the shape and nature of life" (in Burger 2012:63), and argues that this is also true for critique. I am in full agreement with this viewpoint. Arendt's notion of worldliness/love of the word should be recalled here. Below, I elaborate on Arendt's view of judgement – which draws on Immanuel Kant's view of aesthetical judgement – as important for a reflection on critique. Burger (*ibid*), through Kundera, indicates the importance of tradition for the evaluation and consideration of artwork. One should recognise that, in a way, each work of art is in discussion with other works of art. It is also important to note that the undermining and questioning of certain systems usually occurs on a small scale: minor moves, such as the narrative structure of a text, may have specific meaning (*ibid*). Peter Goodrich describes a "minor jurisprudence" in the context of legal critique as "one which neither aspires nor pretends to be the only law or universal jurisprudence" (1996:2). Such a jurisprudence stands as "a challenge to the science of law and a threat to its monopoly of legal knowledge" (*ibid*). In the history of 'minor jurisprudence' one finds "rebels, critics, the marginal, aliens, women and outsiders who over time repeatedly challenged the dominance of any singular system of legal norms" (*ibid*). For Goodrich, thinking about these examples in this way may uncover a multitude of alternative jurisprudences and legal critique.

Following on Goodrich's notion of a 'minor jurisprudence', I want to briefly recall Paul Cilliers' support of what he calls "modest positions" (2005:256) and the recognition of complexity. Cilliers wants to highlight the "limitations of our understanding of this world" and differentiates between "self-confident or assertive positions and modest positions" (*ibid*). Of significance is his view that modesty is important because the failure to acknowledge one's own limitations is not only a technical error, but also an ethical one. Cilliers' call for modesty can also be linked to Ndebele's appeal for humility, referred to earlier. Responding to the claim of relativism, Cilliers explains that a true relativist "is in a way nothing but a disappointed fundamentalist" (*ibid*:260). Bearing in mind Woolman's view of the South African Constitution as the 'last modernist project' and that the task of the legal academic is to find truth, provide final answers and 'fix' things, the support of a 'modest position' is an important counter-position. Cilliers explains:

> [O]ne should realise that the claim that we cannot have complete knowledge does not imply that anything goes. 'Limited' knowledge is not equivalent to 'any' knowledge. If this were so, any modest claim, i.e. any claim with some provisionality or qualification attached to it would be relativistic. The only alternative would be an arrogant self-assurance. Such a self-assured position is deeply problematic since its complacency forecloses further investigation. (Cilliers 2005:260)

Cilliers concludes his argument by saying that exposing the complexity of systems – the limits of knowledge and the fact that understanding cannot be reduced to calculation

– calls for creativity, which for him means "a careful and responsible development of the imagination" (2005:264). For Cilliers, such development relies on reading books, listening to music and appreciating art and film – which, in a sense, brings us to the crux of the *Genres of critique* project: the extent to which an engagement with aesthetics can disclose spaces and possibilities for critique.

Worldliness, tragedy and judgement

In this section, I turn to Hannah Arendt's notion of worldliness as a way of engaging with the question of modernity, which was raised above with reference to the work of Woolman, Le Roux, Du Plessis, and Mbembe and Nuttall. I also refer to Arendt's sense of the tragic as a way of rethinking these authors' calls for complexity, modesty and humility as examples of countering modernist hubris. Finally, I highlight a few aspects that are central to Arendt's understanding of judgement.

In an attempt to place Hannah Arendt in a tradition other than that of interpretations that situate her firmly as anti-modern, exhibiting a nostalgic longing for a revival of the Greek *polis*, Seyla Benhabib describes Arendt as a 'reluctant modernist' in the title of her 1996 book. Many commentators disagree: for Dana Villa, for example, Arendt "barely qualifies as even a reluctant modernist" (Villa 1996:174). Villa follows Kateb's reading of Arendt as a "great anti-modernist" (*ibid*). I elaborate slightly on Villa's argument below, but before doing that, I want to briefly put forward what Benhabib calls "a different genealogy of modernity" in Arendt's writings on the "rise of the social" (Benhabib 1996:22). Modernity and its various meanings – as well as understandings of and engagements with modernity – are central to the reconfiguring of post-apartheid jurisprudence and critique.

Benhabib (1996) finds three dominant meanings of the term 'social' in Arendt, namely the reference to the growth of a capitalist commodity exchange economy, the reference to the rise and growth of mass society, and lastly, the reference to sociability. It is the latter one of sociability that is of relevance for our purpose here of rethinking modernity. Benhabib notes how Arendt exposes the ongoing tension between 'equality' and 'difference' in the social and political realms as a feature of modernity. Difference and otherness in pre-modern societies were less prominent, because of the exclusion of those who did not fall within the ambit of the homogenised city state. The rise of modernity and Enlightenment promises of political and legal equality made difference real. Benhabib refers here to Arendt's work on anti-Semitism and how it brought the dialectic of equality and difference to the fore. Arendt's description of the "complicated and multilayered [...] dynamics of the social" (Benhabib 1996:28) is significant. According to Benhabib, when Arendt refers to 'the social' she means sociability – "patterns of human interaction; modalities of taste in dress, eating, leisure, and lifestyles generally; differences in aesthetic, religious, and civic manners and outlooks; patterns of socializing and forming marriages, friendships, acquaintanceships, and commercial exchanges" (*ibid*). 'The social' designates "civil and associational society, that sphere of human relations that is not economic, or political, or military, or bureaucratic-administrative" (*ibid*).

Arendt, in her biography on Rahel Varnhagen, exposes this notion of 'the social' and sociability (Benhabib 1996:29). Varnhagen ran a Berlin salon in the early nineteenth century – "a space of sociability in which the individual desire for difference and distinctiveness could assume an intersubjective reality" (*ibid*). This notion of sociability as a space that allows difference and plurality and the ability to see the perspective of others also informed Arendt's reflections on judgement later in her life. For Benhabib, Arendt's biography of Rahel Varnhagen hints at different interpretations of her understanding of modernity. It brings to the fore "an alternative genealogy", in which modernity is regarded not only as the rise of commodity exchange relations, capitalism and mass society, but rather is associated with bringing forth new forms of social relations, of being in the world (*ibid*). This take on modernity could connect with the depictions of modernity, Johannesburg as metropolis, and the 'Afro-modern' discussed earlier.

The concepts 'world', 'worldliness' and 'worldlessness' play an important role throughout the writings of Arendt. She was specifically interested in the modern condition of 'homelessness' (Benhabib 1996). In this regard, Arendt was influenced by *Existenz*-philosophy in the work of Kierkegaard, Nietzsche, Jaspers, Sartre and Heidegger, amongst others, naming the loss of human reason, but also the loss of a shared world (*ibid*). Benhabib argues that Arendt brought about a significant shift in Heidegger's concept of the world by making being in the world – and being with others – central to how worldliness is experienced. Her notion of human plurality, which is central to her political and philosophical writings, is, according to Benhabib, a forceful response to *Existenz*-philosophy, most notably the work of Heidegger.

I referred above to Dana Villa's view of Hannah Arendt's anti-modernism. As Villa notes, for Arendt modernity brought about a "limitless instrumentalization of everything that exists" (Villa 1996:171). This instrumentalisation, modern science's treatment of the earth as another object, and the rise of technology resulted in a "pervasive and radical worldlessness" (*ibid*). Villa explains that, in political terms, worldlessness meant the "'atrophy' of the space of appearances and the 'withering' of common sense, a loss of feeling for the world" (*ibid*). On an existential level, worldlessness means the loss of home, a certain homelessness. Villa notes Arendt's agreement here with Heidegger in the 'Letter on humanism'. For Arendt, the modern project was rooted in "existential resentment, a resentment of finitude and limitation as such" (*ibid*:172). Central to modernity is the "'will to will'" – that is, "a will to overcome finitude and contingency, to remake the world and establish man in the position of 'lord and master'" (*ibid*). However, Villa notes the "paradoxical logic of modern existential resentment": that "the age that 'began with such an unprecedented and promising outburst of human activity' may in fact end 'in the deadliest, most sterile passivity history has ever known'" (Arendt 1958:322 in Villa 1996:173). Even though Villa views Arendt as anti-modern, he is cautious not to place her in a tradition that wants to return to the pre-modern. He underscores her refusal of nostalgia and rather views her work as a great attempt of showing why the understandings, morals and politics of a pre-modern world are no longer possible.

Aspects of Arendt's anti-modernism – or perhaps rather critical engagement with modernity – are the limitless instrumentalisation of everything; the rise of technology; the will to overcome finitude, with the resulting loss of the world; the decline of a public sphere of political action; and a loss of common sense:

> Among the outstanding characteristics of the modern age from its beginning to our own time we find the typical attitudes of **homo faber**: his instrumentalization of the world, his confidence in tools and in the productivity of the maker of artificial objects; his trust in the all-comprehensive range of the means-end category, his conviction that every issue can be solved and every human motivation reduced to the principle of utility; his sovereignty, which regards everything given as material and thinks of the whole of nature as of 'an immense fabric from which we can cut out whatever we want to resew it however we like', his equation of intelligence with ingenuity [...] finally, his matter-of-course identification of fabrication with action. (Arendt 1958:306 in Villa 1996:197 – original emphasis in bold)

Villa quite aptly asks about the implications for politics of a tradition that negates all contemplation and replaces it with instrumentalised reality – a question that is of value also for the concern with critique (Villa 1996).

Another aspect before I turn to judgement is Arendt's sense of the tragic. David Scott (2004) pays attention to Arendt's "evocation of tragedy as a mode of remembering the spirit of the revolutionary tradition" (*ibid*:211). For him, Arendt's belief in the virtue of the Athenian *polis* is also due to its being the birthplace of tragic thought, and therefore well aware of contingency, radical plurality and human fragility. Scott traces connections between Arendt's *On revolution* (1963) and CLR James' *The Black Jacobins* (1963 revised edition), specifically their shared sense of the tragic. *On revolution* is not only the third in Arendt's trilogy on political theory, but also a lamentation of the "lost treasure" of the revolutionary tradition (Scott 2004:221). Arendt compares what in her view were the two great revolutions of our age, the French and American revolutions. She famously criticises the French Revolution for not holding on to the ideal of political freedom and allowing economic concerns to displace the ideal of freedom. However, she points out that not even the American Revolution could sustain the revolutionary spirit by constructing a "lasting framework of conceptual notions" (*ibid*:216). Scott notes Arendt's oversight in not engaging with or even mentioning the Haitian revolution, and ascribes this to a Eurocentric view. Of importance is how both Arendt and James end their works on a tragic note. For Scott, this is a fruitful avenue for further engagement with post-colonial theory and critique, in contrast to the pervasive Romanticism associated with the anti-colonial struggle. The sense of tragedy that we find here is also in line with Arendt's critique of modernity's resentment of finitude and belief in rational ability. Tragedy stands in contrast to the optimism associated with the Enlightenment belief in rationality and truth. Below, I turn to Arendt's last project before her untimely death, namely her reflections on judgement.

Of relevance for an Arendtian notion of judgement is not only the substantive content of what Benhabib calls her "alternative genealogy/archaeology of modernity" (Benhabib 1996:94), but also the methodological angle. Benhabib describes her use of fragmentary historiography inspired by Walter Benjamin as "an attempt to think through the human history sedimented in layers of language and concepts" (*ibid*). Language plays a significant role in identifying moments of "rupture, displacement and dislocation in history" (*ibid*). At stake is "a remembering, in the sense of a creative act of rethinking that sets free the lost potentials of the past" (*ibid*).

Arendt shared the views of her life partner, Heinrich Blucher, for whom judgement was not about following rules, but about examples presented in the imagination (Young-Bruehl 2006). She regarded judgement as always exercised in relationship with others: "[...] visiting others – physically or in your mind – consulting them, seeing things from their point of view, exchanging opinions with them, persuading them, wooing their consent" (*ibid*:165). Following Kant, judgement for Arendt meant the reflection of the plurality of possible opinions. She subscribed to a notion of 'common sense' – an experience where an enlarged mentality allows a person to get beyond (transcend) her own subjectivity and reach what could be regarded as a common understanding, or common sense (*ibid*). In contrast to how it is often understood, this notion of common sense is not something unreflective or instinctive, but the outcome of a transcendental thought process.

As noted by Young-Bruehl (2006:166), judgement for Arendt was the way through which a person became a "world citizen". Exposure to and the experience of plurality assist us in seeing the world from another's perspective, and the more positions that can be made present or taken into account, the more representative judgement will be (*ibid*). This kind of judgement, which is possible only through imagination, is neither objective nor subjective, but rather inter-subjective and representative, seeking for a relation between particularity and generality. The notion of aesthetic judgement is therefore never about following or applying general rules, but rather an experiment in imagination (*ibid*). This understanding of reflective judgement is a prerequisite to living in a shared or common world and for the ability to live well. Benhabib also emphasises the importance of worldliness – which she describes as "an interest in the world and in the human beings who constitute the world, and a firm grasp of where one's own boundaries lie and where those of others begin" (Benhabib 1996:191) – in Arendt's notion of judgement. She notes how Arendt, by subscribing to the notion of enlarged thought, returns to the theme of the "perspectivality of the public word" that originated in her biography on Rahel Varnhagen (*ibid*:196).

Concluding remarks

As stated earlier, the broad aim of the *Genres of critique* project and of this chapter is to offer a rethinking of the possibilities for critique in a post-apartheid context. My tentative argument is that critique could be developed in a liminal space or landscape somewhere between law and the humanities and between law and literature, but also between law and philosophy and literature and philosophy. This liminal landscape is not one of transcendence or of abstract thought that is not at all anchored in this world. It is at the same time also not one that is limited to a vision of what is. The possibility of critique lies in ambivalence, unfulfilment and uncertainty.

A few tentative markers for critique can be identified from the various texts and authors mentioned in this chapter. A critical engagement with modernity and the rethinking of possible alternative modernities seem to be central to a critical project. Added to this is Hannah Arendt's notion of worldliness and countering the loss of it – the 'worldlessness' of the modern project. Critique should problematise the hubris of Enlightenment rationality and instrumentalisation and recognise complexity, and with complexity, the significance of plurality. Also as mentioned before, an acceptance of ambivalence and equivocation is an important marker for critique. A sense of tragedy, rather than the Romanticism that often accompanies struggles for freedom, discloses opportunities for critical engagement. Connected to a sense of tragedy could then also stand humility and the acceptance of modest positions; finally an embrace of slowness and, with it, attentiveness. We can recall again Poussin's demand for slowness when viewing his landscapes: complete attention, concentration, emotional engagement.

I leave the last words to Lettie Viljoen:

> It continues to fascinate Lena [...] It draws her attention, the way in which the landscape in Poussin's late work may be portrayed as equivocation. Simultaneously ominous [...] **and** luxuriously fertile. Simultaneously like paradise and sublime, primordial and mysterious – confusing as well as blinding in its abundance [...] In the morning Lena gets up and continues to work in her work room on the vast canvas that she stretched when she thought that everything was possible. She works there with all possible attention.[9] (Lettie Viljoen 1996:206-207 – original emphasis in bold)

9 *Dit bly Lena fassineer [...] Dit boei haar steeds, die manier waarop die landskap in Poussin se laat werk as dubbelsinnig mag uitgebeeld word. Tegelyk onheilspellend [...] én weelderig vrugbaar. Tegelyk paradyslik en subliem, primordiaal en misterieus – verwarrend sowel as verblindend in die oorvloed daarvan [...] Soggens staan Lena op en werk verder in haar werkkamer aan die groot vel wat sy gespan het toe sy gedink het alles moontlik is. Sy werk daar met al die aandag tot haar beskikking.*

Reference List

Arendt H. 1997. *Rahel Varnhagen: The life of a Jewess*. L Weissberg (ed). Baltimore, MD: Johns Hopkins University Press.

— 1963. *On revolution*. London: Penguin.

— 1958. *The human condition*. Chicago, IL: University of Chicago Press.

Ashcroft B, Griffiths G & Tiffin H (eds). 1995. *The post-colonial studies reader*. London & New York: Routledge.

ASSAf (Academy of Science of South Africa). 2011. *Consensus study on the state of the humanities in South Africa: status, prospects and strategies*. Pretoria: ASSAf.

Balibar E. 1994. *Masses, classes, ideas: studies on politics and philosophy before and after Marx*. London: Routledge.

Benhabib S. 1996. *The reluctant modernism of Hannah Arendt*. Thousand Oaks, CA: Sage.

Boyd White J. 2012. Justice in tension: An expression of law and the legal mind. *No Foundations: An interdisciplinary journal of law and justice* 9:1-19.

Breytenbach B. 2009. *Notes from the Middle World*. Chicago, IL: Haymarket Books.

Buchanan R, Motha S & Pahuja S. 2012. *Reading modern law. Critical methodologies and sovereign formations*. London: Glass House.

Burger W. 2012. 'Betrokke kritiek' – Literatuurkritiek wat die wêreld verander? Literatuurkritiek ná teorie. *Tydskrif vir geesteswetenskappe* 52(1):52-67.

— nd. Lettie Viljoen: Landskap met vroue en slang. Unpublished book review. (Text on file with author.)

Carter E, Donald J & Squires J (eds). 1993. *Space and place: Theories of identity and location*. London: Lawrence & Wishart.

Cilliers P. 2005. Complexity, deconstruction and relativism. *Theory, Culture & Society* 22:255-267.

Coetzee JM. 1988. *White writing: On the culture of writing letters in South Africa*. New Haven & London: Radix, in association with Yale University Press.

Constable M. 2012. Speaking of the imperfect: Law, language and justice. *No Foundations: An interdisciplinary journal of law and justice* 9:58-67.

— 1994. Genealogy and jurisprudence: Nietzsche, nihilism and the social scientification of law. *Law and Social Inquiry* 19(3):551-590.

Darian-Smith K, Gunner L & Nuttall S. 1996. *Text, Theory, Space: Land, Literature and History in South Africa and Australia*. London: Routledge.

Du Plessis L. 2008. The South African Constitution as Monument and Memorial, and the Commemoration of the Dead. In: R Christensen & B Pieroth. *Rechtstheorie in rechtspraktischer Absicht*. Berlin: Duncker & Humblot.

Goodrich P. 1996. *Law in the courts of love: Literature and other minor jurisprudence*. New York: Routledge.

Hirvonnen A. 2012. The ethics of testimony: Trauma, body and justice in Sarah Kofman's autobiography. *No Foundations: An interdisciplinary journal of law and justice* 9:144-172.

Human T. 2010. A return to the picturesque: Reading the landscape in Lettie Viljoen's Landskap met vroue en slang. *Journal of literary studies* 26(1):45-66.

James CLR. 1963. *The Black Jacobins*. Revised edition. New York: Vintage Books.

Kateb G. 1983. *Hannah Arendt: Politics, conscience, evil*. Totowa, NJ: Rowman & Allanheld.

Kistner U. 2012. Unchaining the human of the humanities. *Social dynamics: A journal of African studies* 38(1):15-19.

Kitson M. 1966. *The age of baroque*. New York: McGraw-Hill.

Klare KE. 1998. Legal culture and transformative constitutionalism. *South African Journal on Human Rights* 14:146-188.

Kofman S. 2007. *Selected writings*. Stanford, CA: Stanford University Press.

Kundera M. 1988. *The art of the novel*. London: Faber & Faber.

Le Roux W. 2006. The aesthetic turn in the post-apartheid constitutional rights discourse. *Journal of South African Law* 1:101-119.

Mbembe A & Nuttall S. 2008. *Johannesburg: The elusive metropolis*. Johannesburg: Wits University Press.

Ndebele N. 2007. *Fine lines from the box*. Roggebaai: Umuzi.

Rose G. 1996. *Mourning becomes the law: Philosophy and representation*. Cambridge: Cambridge University Press.

— 1992. *The broken middle*. Oxford: Blackwell.

RSA DHET (Republic of South Africa. Department of Higher Education and Training). 2011. *Final Report: Charter for Humanities and Social Sciences*. Pretoria: DHET.

Scott D. 2004. *Conscripts of modernity*. Durham, NC: Duke University Press.

Snyman J. 1998. Interpretation and the politics of memory. *Acta Juridica*:312-321.

Van Alphen E. 2005. *Art in mind: how contemporary images shape thought*. Chicago, IL: University of Chicago Press.

Van der Merwe A. 2011. Justice beyond the law in 'The secret in their eyes': Rights of victims and offenders in the post-sentencing phase. In: F Viljoen (ed). *Beyond the law*. Pretoria: Pretoria University Law Press. 235-252.

Van der Walt AJ. 2006. Legal history, legal culture and transformation in a constitutional democracy. *Fundamina* 1:1-47.

Van Marle K. 2009. Transformative constitutionalism as/and critique. *Stellenbosch Law Review* 20(2):286-301.

— 2003. Law's time, particularity and slowness. *South African Journal on Human Rights* 19:2239-2255.

Viljoen F (ed). 2011. *Beyond the law*. Pretoria: Pretoria University Law Press.

Viljoen L. 1998. Plek, landskap en die postkolonialisme. *Stilet* 10:73-92.

— 1996. *Landskap met vroue en slang*. Kaapstad: Human & Rousseau.

Villa DR. 1996. *Arendt and Heidegger: The fate of the political*. Princeton, NJ: Princeton University Press.

Woolman S. 2008. The South African Constitution as the last great modernist project. In: S Woolman & M Bishop (eds). *Constitutional conversations*. Pretoria: Pretoria University Law Press. 25-35.

Young Bruehl E. 2006. *Why Arendt matters*. New Haven, CT: Yale University Press.

FROM CONFESSION TO CONTESTATION

Critique as witnessing

Patrick Hanafin

[L]e récit est impossible [...] parce que le langage n'est ni expression ni interrogation, mais interrogatoire.

– *Levinas 1975:74*

[A] demand for récit, a violent putting-to-the-question, an instrument of torture working to wring the récit out of one as if it were a terrible secret, in ways that can go from the most archaic police methods to refinements for making (and even letting) one talk that are unsurpassed in neutrality and politeness, that are most respectfully medical, psychiatric, and even psychoanalytic.

– *Derrida 2011a:122*

[I]n their appeal to the narrator's presumed rational capacity (his capacity to furnish a cause for his suffering in the form of rationally ordered facts), we glimpse the violent edge of modern technical reason in the era of biopower.

– *Fynsk 2010:181*

Generation after generation, heroically, our captives refuse to speak to us.

– *Coetzee 2003:70*

[T]he government of men requires, on the part of those who are led, in addition to acts of obedience and submission, 'acts of truth', which have this particular character that not only is the subject required to speak truthfully, but to speak truthfully about himself.

– *Foucault 1999:154*

[W]ho are we, and what, if anything, are 'we' called?

– *Hill 2007:159*

Introduction

In a short essay entitled 'Refusal', written in 1959 in opposition to Charles de Gaulle's capture of power and denigration of democratic citizenship in France, Maurice Blanchot observed that refusal was a means of exposing the perversion of democracy that was being carried out. He noted that "[t]hose who refuse and who are bound by the force of refusal know that they are not yet together. The time of common affirmation is precisely what has been taken away from them" (Blanchot 2010:7). Such a refusal is also a refusal to be constructed as an identity to be managed by the state. Such a strategy of refusal to be constructed as an identity has the advantage of allowing one to remain beyond the grasp of the state's ability to make visible and incorporate such identities into the biopolitical regime. When groups claim the recognition of an identity by the state, such a claim can be used to capture and contain such identities. This mode of claiming identity recognition in the liberal state, as Patchen Markell (2003:31) reminds us, "furthers the state's project of rendering the social world 'legible' and governable; to appeal to the state 'for' the recognition of one's own identity – to present oneself as knowable – is already to offer the state reciprocal recognition of its sovereignty that it demands". The refusal to be formed as an object of governance by the state constitutes an important mode of resistance to biopower. In this chapter, I examine the relationship between modes of refusal and their representation in writing through a reading of JM Coetzee's 1983 novel *Life & Times of Michael K* in order to examine its implications for a critique of the political within writing itself.

Coetzee's writing and characters constitute a stubborn refusal to accept the fixed categories of genre, which, as Gerald L Bruns (2004:125) reminds us, "is always purposeful and just [...] susceptible to formal description and differentiation from an ensemble of alternative possibilities". Coetzee plays with these limitations in order to open another way into writing as a space that refuses to give up its meaning, to give the account demanded of it. Coetzee's writing appeals to an unassimilated community, a community not yet captured by a narrative of identity. As such, one could define his writing as being redolent of what Maurice Blanchot (1993:379) calls the "narrative voice", which, as Derrida notes, "has no fixed [...] place. It takes place place*lessly*, being both a-topical, mad, extravagant, and *hypertopical*, both placeless and overplaced" (Derrida 2011a:130-131). Such a writing marks the refusal of a narrative of fixed identity and history and moves from the comfort of an illusory past to an unknowable future. As such, it becomes, in the words of another of Coetzee's characters, Elizabeth Costello, "a sketchy, bloodless affair" (Coetzee 2003:38). The risk of a future without identity, 'sketchy and bloodless', is the one that Coetzee takes.

Coetzee's unforeseen readings and *détournements* of accepted understandings provide the basis for a rethinking of the relation of writing to the political. In developing this argument, I look at how the relationship between refusal and the narrative voice plays out in Coetzee's *Life & Times of Michael K*. Michael K is exemplary of how, in Coetzee's works, characters emerge who block the possibility of what Mark Sanders (2007:182-183) calls the "ruse of an end". *Life & Times of Michael K* constitutes a mode of thinking another form of community, an 'unavowable community' of the not yet assimilated. Such a thinking of community provides an opening to the future, not a monumentalisation of the past. K as unformed identity provides a means of thinking refusal in both literary and political terms.

Such a model of refusal of identity opposes the model of subject identity formation in the modern state. In post-apartheid South Africa, the model of the Truth and Reconciliation Commission sought to hail forth a new plural political identity by urging public confession and apology as a means of reconciliation and post-conflict resolution. Despite the multiple identities of the new 'Rainbow Nation', the underlying model of the state was one that constructed individuals on the basis of their identity as citizens. Coetzee short-circuits this model and opens up a thinking of community beyond legal identity formation. The refusal to be interpellated by the state does not allow for the neat formation of identity after apartheid which the state desires, and disrupts the neat compartmentalisation of history and marking out of the present.

Narrative voice and writing as effacement

For Maurice Blanchot, the narrative voice is marked by a writing as a form of effacement, which "produce[s] the absence of the work (worklessness)" (1993:424). Such 'worklessness' is the antithesis of the ordered, biocratic, identity-producing state. Being workless and unavowable, it does not impose a form, but can be seen more as, in Foucault's (1998:152) terms, a form of "contestation that effaces". This is a writing that escapes assimilation into a fixed genre or identity. It refuses to produce an account of itself. For Blanchot, the narrative voice conveys what it is ...

> [...] to live once again in another, in a third person, the dual relation, the fascinated, indifferent relation that is irreducible to any mediation, a neutral relation, even if it implies the infinite void of desire; finally, the imminent certainty that what has once taken place will always begin again, always give itself away and refuse itself [...] But who is telling the story here? [...] it is rather the one who cannot recount because she bears – this is her wisdom, her madness – the torment of the impossible narration, knowing herself [...] to be the measure of this outside where, as we accede to it, we risk falling under the attraction of speech that is entirely exterior: pure extravagance. (Blanchot 1993:462)

This 'one who cannot recount because she bears [...] the torment of the impossible narration, knowing herself [...] to be the measure of this outside where [...] we risk falling under the attraction of speech that is entirely exterior', is that singularity (the third person, the *il y a*) which exists outside the frame of legally and politically imposed personhood. In an analysis of Blanchot's notion of the narrative voice, Jacques Derrida observed:

> [It is] a neutral voice that speaks the work from out of this place without a place, where the work is silent. The placeless place where the work is silent: a silent voice, then, withdrawn into its "aphony". This "aphony" distinguishes it from the "narrating voice", the voice that literary criticism or poetics or narratology strives to locate in the system of the récit, of the novel, or of the narration. (Derrida 2011a:130)

This form of writing, like the characters contained within it, performs a stubborn refusal to accept the condition of legal and political subjectification. As Gerald Bruns observes:

[I]t is the unconstructed voice of the singular and the irreducible, that which cannot be assimilated into a system or theory of constituted subjects, objects, and relations. (Bruns 1997:xvi)

Coetzee's writing conveys this 'unconstructed voice of the singular and the irreducible'. It does not come in response to a call, but rather emerges from the margins unsolicited, an instance of "unexpected speech" (Blanchot 2000:36) or speech "that is entirely exterior: pure extravagance" (Blanchot 1993:462). Coetzee's writing has, in the words of his strongly opinionated narrator in *Diary of a bad year*, "a meaning quite different from what the lexicon says, where the metaphoric spark is always one jump ahead of the decoding function, where another, unforeseen reading is always possible" (Coetzee 2008:23). This thinking with and against a law of ordering allows us to think of writing not as a 'work', in the sense of a completed object, a monument to memory, but as an opening to the future. The narrative voice points to a story not yet recorded, to the possibility of a future. In this regard, it opposes such models as that of the apartheid state, based on a mythic national narrative of racial supremacy, as well as the narrative of the post-apartheid state, based on the narrating of a truth or truths about the past with the aim of overcoming conflict and reconciling the nation. Both share a common need to give an account of the nation in the form of a narrating voice. The narrating voice is, as Derrida reminds us, ...

[...] the voice of a subject recounting something, remembering an event or a historical sequence, knowing who he is, where he is, and what he is talking about. It responds to some "police", a force of order or law [...] In this sense, all organized narration is "a matter for the police", even before its genre [...] has been determined. (Derrida 2011a:130-131)

In opposition to this, Coetzee's writing provides an example of the narrative voice undoing or refusing narratives of fixed identity and opposing rigid genre demarcation.[1] This could be seen as an instance of what Gilles Deleuze has termed writing as 'becoming':

To write is [...] not to impose a form [...] Writing is a question of becoming, always incomplete, always in the midst of being formed [...] It is a process [...] Writing is inseparable from becoming [... It] always has a component of flight that escapes its own formalization [...] To become is not to attain a form [...] but to find the zone of proximity, indiscernibility, or undifferentiation where one can no longer be distinguished from a woman, an animal, or a molecule – neither imprecise nor general, but unforeseen and non-preexistent, singularized out of a population rather than determined in a form. (Deleuze 1997:225-226)

1 In another of Coetzee's novels, *Disgrace* (2000), we again encounter refusal as a mode of resistance to subordination, this time not during a state of exceptional civil war, but in a post-conflict liberal order. Such a refusal also points to an undoing of being defined in relation to the state as a victim or as a perpetrator. It is a refusal to be categorised. By refusing to accept a way out of losing his job by issuing an apology – a confession of guilt made publicly to a committee – David Lurie in effect refuses to be interpellated by the post-apartheid liberal state as a particular kind of identity.

Coetzee's writing is not a response to a demand for truth, nor is it a confession. Instead, it engages specifically with the impossibility of a confessional narrative, the impossibility of writing in response to a demand to produce the truth of writing itself. What Coetzee does in his writing is to refuse all entreaties to follow a particular generic mode; instead, what he performs is, to paraphrase Richard Stamelman (1990:143), "writing able to preserve the vivid presence of the word [...] without forcing it to become part of the 'system' of written language".

For Coetzee, forced confession is part of a political apparatus that imposes obedience and order, an apparatus that puts the citizen-subject in his or her place. Words are extracted from one's mouth – not one's own words, but words that represent the 'truth' for the inquisitor: the definitive word, the measurable word, the word that counts as information. In such circumstances, to not speak, to not respond with an account of oneself, would be to produce a rupture in the circuits of biopower. This points to another model of being together in relation with others, one that does not have an end in the sense of extracting a confession, or indeed nation-building. Rather than seeking to be recognised by the state, one refuses it.

Refusing confession or not taking form

In *Life & Times of Michael K*, the eponymous character does not fit into any fixed identity category. He exists in the gaps of society. Set in an unnamed state (which bears a striking resemblance to the South Africa of the 1970s and early 1980s), the novel portrays a state in the grip of civil war and a state of emergency. It is set in a period of *interregnum*, between two orders. In such a state, those who have no fixed 'place' – the homeless, the vagrant, the old, the infirm – are rounded up and put in labour and internment camps. Everyone who is not 'in their place' is viewed with suspicion as an object to be controlled. Michael K, who works as a gardener, is a character who lives on the margins, in a world of silence, perpetually out of place due to his physical deformity (a hare lip) and lack of mental agility. Following an attempt to return with his mother to her place of birth, he exposes himself to suspicion as a would-be aider and abettor of insurgents and finds himself in an internment camp, where the camp commandant and medical officer unsuccessfully attempt to wrestle a narrative from him.

It is perhaps when he disappears into another temporality and space that Michael K takes on some form of sovereignty. To paraphrase Maurice Blanchot (1981:16), it is "as nobody [that he is] sovereign", and it is in this paradoxical state that his power of resistance resides. At one point, after his mother has died on the journey to her home, Michael is left totally alone. He comes across a deserted farm and takes up temporary residence there. Instead of inhabiting the farmhouse, he builds a burrow-like structure in order to be hidden from government soldiers searching for insurgents. Here we see a trace of Kafka's short story *The Burrow,* a story about a creature that has completed an extensive network of tunnels and lives in a state of perpetual anxiety about protecting this burrow against an unnamed 'enemy'. To be sure, it is no coincidence that Coetzee wrote an article on *The Burrow*, which appeared in 1981, two years before the publication of *Life & Times of Michael K*. Coetzee treats this topic from the point of view of the time of the narrative, what he calls "an everlasting present" in the case of *The Burrow* (Coetzee 1981:575). This everlasting present, beyond linear time, also characterises K's stay in his burrow, where he lives "beyond the reach of calendar and clock in a blessedly neglected corner, half awake, half asleep" (Coetzee 1983:116). Like Michael K, Kafka's creature's "whole life is organized around the burrow, his defence against an attack which may come at any moment and without warning" (Coetzee 1981:576). Indeed, in a prescient account of his novel to come, Coetzee writes about time in *The Burrow*, which resembles that in Michael K's burrow:

> Time in 'The Burrow' is discontinuous in a strictly fomalizable sense. Any moment may mark the break between before and after. Time is thus at every moment a time of crisis [...] Life consists in an attempt to anticipate a danger which cannot be anticipated because it comes without transition, without warning. The experience of a time of crisis is coloured by anxiety. The task of building the burrow itself represents a life devoted to trying to still anxiety naturally without success; for without warning 'the enemy' is in the burrow. (Coetzee 1981:575)

This characterisation mirrors the everlasting time of the *interregnum* in *Life & Times of Michael K*: K lives in a similar state, constantly waiting for the enemy, in the form of the state and its agents, to come for him.

Just as Michael K does not fit into the time of society as such, or into the society that the state imposes on him, he also does not fit into the internment camp. K is a character who cannot be pinned down in one identity category or another. He is, as he observes, "out of all the camps" (Coetzee 1983:182). He exists as a sort of unassimable excess, being there and not being there at the same time. According to the camp's medical officer, K does not fit into pre-existing categories of meaning: he is "a human soul above and beneath classification" (*ibid*:151). Instead of narrating himself or providing an account of himself in response to the questioning of the camp authorities, K is unable to give such an account. He refuses to narrate and to be narrated. Here we see a resistant character in a resistant text. What *Life & Times of Michael K* does is provide a detailed fictive reflection on the impossibility of giving a narrative. Michael K's refusal of identity – his very inoperativity – is viewed with suspicion and as a threat to the order of the state, which relies on willing operatives to keep it in motion. As the medical officer asks:

> Did you think you were a spirit invisible [...] a creature beyond the reach of the laws of nations? [...] the laws of nations have you in their grip now: they have pinned you down in a bed beneath the grandstand of the old Kenilworth racecourse, they will grind you in the dirt if necessary. The laws are made of iron [...] No matter how thin you make yourself, they will not relax. There is no home left for universal souls. (Coetzee 1983:151)

During this exceptional state of civil war, what is important at the internment camp is the way in which all aspects of life are governed and behaviour is modified so that internees may become mollified and compliant citizens: as the medical officer observes, the internees "will pass out certified pure of heart and willing of hand" (Coetzee 1983:143). This dictation of what one does in the camp renders all acts predictable. Michael K's silence testifies to a short-circuiting of the order of the camp. In another sense, he exposes the fiction of all power and law in their attempt to create order. The medical officer and the camp commander attempt to make Michael K speak. He is viewed with suspicion as a would-be accomplice to insurgents. To borrow from Branka Arsic (2007:105), the authorities attempt to assign Michael K "a specific place, [to] bring him under its own power by removing him into its very interiority". Michael K's appearance before the representatives of the law mirrors the position of the narrator in Maurice Blanchot's novella *The Madness of the Day*, who is similarly asked to give an account of himself to the representatives of power/knowledge, namely a psychiatrist and an ophthalmologist. Like Blanchot's narrator, Michael K interrupts his own representation by the law. He is asked to explain himself, to relate a narrative that would be useful to the state in its re-imposition of order. The representatives of power attempt to force him to speak in order to form himself as a citizen with an identity. They attempt to form him and make him visible, to identify him. As Deleuze (2006:65) would have it, "[f]ormed substances are revealed by visibility". By not allowing himself to be given form, he remains invisible to the biocratic order.

The law demands everything and demands an identity. It cannot abide non-identity, because non-identity escapes its appropriating grasp. Non-identity is formless and cannot be categorised and therefore contained. In Michael K's encounter with the medical officer, he challenges the medical officer's own legitimacy. The medical officer tries to make Michael K talk: "Listen to me, listen how easily I fill this room with words. I know people who can [...] fill up whole worlds talking" (Coetzee 1983:192). In this way, and similar to the lawmen in Blanchot's novella, the medical officer attempts to announce his ownership of the space and its rules. Indeed, Blanchot's description of the space of the interrogation perfectly describes the encounter between Michael K and his interrogators:

> One is not aware of it, but these men are kings [...] they would say: 'Everything here belongs to us.' They would fall upon my scraps of thought: 'This is ours'. They interpellated my story: 'Talk', and my story would put itself at their service. (Blanchot 1981:14)

Michael K is asked to form himself, to be identified, when he is told: "Give yourself some substance, Man" (Coetzee 1983:192). He is asked to explain himself and make himself appear, but in the end he disappears and does not allow himself to be formed or to inform. K undoes the interrogator-interrogee relationship, and as such, according to Michael Marais ...

> [...] dispossesses the state functionaries of their power without himself assuming a position of dominance. Being silent, he never assumes a subject position in relation to an object: in linguistic terms, he is intransitive [...] his silence can be construed as an anarchic repudiation of all power relations; it is the means by which he resists becoming a character in the text of history, a text characterised by a struggle for power between master and servant on a national scale. (Marais 1989:36)

What occurs here is close to what Maurice Blanchot articulates as the reversal of the ordered dyadic relationship of inquisitor and victim:

> The Powerful One is the master of the possible, but he is not master of this relation that does not derive from mastery and that power cannot measure: the relation without relation wherein the 'other' is revealed as 'autrui' [...] Hence the furious

movement of the inquisitor who wants by force to obtain a scrap of language in order to bring all speech down to the level of force. To make speak, and through torture, is to attempt to master infinite distance by reducing expression to this language of power through which the one who speaks would once again lay himself open to force's hold; and the one who is being tortured refuses to speak in order not to enter through the extorted words into the game of opposing violence, but also, at the same time, in order to preserve the true speech that he very well knows is at this instant merged with his silent presence – which is the very presence of autrui in himself. (Blanchot 1993:132)

Michael K begins to vanish literally and metaphorically out of the story and out of history – if he was ever there. This 'whatever singularity', being without categories of identity, taunts and undoes the state: "It excited him, he found, to say, recklessly, *the truth, the truth about me. I am a gardener*" (Coetzee 1983:181). Michael K finally thinks: "Perhaps the truth is that it is enough to be out of the camps, out of all the camps at the same time" (*ibid*:182). In this move from confession to contestation we see what Judith Butler terms putting "life into truthful form" (Murray & Butler 2007:416). In abnegating the authority of speech, K disappears, is not formed. Of course, his silence does not mean that there is no speech, but such speech emerges elsewhere, not in response to the threatening question that seeks to forcibly extract 'the' truth. When speech comes forth without being forced through torture, then what we have is a breaking of the frame of what is expected and accepted within regimes of war or biopower. That this does indeed undo the conditioned and dictated word of the camp is underlined by the reaction of the camp's medical officer to Michael K's withholding of his narrative. For the medical officer, Michael K's stay in the camp serves an allegory of ...

[...] how scandalously, how outrageously a meaning can take up residence in a system without becoming a term in it. Did you not notice how, whenever I tried to pin you down, you slipped away? (Coetzee 1983:166)

Michael K disappears from the sight of the representatives of the ruling order. He is not visible in their terms; they cannot recognise him. Michael K finds himself in a position similar to that of Blanchot's narrator in *The Madness of the Day*:

[...] when at last nothing was present but my perfect nothingness and there was nothing more to see, they ceased to see me too. Very irritated, they stood up and cried out, "All right. Where are you? Where are you hiding? Hiding is forbidden, it is an offense." (Blanchot 1981:14)

By refusing to be an object, Michael K reverses the power relation. The state officials have no power if there is no object to govern. The state 'disappears' objects and makes them appear; it forms them. However, this does not happen with Michael K, who refuses to make himself appear and resolves to disappear of his own accord. He interrupts the law's representation of itself as well as its representation of him. Being invisible, not being marked with an identity, is an offence. This is what so offends the state. As Giorgio Agamben reminds us:

What the State cannot tolerate in any way [...] is that [...] singularities form a community without affirming an identity [...] The State [...] is not founded on a social bond, of which it would be the expression, but rather on the dissolution, the unbinding it prohibits. For the State [...] what is important is never the singularity as such, but only its inclusion in some identity, whatever identity [...] Whatever singularity [...] rejects all identity and every condition of belonging, is the principal enemy of the State. (Agamben 1996:84-86)

The attempt by the law to fit Michael K's account into an ordered narrative frame, to form his words to their ends, fails. The law wants to make of Michael K an object, a pure mask resounding with the magisterial voice, the perfect persona. However, he contests this attempt to extract an account from him. Like the narrator in *The Madness of the Day*, Michael K "was not capable of forming a récit" (Blanchot 1981:18). To paraphrase Leslie Hill, Michael K is ...

> [...] other than the law [...] because of [his] refusal, on grounds of impotence, impossibility, and weakness, to allow [himself] to be addressed by the language of the law and constituted by the law as a subject or hostage of that law. (Hill 1997:187-188)

To paraphrase Jacques Derrida, by not giving a satisfactory account of himself, Michael K ...

> [...] not only troubles the representatives of the law [...] who demand of him, but are unable to obtain, an organized récit, a testimony oriented by a sense of history or his story, ordained and ordered by reason [...] he alarms [...] the lawmen, he radically persecutes them and [...] conceals from them [...] the truth they demand and without which they are nothing. (Derrida 2011b:245)

Michael K has a profound psychic impact on the camp's medical officer, making him rethink his position in the biocratic regime. The medical officer after the encounter reflects that "I was wasting my life [...] by living from day to day in a state of waiting [...] I had in effect given myself up as a prisoner to this war" (Coetzee 1983:157). He is forced to admit to himself that K exists beyond all camps, all histories and texts. In addition to not giving an account of himself, Michael K also refuses to eat in the camp. He wants to disappear both in vocal and visual terms. Such refusals to speak and to eat are the last vestige of power as non-power that those in the abject position of the excluded retain. Yet, in his reduced, emaciated form, Michael K represents a certain hope for the future, a confused beacon of resistance to the moulding of the individual will to the state's desires. This negative affirmation of agency by those not deemed worthy of full citizenship can be seen as an instance of the stubborn refusal of mere life to be categorised and ruled. Indeed, to borrow Judith Butler's phrase, such refusals can be seen as "critical acts of resistance [...] incendiary acts that somehow, incredibly, live through the violence they oppose, even if we do not yet know in what ways such lives will survive" (Butler 2009:62).

Conclusion

Besides being a stubborn refusal to submit to the order of the camp – to be 'out of all the camps' – the performance of Michael K is also a testimony to a being beyond the order of law. It is a refusal to surrender to the role imposed on the detainee as source of information. If, as Jean-Michel Landry (2009:112) has noted, "to confess, to seek to know, and to produce the truth concerning oneself, amounts to submission", then the refusal to divulge is a form of power as non-power, an act of insubordination.

Confession, then, is a mode of governance, behind which, as Landry points out, "lies a political technology of obedience" (*ibid*:122). By refusing to allow the law to have what it wants, Michael K attempts to counter this violent authority of the interrogating state. He exists in "the interval *between* speech and violence" (Blanchot 1993:62). At the end of the encounter between Michael K and the medical officer it is the medical officer who is temporarily disarmed. By inhabiting 'the interval between speech and violence', Michael K leaves traces, both on the law and its agents, rather than being traced and formed by the law. Michael K exposes the paradoxical nature of the political technology of obedience that contains within it its own undoing in the form of disobedience. As Etienne Balibar has argued, disobedience may be considered the only possible positive condition of law:

> [...] there is no political community **without** the inclusion of a principle of disobedience or dissidence **within** the legal frame of obedience itself, which radically challenges the purely **legal understanding of the law** [...] What is strange, indeed remarkable, is that the "negative" argument provides the institution with its only possible **positive** condition, and the positive argument entirely concerns a "dialectical" inclusion of the negative within the positivity of the law, albeit not in order to overcome it, rather in order to give it **life**. (Balibar 2007:737 – original emphasis in bold)

Coetzee evokes the complex, paradoxical nature of obedience wonderfully in a scene where the medical officer contemplates Michael K's unique form of resistance:

> You were not a hero and did not pretend to be, not even a hero of fasting. In fact you did not resist at all. When we told you to jump, you jumped. When we told you to jump again, you jumped again. When we told you to jump a third time, however, you did not respond but collapsed in a heap; and we could all see, even the most unwilling of us, that you had failed because you had exhausted your resources in obeying us [...] Your body rejected the food we fed you and you grew even thinner [...] I slowly began to understand the truth: that you were crying secretly, unknown to your conscious self (forgive the term), for a different kind of food, food that no camp could supply. Your will remained pliant but your body was crying to be fed its own food, and only that. (Coetzee 1983:163-164)

Disobedience, then, does not lead to an overcoming of law, but rather creates the possibility for action and for the cultivation of freedom. As Balibar notes:

> [W]ithout a possibility of disobedience there is no legitimate institution of obedience – a thesis [...] rooted in the pragmatic understanding of how democratic regimes, 'constitutions of liberty,' emerge and collapse in history. (Balibar 2007:735)

As such, Michael K allows us to think of the paradoxical nature of political obedience and the subject's willed servitude to order. The action of refusing such servitude points to the beginning of resistance to biopolitical modes of production. Indeed, as Michael Hardt and Antonio Negri observe in their analysis of Michael K's particular model of refusal:

> Michael K [...] is [...] a figure of absolute refusal [...] he is continually stopped by the cages, barriers, and checkpoints erected by authority, but he manages quietly to refuse them, to keep moving [...] The barriers [...] seem to stop life, and thus he refuses them absolutely in order to keep life in motion [...] K's refusal of authority is as absolute as Bartleby's, and that very absoluteness and simplicity

situate him, too, on a level of ontological purity. K also approaches the level of naked universality. (Hardt & Negri 2000:203-204)

Hardt and Negri link Michael K's refusal to Etienne de la Boetie's politics of refusal, where resistance can be performed as much in a deliberate refusal to support the tyrant as in the violent toppling of the tyrant. As De la Boetie exhorted: "Resolve to serve no more, and you are at once freed" (1975:52). In such a refusal, Hardt and Negri see the beginning of a liberatory politics. However, it is only the beginning. The larger project requires for them the creation of ...

> [...] a new social body, which is a project that goes well beyond refusal. Our lines of flight, our exodus must be constituent and create a real alternative. Beyond the simple refusal, we need also to construct a new mode of life and above all a new community. (Hardt & Negri 2000:204)

The beginning of the outline of such a coming community can be seen in figures of refusal such as Michael K. Michael K's Bartleby-like work-to-rule demonstrates the inoperativity of all attempts to resist power while at the same time noting the impossibility of doing otherwise. Indeed, in the mode of De la Boetie, the medical officer sees the significance of Michael K's resistance in terms beyond the toppling of one power and its replacement with another, equally violent, one:

> [...] as your persistent No, day after day, gathered weight, I began to feel that you were more than just another patient, another casualty of the war, another brick in the pyramid of sacrifice that someone would eventually climb and stand straggle-legged on top of, roaring and beating his chest and announcing himself emperor of all he surveyed. (Coetzee 1983:164)

Michael K, in effect, performs what Michel Foucault (2002:33) calls "the right to bear witness, to oppose truth to power [...] That right to set a powerless truth against a truthless power". In our role as either citizens or rights-claiming subjects in contemporary liberal democracies the efficacy of our speech is limited, because, to paraphrase Foucault (1990:61), we, as speaking subjects, are also the "subject [matter] of the statement". The interlocutor (the lawman) is always in the position of authority. The refusal to divulge in such circumstances is a form of power as non-power, a non-positive affirmation rather than a withdrawal into silence. The uncalled for 'No' is an affirmation of a provisional non-power that contains the possibility of the beginning of a liberatory politics. Nothing is ostensibly changed – the institutions continue – but something will never be the same. This is the imperceptible moment of subversion, which, as workless, as pure excess, achieves nothing. Yet this is its very force. It counterposes worklessness to the work of power, non-identity to identity, responsibility to one's own non-responsibility. This "counter-law" is "the condition of the possibility of the law [...] an axiom of impossibility [... which] confound[s] its sense, order and reason" (Derrida 2011b:220).

Reference List

Agamben G. 1996. *The coming community*. Minneapolis, MN: University of Minnesota Press.

Arsic B. 2007. *Passive constitutions or 7½ times Bartleby*. Stanford, CA: Stanford University Press.

Balibar E. 2007. (De)Constructing the human as human institution: A reflection on the coherence of Hannah Arendt's practical philosophy. *Social Research* 74:727-738.

Blanchot M. 2010. *Maurice Blanchot: Political writings, 1953-1993*. New York: Fordham University Press.

— 2000. *Les intellectuels en question*. Tours: Farrago.

— 1993. *The infinite conversation*. Minneapolis, MN: University of Minnesota Press.

— 1981. *The Madness of the Day*. Barrytown, NY: Station Hill Press.

Bruns GL. 2004. Anarchic temporality: Writing, friendship, and the ontology of the work of art in Maurice Blanchot's poetics. In: K Hart & G Hartman (eds). *The power of contestation: Perspectives on Maurice Blanchot*. Baltimore, MD: The Johns Hopkins University Press.

— 1997. *Maurice Blanchot: The refusal of philosophy*. Baltimore, MD: The Johns Hopkins University Press.

Butler J. 2009. *Frames of War: When is Life Grievable?* London: Verso.

Coetzee JM. 2008. *Diary of a bad year*. London: Vintage Books.

— 2003. *Elizabeth Costello*. London: QPD.

— 1983. *Life & Times of Michael K*. London: Vintage Books.

— 1981. Time, Tense and Aspect in Kafka's 'The Burrow'. *MLN* 96(3):556-579.

De la Boetie E. 1975. *The politics of obedience: The discourse of voluntary servitude*. New York: Free Life Editions.

Deleuze G. 2006. *Foucault*. London: Continuum.

— 1997. Literature and life. *Critical Inquiry* 23:225-230.

Derrida J. 2011a. Living on. In: JP Leavey (ed). *Jacques Derrida, Parages*. Stanford, CA: Stanford University Press. 103-191.

— 2011b. The law of genre. In: JP Leavey (ed). *Jacques Derrida, Parages*. Stanford, CA: Stanford University Press. 217-249.

Foucault M. 2002. Truth and juridical forms. In: J Faubion (ed). *Michel Foucault: Essential Works 1954-84. Vol 3: Power*. London: Allen Lane the Penguin Press. 1-89.

— 1999. On the government of the living. In: JR Carrette (ed). *Religion and culture*. New York: Routledge. 154-157.

— 1998. The thought of the outside. In: J Faubion (ed). *M Foucault: Aesthetics, Method and Epistemology. Vol 2 of The Essential Works of Michel Foucault*. London: Allen Lane the Penguin Press. 147-169.

— 1990. *The history of sexuality. Vol 1*. New York: Vintage Books.

Fynsk C. 2010. Writing and sovereignty: La folie du jour. In: K Hart (ed). *Clandestine encounters: Philosophy in the narratives of Maurice Blanchot*. Notre Dame: University of Notre Dame Press.

Hardt M & Negri A. 2000. *Empire*. Cambridge, MA: Harvard University Press.

Hill L. 2007. Not in our name: Blanchot, politics, the neuter. *Paragraph* 30:141-159.

— 1997. *Maurice Blanchot: Extreme contemporary*. London: Routledge.

Landry J-M. 2009. Confession, obedience, and subjectivity: Michel Foucault's unpublished lectures on the government of the living. *Telos* 146:111-123.

Levinas E. 1975. Exercices sur 'La folie du jour'. In: E Levinas. *Sur Maurice Blanchot*. Montpellier: Fata Morgana. 53-74.

Marais M. 1989. Languages of power: A story of reading Coetzee's Michael K. *English in Africa* 16(2):31-48.

Markell P. 2003. *Bound by recognition*. Princeton, NJ: Princeton University Press.

Murray S & Butler J. 2007. Ethics at the Scene of Address: A Conversation with Judith Butler. *Symposium: Review of the Canadian Journal for Continental Philosophy* 11:415-445.

Sanders M. 2007. *Ambiguities of witnessing: Law and literature in the time of a truth commission*. Stanford, CA: Stanford University Press.

Stamelman R. 1990. *Lost beyond telling: Representations of death and absence in modern French poetry*. Ithaca: Cornell University Press.

JOYCE'S POLITICS IN EXILE

Music and motif between two nations

Richard Bowyer

The long-held view that James Joyce was apolitical or otherwise disinterested in politics, which was, as Seamus Deane (1985:92) put it, "one of the more secure assumptions about his life and work", is no longer credible in the light of recent research on Joyce and his politics. Deane was amongst the first, in 1985 – relatively late in the history of the 'Joyce Industry' – to challenge this assumption and offer an account of Joyce that is heavily politicised and based upon a repudiation of imperium. Others have subsequently followed and pursued the question of Joyce's politics energetically.[1] The repudiation of imperium in Joyce included both that of the British and Roman (Catholic) imperialisms, but also, crucially, included a rejection of existing cultural and political narratives of the Irish (Fenian) nationalist sort, exemplified in literature by the Irish Literary Revival (*ibid*). Joyce's self-exile to continental Europe from around the time of the foundation of Sinn Féin until his death is not – as was believed by Joyce scholars before the 1980s – a turning of his back on Irish nationalist causes. Rather, Joyce's self-exile provided a critical standpoint from which to critique colonial rule and advance a politics.

1 Cheng 1995; Gibson 2002; Kiberd 1995; Manganiello 1980; McCabe 2003; Nolan 1995.

The position of the exiled writer in the twentieth century literary canon is a formidable one.[2] In his book on the subject, Terry Eagleton (1970) identifies and relates the rise of the literary exile to the collapse of productive and meaningful correspondences between the 'particular' and the 'social' – the mainstay of nineteenth century literature. In lieu of this vigorous relationship between the particular and the social, the exile brings new traditions and perspectives to a situation which is "in no full sense their own": "In each case, great art is produced, not from the simple availability of an alternative, but from the subtle and involuted tensions between the remembered and the real, the potential and the actual, integration and dispossession, exile and involvement" (*ibid*:18). In the case of Joyce, his personal self-exile to Europe to write about the home he left, his exile from Irish politics "as practiced", his exile from the literary culture, from the Church, from the languages of Gaelic and English – in short, what Cixous calls an "absolute exile" (1976:437-438) – provided Joyce with a unique critical perspective of 'home'. But this perspective is not just a view of Irish politics from afar. The critical movement that is exile is a movement that effects certain aesthetic phenomena too. From the position of exile, the exiled writer is engaged in the processes of remembering and forgetting, creating and destroying, as they relate to 'home'. Under the conditions of exile, these processes extend to the grand narratives and mythologies prevalent in the 'home' culture. The exiled writer, by virtue of being in exile, assumes the position of myth-maker, displacing 'home' myths in their writing, thus exposing the mythical or fictive nature of 'home' myths.

One of the 'home' myths Joyce takes up repeatedly in his oeuvre is the mythology of Irish nationalism conceived of through heroic Fenian legends.[3] Nowhere is this more explicit than in the 'Cyclops' episode of *Ulysses*, which takes as its subject matter Fenian nationalism and the origins of the Irish nation. The main action takes place in a pub in the legal district of Dublin. Twelve pub-goers discuss a range of political issues, espousing nationalist sentiments. One character, known simply as 'the Citizen' and modelled on Michael Cusack, founder of the Gaelic Athletic Association, represents one extreme of nationalist opinion, and he is posited against the book's protagonist, Leopold Bloom. Bloom, who is half-Jewish and half-Irish, and consequently neither Jew nor Irish,[4] becomes the Citizen's adversary, as each adopts opposing positions on various subjects, including, for example, the virtues of lawn tennis.[5] Of course, even this is a political matter, since lawn tennis is not an Irish sport. Joyce shows how the one-eyed Cyclops of the Homeric legend coincides with the narrow-sightedness of

2 See, in particular, Eagleton 1970; Said 2001.

3 Especially in *Finnegans Wake* (Joyce 1939).

4 This precise point is taken up in the 'Circe' episode, where Bloom fails to pronounce 'shibboleth' correctly (he says "shitbroleeth"), thus ruling out his membership to the community of Irish Dubliners (the context at that moment of the novel) and Judaism (the Biblical context discussed in *Judges* 12:4-6). See Joyce 1986:15.765-770. (The following abbreviation applies throughout: *U* 15.765-770, where the first digit refers to episode number, the second to line number.)

5 *U* 12.952.

the Citizen, who has his eye on only one thing: a nationalism based on a particular Gaelic history and culture, whether real or imagined.

The work of this chapter is not aimed at reconciling the question of what Joyce's political position was in relation to Irish nationalist causes. On this, Emer Nolan (1995) has shown how the reception of 'Cyclops' has been overly sympathetic towards the position adopted by Bloom in the episode, when in fact Joyce's own position was more ambiguous. Rather, this chapter deals with a particular aesthetic dimension to Joyce's politics: Joyce's use of music in the 'Cyclops' episode to convey ideas of or about nation. In particular, the chapter looks at the use of a motif: the motif of a biscuit tin – an object which, from time to time, appears throughout the episode. The biscuit tin has a history beyond Bloom's encounter with the Citizen: since the biscuit tin is a *Jacob's* biscuit tin, it recalls the transaction of birthright between Jacob and Esau in *Genesis*, where a starving Esau sells his birthright to Jacob in return for pottage, or a bowl of lentils. The pottage becomes a biscuit tin in *Ulysses*, but nevertheless performs the same function in transacting birthright between two nations. Since the motif form is principally a musical device, the relationship between music and law is analysed and an account of law *as* music in Joyce is asserted. The chapter proceeds by looking first at that relationship between law and music, and the role of music in the state, beginning with Plato. Then, the chapter looks at Joyce's particular use of music in his writings. The motif of the biscuit tin in 'Cyclops' is analysed in the third and final part.

Law and music

The relationship between law and music was recognised in antiquity: Plato's Book IV of *The Republic* outlines the significance of music in the functioning of the state, and the threat posed to the state by musical 'innovations'. In Plato, it is recognised that "musical innovation is full of danger to the whole state, and ought to be prohibited", but also that, "when the modes of music change, the fundamental laws of the state always change with them" (1888:424c). Music, then, is what supports the state in antiquity, but also that which poses a threat to the existence of the state. The origin and thus existence of the state is therefore identified with music: "[...] our guardians must lay the foundations of their fortress in music" (*ibid*:424d). The function of music *vis*-à-*vis* the state is, in Plato, one which "penetrates into manners and customs; whence, issuing with greater force, invades contracts between man and man, and from contracts goes on to laws and constitutions" (*ibid*:425a). Music is especially powerful in Plato because of the way in which it affects the soul: "[M]usical training is a more potent instrument than any other, because rhythm and harmony find their way into the inward places of the soul" (*ibid*:401d).

The presence of another, non-state, music is, as Plato/Socrates describes, "lawlessness" (Plato 1888:425a). Thus, the very thing that binds a people in a social contract, and which generates laws and constitutions, is music. Music is generative of both community and law in Plato.

Reference to Books III and X of *The Republic* might suggest a similar role for the poet and poetry: the significance of poetry in praising heroes and gods in the functioning of the state, and the expulsion or censorship of poets who might want to say something else.[6] Whilst an analysis of the differences between music and poetry in Plato is beyond this work, for present purposes it is sufficient to recognise the special significance of music in the foundation and continuation of the state. It should be noted too, however, that what was considered 'music' in ancient Greece included music as we know it today, but also poetry and dance: the separation between the three is a modern phenomenon.

The case for censorship in Plato is a famous one: the poet – except where limited to imitative poetry, imitating and thus 'educating' in the ways of the state – is a dangerous soul who must be banished. The irony is that Plato's own poetry – *The Republic*, for example – ought not to be tolerated according to Plato's own injunction, for he too is creating poetry and music other than mere idolatry of the state and of the gods. This irony is dealt with by Nietzsche in *On the genealogy of morality* (1994), where Nietzsche identifies the competitive spirit in Plato, and the Greeks generally. By affirming the singularity and exclusivity of the state poetry, Plato is there aspiring to take that position, competitively, as if to say, in Nietzsche's words:

> I can do it better than them. No Protagoras has written myths as beautiful as mine, no dramatist has written such a lively and fascinating whole as the Symposium, no orator has composed speeches as I present in the Gorias – and now I reject all of that and condemn all imitative art! (Nietzsche 1994:193)[7]

With Nietzsche's intervention in mind, the Platonic discourse on music and poetry stresses the innate power of music – its force, its force as state force, or its force in a displacement of the state.[8] This is also a force that is exceptional in nature and asserts its exclusivity as such.[9]

In a remarkable book from 1928, the English composer Cyril Scott sets out to show how music is the driving force behind transformations in moral values throughout history. He identifies in Beethoven, for example, the "first psychoanalyst" (Scott 1928:32), who introduced to the world, for the first time, the full spectrum of the emotions – "especially the lower ones" (*ibid*). This would consequently have an impact on areas of life such as criminology, where, thanks to Beethoven, one could now, and only now, "feel 'with' the criminal" (*ibid*:35). Moreover, and possibly more importantly to Scott, Beethoven's presentation of the emotions improved the psychological well-being of society generally, and brought a whole host of benefits. For example, by experiencing the emotions through music, "women gradually became less hysterical

6 Plato's account of censorship is contested. See Naddaff 2002; Church 1941.

7 See also Naddaff 2002:6: "The infamous action of competition in *The Republic*, namely the poets' exile and ostracism [... is] an attempt to break down the poets' exclusive control, their totalizing cultural, social, literary power [...] The censorship of poetry opens up rather than closes down the possibility of new forms of discourse."

8 Cf Walter Benjamin's (1996) essay 'Critique of violence'.

9 Jacques Derrida (2007) has written about the force of music in 'What remains by force of music'. The force of music is carried by the rhythm of music, which imposes itself with or without content. The rhythm "counts more than all the themes it carries off" (*ibid*:88-89).

and less subject to fainting and tearfulness" (*ibid*:38-39). However far-fetched Scott's appropriation of both Beethoven and psychoanalysis, the general thesis that music performs some sort of constitutive function – of moral values, or indeed the state – is one that is compelling.

Whilst it may be difficult to identify the 'music' of the state in modernity, Plato's/Socrates' invocation of the function of music in the state is still relevant when one considers, for example, the importance of music in protest, the role of the brass band in trade union marches, and other resistant uses of music. With the state itself, music has become largely symbolic in use. But that is not to say that the state does not employ music in its functioning: it might be that one has to look for it in different places, or recognise it in different ways. Plato/Socrates sees music in the "habit of order" (Plato 1888:425a), and so it may be that the fissiparous institutional and normative aspects of the state have music in their sense or habit of order. In relation to music and sound specifically, the regulation of radio broadcasts and the primacy of the state broadcasters could be contrasted with the advent and continued presence of pirate radio stations on the airwaves as two sides of the state/non-state competition to govern (state broadcaster), and resist (pirate radio), with music.[10] Further, it was until recently the practice of the London Metropolitan Police to ask, when carrying out a risk assessment for the public performance of music, what style, type or genre of music was to be played.[11] One can also point to more overtly state-based examples. Tan Dun's *Symphony 1997: Heaven, Earth, Mankind*, written on the occasion of Hong Kong's reunification with China, makes use of Chinese instruments, but consists of a distinctly Western composition. As John Sallis (2008:110) notes, the performance of the music "attests to – and projects hope for – a union without reduction", a reduction of Hong Kong to simply another part of China. This music is, for Sallis, not just symbolism detached from politics: "[...] the power of music to insinuate itself into the soul so as to shape its dispositions, thereby determining human practices, is what renders music politically effective and hence potentially dangerous" (*ibid*:115).

Music is also fundamentally important in the context of memory. The human capacity to remember music is well documented.[12] But music remembered can also signify, beyond the music itself, other objects of memory. The Wagnerian leitmotif, or motif – which is discussed later in this chapter – is one example: the motif signifies a character, theme or idea that is invoked in the minds of the audience whenever the motif is played. But music can also signify a moment in history, remembered by those who were part of that history. Milan Kundera has written recently on the significance

---

10 See, for example, Johns 2011.

11 The infamous form is Form 696, branded by many as 'racist' for identifying, in particular, black and Asian music. See http://www.guardian.co.uk/society/2009/sep/07/met-police-form-696-clubs (Access date: 3 June 2011).

12 The relationship between music and memory is explored comprehensively in Snyder 2000. Snyder shows how music is remembered, cognitively, but also how music takes many of its concepts and features from how one remembers.

of music in the memory of the Holocaust. Jewish people in the Czech city of Terezín were used to show the world – via the Red Cross – the good treatment they were receiving at the hands of the Nazis by allowing them to have certain freedoms, including the occasional concert. "Under the executioners' watch", writes Kundera (2010:152), "the condemned played condemned music." The music included that of Mahler, Zemlinsky, Schoenberg and Haba. The efforts of the people of Terezín were to "preserve the memory of Mahler and Schoenberg", and so it is fitting that Kundera finds in Schoenberg's *A Warsaw survivor* "the greatest monument ever dedicated to the Holocaust" (*ibid*:153). The memory of the music that was kept alive during the Holocaust then becomes the music that memorialises the Holocaust. It can be said, then, that music functions as something that preserves and recalls memories.

The power or force of music, then, can be identified in the Platonic tradition as the use of, or displacement of, the exclusivity of the state's musical hegemony – competitiveness in Nietzsche's reading of Plato. One can see in music both a 'constructive' force and a 'destructive' force, and this force constructs and drives – if we take Scott's more general thesis on this – historical and normative sensibilities, and possibly even institutions. One can furthermore identify the use of music by the state, and by people acting against the state. And finally, one can note the significance of music in the context of memory, including music signifying an object of memory other than the music itself. Given all of this, the relationship between law and music is an important object of enquiry in the study of law.[13] In the context of Joyce as an exiled writer, music becomes one of the principal modes by which Joyce engages in the processes of remembering and forgetting, creating and destroying – also in relation to conceiving of the Irish nation.

Music and Joyce

Joyce's second talent was as a tenor, and he was known to have an excellent voice. He also had a go at composing music himself, writing music for two of James Clarence Mangan's poems, as well as for Yeats' *Who goes with Fergus*.[14] He was known to have frequented opera houses in Dublin, and later, on the European continent. Opera in late nineteenth century Ireland was not the bourgeois interest that it arguably is today: arias were often sung throughout the city by all social classes – as we know from Joyce's own writings, including *The dead* (middle classes) and *Ulysses* (working classes). A survey of opera performances in Dublin from 1888 to 1904 further shows the prolific interest in the form, and evidences Joyce's early exposure to opera, including Wagner, Mozart and Verdi.[15] Music, as we shall see, had a great influence on Joyce, evidenced in his writings.

13 Studies on law and music include: Frank 1948; Frank 1947; Grossfeld & Hiller 2008; Levinson & Balkin 1991; Llewellyn 1942; Manderson 2000; Posner 1990. See also a special edition of the *Cardozo Law Review* dedicated to 'The modes of law: Music and legal theory, an interdisciplinary workshop' ((1999) 20:5 and 6), edited by Desmond Manderson and David Caudill.

14 As identified by Martin 1991:7.

15 A historical study of opera in Dublin is provided in Reilly 1999.

Joyce's writings have in turn influenced music. Joyce has been explicitly associated with the work of John Cage, by Cage himself.[16] And the words of Joyce have been adapted for music, notably in Luciano Berio's *Sinfonia*, but also on Kate Bush's 2011 release, *Director's Cut*.[17] Joyce's collection of poems, *Chamber music*, likewise has been adapted or put to music on several occasions.[18] The force of Joyce's music has therefore, in turn, been appropriated by other musicians.

Scholarship on the use of music by Joyce in his writings is vast. There are now several monographs[19] on the subject, as well as catalogues[20] of musical references, edited collections[21] and special editions of journals.[22] On what one might mean by Joyce's 'music', it might be useful to consider Knowles' point that "Joyce attempts to create a musical language"; that is, words that are musical in their phonetics, in their rhythm, tempo, style, and so forth (Knowles 1999:xxix). Knowles offers an analysis of a few lines in the 'Cyclops' episode of *Ulysses*. He notes that the following – from Bloom in response to the Citizen's anti-Semitic jibes – is written in the style of, and with the stresses of, a waltz:

> Mendelssohn was a jew [...] And the Saviour was a jew and his father was a jew. Your God [...] Well, his uncle was a jew [...] Your God was a jew. Christ was a jew like me. (*U* 12.1804-1809)

The significance of Bloom responding in the rhythm of a waltz and affirming his Jewish identity is to stress that Bloom and the Citizen could not be further apart from one another in terms of their thought, ideas and values: the Citizen shouts abuse, and Bloom responds with music. With Bloom's invitation to dance – his music – the Citizen gets up, hobbles over the door, and throws a biscuit tin at Bloom as he rides off down the street.

Joyce's 'music' can also be seen elsewhere in *Ulysses*, in 'Sirens', where we can see or hear the sounds of Joyce's language – the repetition and rhythm and indeed playfulness of the language, which cannot resist a musical reading:

> Bald Pat who is bothered mitred the napkins. Pat is a waiter hard of his hearing. Pat is a waiter who waits while you wait. Hee hee hee hee. He waits while you wait. Hee hee. A waiter is he. He waits while you wait. While you wait if you wait he will wait while you wait. Hee hee hee hee. Hoh. Wait while you wait. (*U* 11.915-919)[23]

---

16 See Klein 1999:152-170.

17 On Berio's *Sinfonia* and Joyce, see Eyuboglu 2002:177. Kate Bush's single, *Flower of the mountain*, takes much of the lyrics from Molly's soliloquy in the final episode of *Ulysses*. When Bush's song was written in 1989, the Joyce estate refused permission.

18 For example, Frost 1947; Kauder 1955; Treacher 1963.

19 Bowen 1995; Bowen 1975; Bucknell 1995; Burgess 1973; Burgess 1965; Hodgart & Bauerle 1997; Martin 1991; Myers 1992; Weaver 1998.

20 Bauerle 1982; Hodgart & Worthington 1959.

21 Bauerle (ed) 1993; Knowles (ed) 1999.

22 For example, *James Joyce Quarterly* 38(1) and 38(2) on 'Joyce and Opera'. There are dozens of individual journal articles on Joyce and music throughout this and other titles.

23 Bowen 1967:250.

Joyce's interest in music was by no means unique amongst his Irish contemporaries. Music was of great interest to nineteenth and early twentieth century Irish writers.[24] But what was proving to be absolutely vital in the writers' relationship with music was the simple but important fact that Ireland had no contemporary leading musical figures of their own. If such a thing as 'Irish music' existed, it would have to be sought through a historical and indeed romantic turn to early Irish folk music. This endeavour, although attempted, is problematic in the Irish experience, because early forms of Irish music were not readily available to the population at large. Early Irish music and poetry, written in Gaelic, struggled to find listeners who could speak the language. Because the potato famine of the 1840s killed much of the rural population, the Gaelic language towards the end of the nineteenth century was a dying language, and it would require a political effort – such as the establishment of the Gaelic League – to create anew a body of Gaelic speakers. Whilst figures such as Tom Moore made available Irish language poetry and music in English translation, the requirements of English necessitated a transformation of the music and poetry, so that it lost much of its essentially Irish character. Besides, such an enterprise does not sit easily with the ideas and ideals of literary modernism, where the emphasis is on creation, including the creation of new forms. Irish modernists would have to forge a new relationship with music in these circumstances, there being no national music that is authentically rendered or available to the population at large.

Harry White's recent book, *Music and the Irish literary imagination*, identifies a new home for an Irish music – or at least something that retains the "fundamental properties of music, its connotations of order, language, form, and meaning" (White 2008:8). Because Ireland had no leading musical figures of its own, Irish writers would aim at music in their writing: "[...] language could aspire to the condition of music itself" (*ibid*). And in terms of musical form, "Irish literary discourse could perform the function of musical genres" (*ibid*). The ensuing mantra is *words for music* – a substitution of words for the style, form or effects of music. One can see this first in the writings of George Bernard Shaw, who insisted that his writing is founded upon music,[25] but also in the writings of James Joyce.

One of the most illuminating points White makes in his book is the way in which Joyce weaves musical memory into his writings: he presents a distinctly Irish novel (*Ulysses*) that is laced with so much music and so many references to music that the memory of Dublin music (whether from Ireland or not) in 1904 is archived in his "monumental instance of words for music" (White 2008:16). The question of whether there was an 'Irish music' or not is bypassed by presenting music in all its profuseness, its intimacy with the lives of Dubliners.

If *Ulysses* is musical remembrance, one can recall Kundera on Schoenberg: the music that recalls a memory other than the music itself. Here, then, it is possible to see how the vast referencing of music in *Ulysses* recalls something other than the music

[24] See White 2008.

[25] As Shaw said: "[...] my method, my tradition, my system is founded upon music" (quoted in White 2008:15).

referenced – the state of Irish music in 1904, for example. It might be that music remembered is in fact a signifier for a music lost: Ireland's music before the potato famine, the Irish language, and so forth.

In thinking of both Ireland's lost music and the desire to create music in the *words for music* substitution, Walter Pater's famous statement that "all art aspires to the condition of music" (1932:90) may offer some insight into Joyce's method. Pater continues: "[...] for while in all other kinds of art it is possible to distinguish the matter from the form [...] it is the constant effort of art to obliterate [the distinction]" (*ibid*). Pater distinguishes poetry from music. Behind every poem there is an occasion or event – the occasion of the poem – which relies upon the form to deliver it. What if the deliverance of the poem became the end itself? What if the poem conveyed the aesthetic qualities of the poem quite separate from the occasion of the poem, as if the occasion of the poem was veiled by the aesthetic effects of the form? The poetry of William Blake, for Pater, achieves something like the status of music: the poem carries itself without relying on the occasion of the poem. Music carries itself without relying on the matter of its occasion. The point Patter makes is that not all art forms are the same in terms of the way in which they convey matter; a romantic landscape painting, for example, is tied to the aesthetics of the 'matter,' the landscape.

Pater's aesthetic theory and his statement regarding the special position of music is often criticised for presenting a dogmatic "hierarchy of arts", with music at the top, and poetry probably close behind (Bucknell 1995:37). The irony is that Pater, in being modern, had to appeal to "19th century doxa" of one art above them all (*ibid*). Whilst Bucknell recognises this as an antiquated approach to the arts, he nevertheless points to modernism's, and Pater's, interest in music as somehow symptomatic of modernity itself. Music, for Bucknell, is "the articulation of modernity's dis-ease" (*ibid*:24). Modernism not only aims at a meaning beyond the work of art itself, but includes "the hope of making new meaning as well" (*ibid*:1-2). Thus, "[b]ehind the prevalent 19th century conception of music as the highest of art forms, possessing, as Pater contended, an exquisite balance between form and content, there also lurks the sense that the realm toward which music tends may also be one of disturbing plenitude or excess" (*ibid*:24).

This excessive search for meaning beyond the discursive is therefore an essential feature of modernist art. Pater recognises this too, but identifies it solely with the condition of music – the collapse of the distinction between matter and form. Interestingly, for present purposes, Pater not only identifies in music this exceptional, excessive force of pure art – without distinction between matter and form – but also that this force, to which all art aspires, is also a *law*:

> It is the art of music which most completely realises this artistic ideal, this perfect identification of matter and form [...] In music, then, rather than in poetry, is to be found the true type or measure of perfected art. Therefore, although each art has its incommunicable element, its untranslatable order of impressions, its unique mode of reaching the 'imaginative reason,' yet the arts may be represented as continually struggling after the law or principle of music, to a condition which music alone completely realises, and one of the chief functions of aesthetic

> criticism, dealing with the products of art, new or old, is to estimate the degree in which each of those products approaches, in this sense, to musical law. (Pater 1932:92)

Musical law, then, is the law of excessive meaning – of aiming beyond the discursive and of presenting an art form whose aesthetic force is beyond the matter of its form. Pater's aesthetic theory can be compared with the earlier invocation of Plato: the "centripetal force", to use a Pater term, of state music (Pater 1896:18). The aspiration or tendency towards singularity, towards the existence of state music and imitations and repetitions thereof, is similar to Pater's artistic force towards collapsing the matter and form distinction. In the Platonic state, the expression of a state music denies or prohibits the possibility that form might be filled with a different content: music is thus the expression of a form which must necessarily, and simultaneously, also be the matter. Music is the form and matter of this excessive law, this sovereignty. The next section in this chapter examines Joyce's use of music in the context of this form and matter distinction by offering a reading of the 'Cyclops' episode of *Ulysses*.

The motif of Jacob's biscuit tin in 'Cyclops'

'Sirens' testifies to the proposition that literature can be music. Conversely, music can give rise to narrative. The opera of Richard Wagner is an obvious reference point for this 'music for narrative' – in particular, the use of narrative-driving techniques in music, such as the leitmotif. This part of the chapter examines the Wagnerian leitmotif and, in particular, Joyce's appropriation of this musical device in the 'Cyclops' episode of *Ulysses*. Joyce's writing may be seen, therefore, not only as 'words for music', but also 'music for words'. The significance of this 'words for music for words' is set out here.

Wagner's famous leitmotif, or motif, describes a short piece of music – a few bars or even a few notes – within a larger work or opera; the motif signifies a motive or leading motive (*Leitmotiv*), which could include a theme or idea, a character, or an emotion. A motif typically occurs more than once in an opera, but may also appear across different operas, particularly in Wagnerian opera. It is a useful narrative technique in opera, because it announces the arrival or recurrence of the signified character, theme or emotion. Its recurrence in a particular part of the opera also develops what the motif is or means; the motif, therefore, whilst referencing or signifying its 'motive', can also develop its meaning in the context of its appearance in the larger work. This often forgotten dynamism of the motif is important to consider in the context of Wagner's work, including the history of its reception and (mis)use. As Hilda Brown says of Wagner's writings on motif:

> [...] whenever he is expounding the theory of the leitmotiv, or Grundmotiv (primary motive) [...] Wagner emphasises its functionality – the way, that is, that it is both promoted by dramatic events and fully integrated into the dramatic action. (Brown 1991:48)

The motif, therefore, is not transcendental to the dramatic action of the opera.

The significance of the motif, and the relative weight to be attached to it in relation to the work as a whole, is contested. Wagner himself stated its structural importance, and spoke of a "harmony" between structure and music (in Brown 1991:52,67). As to the significance of this structuring force, Wagner would sometimes glorify this "process of judicious repetition", producing a "truly unified musical form", but at other times, he would play down the role of the motif, rather dismissively, calling them no more than "emotional signposts" (*ibid*).

Whatever the intended function of the motif, the technique has attracted criticism, particularly in the context of its function during the rise of National Socialism in 1930s Germany. Theodor Adorno, in his text *In search of Wagner*, written in 1937-8, characterised Wagner's motif as a "gesture [...] striking a blow" with the audience (Adorno 2005:20). Adorno argues that the use of the motif, and its repetition, is a violent gesture on the part of the composer/conductor; the violence of the gesture is a public violence that assimilates the audience with the aggressor striking the blow (*ibid*). Not only is the public assimilated with the aggressor of the gesture – the repetition of the motif – but that very gesture adopts a "commodity-function [...] the music is designed to be remembered, it is intended for the forgetful" (*ibid*:21). The motif thus assimilates the public with its blows, but then comes to be one of the most remembered aspects of the opera. In Adorno's terms, then, the gesture of the motif becomes "the" expression of the artwork (*ibid*:34). The motif conveys the emotional content of the drama, but it does so under the auspices of the motif and not as emotion *per se*: "[...] its expression [for example, of emotion] does not present itself, but is itself the object of presentation" (*ibid*:34-35).

Adorno thus argues that the motif comes to dominate the meaning of Wagnerian opera, that the emotional content of the drama is encapsulated and conveyed in the commodity form of the motif and not the performance or experience of emotion itself, and that the expression of the motif precludes the possibility of a signified meaning other than in the expression of the motif (Adorno 2005:35).[26]

Adorno later qualified his criticism of Wagner by stressing the essentially historical nature of interpretation of Wagnerian opera, and opened up the possibility of Wagner's motifs having a more nuanced and open meaning. He said of Wagner's artworks:

> They are not complete in themselves. They create a magnetic field of all possible intentions and forces, of inner tendencies and countervailing ones, of successful and necessarily unsuccessful elements. Objectively, new layers are constantly detaching themselves, emerging from within; others grow irrelevant and die off. One relates to a work of art [like Wagner's] by deciphering within it things to which one has a historically different reaction. (Adorno in Leppert 2002:535)

Thus, whereas Adorno once criticised the use of the Wagnerian motif as closing down the possibility of multiple and differing interpretations of the artwork, here he states that this is largely historically contingent. What one might identify in the critical appraisal of the motif is the question of whether, and to what extent, the motif conveys meaning in its expression. Whilst this, in the later Adorno, might be historically contingent, the motif does seem to promote a narrative meaning in its expression in a way that is not normally associated with music. Walter Pater's

26 "[...] a process in which signifiers and signified are interchangeable."

aesthetic theory, for example, could be used to criticise the use of the motif in music as promoting emotional or aesthetic content or matter through a narrative form, opening up a distinction between matter and form in music. This narrative function of the motif is affirmed when one considers the process of naming motifs: love, servitude, sword or ring, to give some Wagnerian examples.

The motif form has been used outside of music and opera – in literature especially. The motif conceived of – in Wagner's own terms – as a structuring force, lends itself well to modernist literature, because, as Clive Hart argues, modernist writers were very much engaged with the question of remaking order out of "fragments" (Hart 1962:162). But in the context of literature, if we conceive of the motif as simply a signifier for some emotion, theme or idea, then literature is full of motifs, and there is nothing particular in Wagner's motif that warrants its appropriation by writers of fiction. Symbolism, or symbolism in repetition, has been used in literature for millennia. If motif – which arose in Wagner – is to mean anything more than mere symbolism, criticism therefore calls for a refining of the motif and its definition. Hart's book, *Structure and motif in Finnegans wake*, offers a useful interpretation. He proposes that mere repetition of a motif in literature is not enough; the motif must act dynamically:

> Real leitmotiv entails a use of statement and restatement in such a way as to impel the reader to relate part to part; each recurrence of such a motif derives in some necessary way from all its previous appearances and leads on to future resurgences, pointing to correspondences and relationships far beyond those that hold between the individual motif and its immediate context. (Hart 1962:165)

Hart's concept of the motif is thus radically different to the early Adorno: motifs do not function to reference a common theme or emotion, but work dynamically as part of some sort of sub-narrative on that common theme or emotion. The recurrence of a motif must, according to Hart, ...

> [...] grow functionally from the evolving material, yet not recur regularly in a wholly predictable way; it must arouse expectations of its reappearance and yet give new insights when it does recur; it must be a shaping influence, not the fulfilment of predetermined formal requirements; it must be an active, rather than a passive, function. (Hart 1962:165)

Joyce scholars have identified certain common motifs covering the main themes of *Ulysses* throughout the book: the motifs of paternity, fidelity, wandering, displacement and usurpation.[27] Taking Hart's account of the motif, these active and dynamic reference points develop in relation to the main narrative of the work. Timothy Martin points more exactly to the workings of the Joycean motif: he argues that since Joyce's writings are so rich and nuanced, the motif works in a way which is essentially Wagnerian in that it aids the audience/reader to pinpoint meaning and guides them through the work (Martin 1991:155). This reading of the motif is quite standard in Wagner studies, but Martin continues with his argumentation, adding that the particular use of the motif by Joyce is part of the "stream of consciousness"

[27] See Martin 1991:154 and Gilbert 1993:616.

technique: Joyce is actually offering his own stream of consciousness, as author, in the development of the novel (*ibid*). The Joycean motif therefore gives us access to what Joyce was thinking as he wrote the novel, to the development of his thought as some sort of sub-narrative to the novel itself.

With these accounts of the motif in mind, I will analyse the use of one particular motif in the 'Cyclops' episode of *Ulysses*. The chosen motif is that of a biscuit tin: a Jacob's biscuit tin.[28] The tin makes its appearance on several occasions during the episode. The biscuit tin as motif passes Hart's criteria – as I will show – for it arises out of the evolving material, and functions in an active and dynamic sense in that it contributes to a sub-narrative that is neither predetermined, nor of a static meaning. The motif of the biscuit tin also references a previous occurrence outside the text of *Ulysses*, in the *Book of Genesis*, so that the Wagnerian use of motif across different operas is invoked in this continuing narrative created by the motif across different works, albeit here across works by different authors.

The 'Cyclops' episode takes place at around five o'clock in the afternoon and most of the action is centred in and around Barney Kiernan's pub, in the legal district of Dublin. The episode features conversations between twelve drinkers and Bloom, who is there to meet Martin Cunningham to discuss the estate of Paddy Dignam. Bloom is generally treated badly, and the twelve drinkers, almost without exception, espouse anti-Semitic opinions on subjects such as law, finance, nation and religion. Bloom is personally vilified. The motif of the biscuit tin is invoked throughout the episode, and its appearance and function recalls, but also gives effect to, questions of nationhood and birthright. There is a clear opposition between the novel's hero, Bloom, and a character known only as 'the Citizen', who represents the extremity of the anti-Semitic, but also Irish nationalist, sentiments.

The first invocation of the biscuit tin is a seemingly modest and unimportant one: a Jacob's biscuit tin is brought over to the Citizen's dog, Garryowen, so that it may have the last remaining biscuits and crumbs (*U* 12.495), and is later also used to hold water to satisfy the dog's thirst (*U* 12.748). The significance of these uses of the tin is apparent only later. The biscuit tin features more prominently at the episode's conclusion. In the mistaken belief that Bloom has won a bet on a horse called Throwaway, the Citizen, thirsty for another drink, seizes the empty biscuit tin and throws it at Bloom as he makes his departure from the pub (*U* 12.1812). This act follows a debate with Bloom in which the question of his nationhood was raised and in which Bloom defended his Irishness and appealed to his rights not to be persecuted as a Jew. The presence of the biscuit tin throughout the episode, and especially its appropriation towards the end, is significant when one considers the origins of nation and birthright in *Genesis* and the role of Jacob's 'biscuit tin' in *Genesis* 25:19-34.

In the Biblical context of Abraham and Rebekah's two sons, and Rebekah's pregnancy, the Lord said:

[28] *Jacob's* is a brand of biscuit or cracker common in Ireland and elsewhere in 1904.

> Two nations are in your womb, and two peoples, born of you, shall be divided; the one shall be stronger than the other, **the elder shall serve the younger**. (*Genesis* 25:23 – my emphasis in bold)

The elder, Esau, "came forth red", whilst the younger came with "hold of Esau's heel" – the younger was called Jacob, which means 'foot holder'. Esau, as the eldest son, had the birthright. He is characterised as "a skilful hunter", a "man of the field". Jacob, on the other hand, was "a quiet man", who liked "dwelling in tents". The Lord's decree that 'the elder shall serve the younger' was realised one day when Esau came home from the field and, starving, pleaded with Jacob for some of his "red pottage" – 'red pottage' referring both to a red lentil food and the vessel in which the lentils were contained. Jacob agreed to give Esau the pottage, but on condition that Esau give his birthright up to him. Since Esau was starving, he agreed, and thus Jacob, the younger, obtained his brother's birthright through this transaction of pottage (*Genesis* 25:29-34).

In 'Cyclops', the Jacob's biscuit tin is a motif referencing directly the transaction between Jacob and Esau of birthright and pottage. Joyce moreover intended this reference, because he also models the characters of the Citizen and Bloom on Esau and Jacob, respectively. The Citizen is red-haired and his dog is an "Old Irish Red Setter" (*U* 12.715). The Citizen is likewise into Gaelic sports (a 'man of the field'), whilst Bloom is more of 'a quiet man'. There are also specific references in the narrative: Bloom, playing Jacob, obtains tins of "Neave's food"[29] six weeks prior to the birth of his son – that is, Bloom is careful to keep food stocks (*U* 12.1650-1652) – and the Citizen and his dog drink with great thirst from the pint glass (the Citizen) and Jacob's biscuit tin (Garryowen).[30]

The biscuit tin comes to represent the transaction of birthright and the antagonism between Bloom's and the Citizen's claims to nationhood. This is no minor reference: in the final moments of the episode, the tin – the motif taken as an object – is picked up by the Citizen and hurled towards Bloom, causing a ...

> [...] seismic disturbance [... not seen] since the earthquake of 1534 [...] All the lordly residences in the vicinity of the palace of justice were demolished and that noble edifice itself, in which at the time of the catastrophe important legal debates were in progress, is literally a mass of ruins beneath which it is to be feared all the occupants have been buried alive. (*U* 12.1860-1869)

The use of motif by Joyce is a use of a musical form that recalls an originary, state-like performance of music. The motif literally levels the legal and colonial district of Dublin and inaugurates a new nation. This is suggested by the nature of the conversation during the transaction between the Citizen and Bloom: Bloom, readers are told, was responsible for drawing up the plans for Sinn Féin (*U* 12.1574). The Citizen, likewise, has his own plans. But it is Bloom who has transacted and secured his birthright.

29 "[...] advertised as a health food for 'infants, invalids, growing children and the aged'" (Gifford 2008:368).

30 See, for instance, *U* 12.120-121, 709-711, 748-749. The Citizen "waiting for what the sky would drop in the way of drink" (*U* 12.120-121)

Amongst the dead, as the legal district is brought down to rubble, is the infamous Recorder of Dublin, Sir Frederick Falkiner. Falkiner, who served as the real Recorder of Dublin from the late nineteenth century into the twentieth, was renowned for his anti-Semitic approach to Jewish settlers in Dublin when hearing cases involving Jewish defendants, and it is thought that the character of Bloom was based on a real Jewish Dubliner who had been handed a harsh sentence by Falkiner in 1904.[31] When Bloom later imagines his own trial in 'Circe', it is Falkiner who tries him.

Although there has been – as Zack Bowen (1967:257) said – "lavish" claims about the use of music in *Ulysses*, there is evidently a conscious attempt by Joyce to use musical techniques in his writings, or to write musically. In the case of the motif of the biscuit tin in 'Cyclops', Joyce invokes the music of *Genesis* to inaugurate a new music: Bloom's music. Bloom's response to the Citizen shortly before the biscuit tin is thrown is an invocation of music, an invitation to dance.[32] The 'Cyclops' episode of *Ulysses* marks the beginning of Joyce's more considered approaches to writing music – and writing music as law and law as music.

A tranche of scholarship on Joyce's politics identifies him as a politically uninterested writer, politically and physically exiled from the Irish nationalist cause. This chapter has shown how Joyce was, to the contrary, politically engaged with Irish resistance. This chapter has also threaded together themes and ideas around the coincidence of law and music: the force of music, music in memory, music and meaning, and the musical origins of the state and uses of 'state music'. Through the processes of remembering and forgetting, the critical standpoint of exile offers a privileged position from which to challenge and displace dominant myths. That Joyce should use music and musical forms such as the motif in displacing the more imperialistic[33] versions of Irish nationalism dominant in Ireland in 1904 – and seen in Barney Kiernan's pub in 'Cyclops' – raises the question not only of myth, but also of the musical origins of nation. These musical origins, which take on an object form, signify some mythical past (*Genesis*), yet they function dynamically within and across artworks to create new meaning. The transaction and usurpation of birthright in *Genesis* and *Ulysses* – the movement from Jacob to Bloom, from Esau to the Citizen, from pottage to biscuit tin – is politics 'in exile'. It consists in a struggle between remembering and forgetting in an exiled political imagination.

---

31 See, for example, Goldberg 1982:6-7.

32 As discussed earlier, the waltz of Bloom's words "Christ was a Jew, like me ..." (*U* 12.1804-1809).

33 As Declan Kiberd has said: "the militants [Irish republicans and revivalists] were at grave risk of embracing the imperial psychology in a reworked form. Joyce heaped mockery on the imitation of English models by Irish revivalists." Kiberd 1995:335.

Reference List

Adorno T. 2005. *In search of Wagner*. London: Verso.

— 2002. Wagner's relevance for today. In: R Leppert (ed). *Essays on music*. Berkeley, CA: University of California Press. 584-603.

Bauerle R (ed). 1993. *Picking up airs: Hearing the music in Joyce's text*. Urbana, IL: University of Illinois Press.

Bauerle R. 1982. *The James Joyce songbook*. New York: Garland Press.

Benjamin W. 1996. Critique of violence. In: M Bullock & MW Jennings (eds). *Walter Benjamin: Selected writings: Volume 1*. Cambridge, MA: Harvard University Press. 236-252.

Bowen Z. 1995. *Bloom's Old Sweet Song: Essays on Joyce and music*. Gainesville, FL: University of Florida Press.

— 1975. *Musical allusions in the works of James Joyce – Early poetry through Ulysses*. Albany, NY: State University of New York Press & Dublin: Gill & Macmillan.

— 1967. The Bronzegold Sirensong: A musical analysis of the Sirens episode of Joyce's Ulysses. In: E Rothstein & TK Dunseath (eds). *Literary monographs: Volume 1*. Madison, WI: University of Wisconsin Press.

Brown HM. 1991. *Leitmotiv and drama – Wagner: Brecht and the limits of epic theatre*. Oxford: Clarendon.

Bucknell B. 1995. *Literary modernism and musical aesthetics: Pater, Pound, Joyce, and Stein*. Gainesville, FL: University of Florida Press.

Burgess A. 1973. *Joysprick*. London: Andre Deutsch.

— 1965. *Re Joyce*. New York: WW Norton.

Cheng VJ. 1995. *Joyce, race, and empire*. Cambridge: Cambridge University Press.

Church R. 1941. *Plato's mistake: On the place of the poet in society*. London: Allen & Unwin.

Cixous H. 1976. *The exile of James Joyce*. London: John Calder.

Deane S. 1985. *Celtic revivals*. London: Faber.

Derrida J. 2007. What remains by force of music. In: P Kamuf & E Rottenberg (eds). *Psyche: Volume 1*. Stanford, CA: Stanford University Press. 81-89.

Eagleton T. 1970. *Exiles and émigrés: Studies in modern literature*. London: Chatto & Windus.

Ellmann R. 1959. *James Joyce*. Oxford: Oxford University Press.

Eyuboglu M. 2002. Davies, Berio, and 'Ulysses'. In: S Knowles (ed). *Bronze by gold: The music of Joyce*. London: Garland.

Frank J. 1948. Say it with music. *Harvard Law Review* 61:921-957.

— 1947. Words and music: Some remarks on statutory interpretation. *Columbia Law Review* 47:1259-1278.

Frost J. 1947. *Chamber music: Opus 12: A cycle of thirty-six songs for tenor and bass-baritone, with accompaniments and preludes for the pianoforte*. London: John Frost.

Gibson A. 2002. *Joyce's revenge: History, politics and aesthetics in Ulysses*. Oxford: Oxford University Press.

Gifford D. 2008. *Ulysses annotated*. Berkeley, CA: University of California Press.

Gilbert S. 1993. *Reflections on James Joyce*. Austin, TX: University of Texas Press.

Goldberg G. 1982. Ireland is the only country ... Joyce and the Jewish dimension. *The Crane Bag* 6:5-11.

Grossfeld B & Hiller JA. 2008. Music and law. *The International Lawyer* 42:1147-1180.

Hart C. 1962. *Structure and motif in Finnegans wake*. London: Faber.

Hodgart MJC & Bauerle R 1997. *Joyce's grand operoar: Opera in Finnegans Wake*. Urbana, IL: University of Illinois Press.

Hodgart MJC & Worthington MP. 1959. *Song in the works of James Joyce*. New York: Columbia University Press.

Johns A. 2011. *Death of a pirate: British radio and the making of the information age*. New York: WW Norton.

Joyce J. 1986. *Ulysses*. (Gabler Corrected Text). London: Bodley Head.

— 1939. *Finnegans Wake*. London: Faber.

Kamuf P & Rottenberg E (eds). 2007. *Psyche: Volume 1*. Stanford, CA: Stanford University Press.

Kauder H. 1955. *Ten poems from James Joyce's chamber music: For soprano, alto, tenor and string quartet*. New York: Boosey & Hawkes.

Kiberd D. 1995. *Inventing Ireland*. London: Jonathan Cape.

Klein SW. 1999. The Euphonium Cagehaused in Either Notation: John Cage and Finnegan's Wake. In: S Knowles (ed). *Bronze by gold: The music of Joyce*. London: Garland. 151-170.

Knowles S (ed). 1999. *Bronze by gold: The music of Joyce*. London: Garland.

Kundera M. 2012. *Encounter*. London: Faber.

Leppert R (ed). 2002. *Essays on music: Theodor W Adorno*. Berkeley, CA: University of California Press.

Levinson S & Balkin JM. 1991. Law, music and other performing arts. *University of Pennsylvania Law Review* 139:1597-1658.

Llewellyn K. 1942. On the good, the true, the beautiful, in law. *University of Chicago Law Review* 9:224-265.

Manderson D. 2000. *Songs without music: Aesthetic dimensions of law and justice*. London: University of California Press.

Manganiello D. 1980. *Joyce's politics*. London: Routledge.

Martin T. 1991. *Joyce and Wagner: A study of influence*. Cambridge: Cambridge University Press.

McCabe C. 2003. *James Joyce and the revolution of the word*. 2nd Edition. Basingstoke: Palgrave Macmillan.

McHugh R. 1976. *The Sigla of Finnegans Wake*. London: Edward Arnold.

Myers P. 1992. *The sound of Finnegans Wake*. London: Macmillan.

Naddaff RA. 2002. *Exiling the poets: The production of censorship in Plato's Republic*. London: University of Chicago Press.

Nietzsche F. 1994. *On the genealogy of morals*. Cambridge: Cambridge University Press.

Nolan E. 1995. *James Joyce and nationalism*. London: Routledge.

Pater W. 1932. *The School of Giorgione, from the Renaissance*. London: Birmingham School of Printing.

— 1896. *Plato and Platonism*. London: Macmillan.

Pearse D & Taylor M. 2009. Met police bow to pressure to drop question on 'racist' form 696. *The Guardian*, 8 September. 10.

Plato. 1888. *The Republic*. Oxford: Clarendon.

Posner R. 1990. Bork and Beethoven. *Stanford Law Review* 42:1365-1382.

Reilly S. 1999. James Joyce and Dublin Opera. In: S Knowles (ed). *Bronze by gold: The music of Joyce*. London: Garland.

Said E. 2001. *Reflections on exile and other literary and cultural essays*. London: Granta.

Sallis J. 2008. *The verge of philosophy*. London: Chicago University Press.

Scott C. 1928. *The influence of music on history and morals: A vindication of Plato*. London: Theosophical Publishing House.

Snyder B. 2000. *Music and memory: an introduction*. Cambridge, MA: MIT Press.

Treacher G. 1963. *Bright cap and streamers: From chamber music by James Joyce: Two part children's choir and piano*. London: Schott.

Weaver JW. 1998. *Joyce's music and noise: Theme and variation in his writings*. Gainesville, FL: University of Florida Press.

White H. 2008. *Music and the Irish literary imagination*. Oxford: Oxford University Press.

INDEX

E

F

G

H

I

J

K

L

M

N

O

P

Made in United States
Troutdale, OR
11/03/2026

56845377R00093